The Theory of E
A Journey of the Mind

Yvonne Bailey

www.capallbann.co.uk

The Theory of Everything
A Journey of the Mind

ISBN 186163 314 9
ISBN 13   9781861633149

Cover design by HR Design
Cover artwork by Yvonne Bailey

Published by:

Capall Bann Publishing Ltd
Auton Farm
Milverton
Somerset
TA4 1NE

Contents

www.yvonnebailey.co.uk

Acknowledgements

There are so many people I would like to acknowledge who have helped me in the process of writing this book.

My amazing son Kristian Bailey, who has never doubted me or my work and has supported and encouraged me along the journey, he's always let me know he is proud of me and loves me; his lovely partner Katy Gilvear who has accepted me and my work wholeheartedly; the wonderful Neil Craven-Lashley whose positive energy has always been present and his equally wonderful partner Richard Lashley.

A special thank you to a lady who is a true earth angel, Joyce Welch from Cardiff, who introduced me to the universal language of symbols and dreams.

To the many, many people who have sat my courses, and contributed to my market research. You have truly been an inspiration and a delight to teach and I want to thank you all. You are true warriors and have taught me so much, but there are so many of you I cannot mention you all and so please forgive me if your name is not included in the following: Dawn Burns [who has kept pace with me throughout the process of writing the book], Beverley Jones, Laura Peterson and Martin Moloney [parents to Theo Moloney whose birth I witnessed], Paula Bartram, Julia and Jonathan Latchem-Smith, Nicola Schramm, Gill Jones, Gemma Rees and Safiya Sayed Baharun [my little stars], Paula Williams, Lois Eckley, Jason Roberts, Claire Hobbs, Ann Sibley, Matthew Dennis, Wendy and Victoria Payne, Ros Wilson, Helen Gunter, Janet Sweeting, June Wesley, Sophie Cobb, Mererid Wigley, Gail Andrews, Debbie Mackay, Linda Proctor, Cheryl Peterson, Hilary Williams, Richard Williams, Sharon Fry, Jane Davies, Kelly Davies, Elin Forster, Maureen and Jonathan Booth-Martin, Andrea Jones, Marion Nao, Angela Pook, Natalie McKendrick, Kay and Rex Greatrex, Kim Saunders, Keith Crudgington, Annette Monks, Jill Yeandle, Phil Fletcher, Lesley Robinson, Nicola Crawford, Jennifer Meah, Elaine Toft, Wendy Hale, Sara Baldwin, Stephen Cordle, Cheryl Bowden, Jan Abbott, Sheryl Paterson, Juliana Bowden, Michael Limbrick, Irene Matthew, Darren Hamer, Eileen Ruck, Nicola Jones, Danny Pinto, Claire Woollacott, Susan Hughes[mum of Amy now in spirit], Maria Akbas [mum of Leah now in spirit], Paul Hayes, Joel and Hayley Ingram, Karen Barker, Nina Stedman, Sara Rees, Jenny Henn, Sarah Tutssel, Linda Wong, Nicola Ham, Jean Branson, Joanne Rees [mum of Catrin now in spirit], Nicola Steele, Kay O'Shea, Anne Huxtable [mum of Dan Logan now in spirit], Janice Harris, Tina Griffiths, Janet Nute, Jacqui Malpass, Valerie Burnell, Hannah Raffour, Fiona Akpinar, Karen Parker, Susan Mortimer, Sue Da'Casto, Maria Quinn, Eiris Watkins, Sharon Stanton, Leanne Walley, Angela Palfrey, Jacqueline Taylor, Lorraine Jones, Wendy Gonzalez, Sandra Pengilley, Mark Jones, Philip Thomas, Suzanne Clarke, Berny Connolly, Michelle Gill, Keely Burrows, Kim Davies, Dee Copley, Alison James, Geraldine Evans, Naomi Somers, Phillip Morris, Jeanette Thomas, Helen Summers, Amira Alam, Lesley James, Cathy McGrath, Yvette Marshall, Clare Matthews, Lou Lockwood [mum of Bill now in spirit], Bola Yesufa, Chris Watkins, Helen Davies, Yomi Yesufa, Gail Hagerty, Catrin Jones, Dawn Blower, Emma Ward [now in spirit], Anita You, Liz O'Connor, Maria Pritchard, Di Wookey and Anita Salter [Anita is the messenger/earth angel who brought the name of the publisher for this book].

I would also like to acknowledge the South Wales Echo, BBC Radio and Radio Cardiff. A special thank you must go to Enid Price, a teacher of psychology who for years has invited me to her classes as a guest speaker to offer the students a different perspective on the mind, 'Enid, you really are a special educator'. I am particularly grateful to Gary King for advising me on the circles appearing on the face of the earth, as well as all the people who have written to me and visited me over the years and have shared their lives with me. Also Joanne Wesley-Williams a fellow writer, my friends and colleagues at Beech Jones de-Lloyd Solicitors, and how could I forget the original crew at the start of my spiritual journey Andy, Gail, Hazel and Phil.

A very special thank you to all the researchers and writers whose work I have relied on and referred to in this book. Your work is amazing and you have helped to educate me.

Also thank you to Julia and Jon of Capall Bann who were chosen by the universe to publish this book. It feels great to be working with you.

And finally I would like to say the biggest thank you ever to those unseen workers out there in the universe who are the real authors of this book, and for whom I have worked as a ghost writer. Thank you for ensuring I got it right, even though I must have tried your patience. xxx

CAUTION!!!

CAUTION!!!!

CAUTION!!!!!

".....................I should introduce a note of caution at this point. I think the book you are reading might accelerate and raise the consciousness of you the reader, and the more people that read it, the faster and greater the impact will be on the whole. This heightened awareness brings with it a responsibility so be warned, as once you know better you are more accountable."

1

Yvonne Bailey
Photograph courtesy of Natalie McKendrick Photography

Foreword

I am not a scientist, physicist or mathematician and neither do I claim to be. I have had a basic education and no higher education. I am not religious but I am spiritual, although I am not a spiritualist. Rather I am a student of life, symbolically enrolled in a distance-learning programme. Most of all I am an ordinary middle aged woman, a mother, daughter, sister and universal family member, and that means I am related to you. I am related to you and the whole by a single organism of interconnected energy fields designed by and connected to a Creative Designer/God.

Having had the less than ordinary experiences which you will read about in this book, I could do no other than look for answers as what I was experiencing defied my concept of reality.

Early on in my life I recognised my thoughts and feelings were not developed making it impossible for me to evaluate my situation and the greater meaning of life. I was like a radio or television that was not properly tuned in, only connecting with those who were also out of sync, and I needed to make adjustments in order for me to hear and see with clarity.

And no wonder, because our world is like a big cooking pot and we humans with our differing religions, cultures, belief systems, prejudices and history can be likened to lots and lots of different ingredients and mixes. Some of these ingredients and mixes might not blend as well with some as they do with others, some need more developing, and some can leave a bitter taste in your mouth.

To make sense of this world and the things I was experiencing, I have embarked on a road of self-development and mind expansion to change my frequency, tutored by a force I cannot see. This force had made itself known to me in many different ways and at first, out of ignorance, I ignored it and when I did, things would go badly for me and I would experience emotional hurt and pain, or setbacks in one way of another.

Eventually I began to get the message and started to strengthen. I learnt to say 'no' and to modify my behaviour. I began to change my way of thinking and acting by standing back, observing, listening, learning, following my 'gut' instinct and reading the signs, and I began to resonate differently and found my way back to the whole. I recognised by experience there really was a power greater than me, and I tested this power and began to interact with it, asking questions and being blown-away when I would get answers in a universal language that was cryptic and subtle and I took to with ease.

Once I was confident in what I was experiencing and deciphering I decided to run workshops and courses to help others expand their mind to change their frequency, and teach them about the universal language so they too could communicate with this power. I have also written books on this subject, have had a column in a daily newspaper, as well as a regular radio slot. I have spoken at psychology classes and many other venues, and as word of my work has spread many, many people have shared their unexplained experiences and happenings with me.

It is as though I have been doing market research and the results have been truly stunning and I can say with confidence something huge is going on to people individually and somehow we have missed this collectively. It has sneaked under the radar because what is happening is not tangible. It is cryptic and subtle and we have been too busy to 'see' it, but it is what this new Age of Aquarius is all about.

These things of the air cannot be seen and can be likened to the wind, it is a force that can make itself known without being seen and occupies the empty space which is all around us, and this force is here now and is getting stronger and stronger, and it seems now is the time for it to be heard. It is this that has given me the confidence and desire to reach a wider audience and to get the message across there is a Creator, and there is a plan for our lives, the Earth and the universe; we are pre-programmed to receive symbolic communication from our subconscious and beyond, and we can also communicate with people who have 'died' but live on in the spirit form, and by understanding their language we can be helped on our journey.

We can ask for guidance from our subconscious, the wider universe and these spirit workers to help with our development and to help us achieve what is in our plan and what we have come here on Earth to experience and achieve. The guidance comes in many different forms such as dreams, symbolic happenings, coincidence, intuition and so on, and has to be interpreted via the universal language, but in order to benefit fully from this guidance our thoughts and feelings have to be balanced.

There are many, many spirit workers living in parallel universes composed of different forms of matter who know so much more of the plan for our lives, for the Earth and universe and they are part of the whole, linked by the interconnected energy fields, and they are fully briefed and are waiting to work with you, and **you** are so much more than you know.

In writing this book I have no wish to offend you the reader and I do realise my words are open to question and I think that is positive and questioning is a good thing. Ours is still an immature civilization and we are living in chaos and pain, and it will probably take centuries before we are able to look at our actions and ourselves with complete honesty.

We need to question our journey individually and collectively and we need to understand we are spiritual beings living a life in a physical body to learn lessons and grow spiritually.

In order to grow spiritually we have to develop our mental and emotional maturity so we operate on a different frequency, and this comes with awareness and understanding, when we are concerned with facts and experience rather than belief systems, when we use reasoning rather than emotions, when we think without acting on impulse so we listen to our inner voice or sixth sense, and when we are able to read the signs in an unbiased way.

The famous Greek philosopher Socrates once said 'The only good is knowledge and the only evil is ignorance', so with this in mind perhaps we should teach our children not what to think about life, Mother Earth, the wider universe and the Creator, but how to think about these things by presenting them with facts and allowing them the opportunity to question, experience and interpret for themselves. It is only then, collectively, the coming generations will understand their thoughts, feelings and actions which will create the future for themselves and everything they are connected to. It is only then they will have a sense of personal responsibility and become a true universal citizen.

Over the past century, science has unlocked the secrets behind radio and television, nuclear energy and the power of the sun, and those working in this field of the intangible are seeking the ultimate, a 'theory of everything'. The work of these pioneering scientists is invaluable, however, it is clear to me a theory of everything at this point in time cannot be based on science alone. We have to look at other pieces of the jigsaw the Creator has designed, that can be found in ancient monuments and civilisations, historical writings, religion, symbolism, astrology and the astrological ages, as well as expressed in the individual by way of symbols, dreams, coincidence etc. that should be interpreted via the universal language. However the Creator's words are at the mercy of the interpretation of man and through ignorance and self-interest can, and historically have, been used as a form of control and manipulation.

In writing this book I have mapped the path I have taken on my journey of mind expansion and self-development, and I emphasise I still have a long way to go, I have so many questions to ask and I am a work in progress.

This book will help you to understand the mechanisms behind the universal language and demonstrate the style of the language to you. It also contains pieces of the jigsaw I am putting together to help me achieve a higher state of consciousness and make sense of my journey so I can interpret the guidance received in a more balanced way. As I have witnessed the positive effects when sharing what I have learnt with others, I am happy to share these thoughts and theories with you, as I think this will influence and benefit the whole and will help to raise consciousness for this new age.

I do not present anything as fact, other than what I have personally experienced, and just as you would with a balanced meal, you the reader might want to chew over these thoughts and theories and swallow what is acceptable to you and put aside that which is not. However, as the meal is balanced, what you have not swallowed will need to be replaced with some other ingredient, thought and theory so you too can benefit from the whole.

There are many, many ingredients to think about that make up the total and many of these ingredients need to be sourced from other places, countries, religions, cultures, civilisations, science etc. and so there is a journey of the mind to be undertaken and I wish you well on your journey and, who knows, we might meet at some point on the road.

2

My story

I started to write 'The Theory of Everything – A Journey of the Mind' when I was fifty four, and I completed it just as I neared fifty seven. Looking back I can see my date of birth, parents, environment etc. were chosen for me for this lifetime, to enable me to develop and to see clearly, to better understand people and life. This has enabled me to achieve what I see as my life's work, this book.

I view myself as being similar to a computer with a wireless connection and it has taken me many years to understand I am a transmitter and receiver of subtle energies/information that cannot be seen but have influenced me hugely. I was born with a bespoke software programme, and from the moment of conception everything I have felt, thought, learnt and experienced has been entered, filed and saved in to the database of my mind. I view not just me in this way, but every living thing – **and that includes you!!!**

I believe in writing this book I am a ghost-writer/medium for a higher power but in order for this higher power to influence me, my database had to be populated with the right data/information. Now this book is finished, I will be relinquishing it to those unseen workers who work with me with the confidence they will show me where it is to go, as it is all very well to 'talk the talk' but the real test is to 'walk the walk'. Whilst writing this book the guidance received via the universal language has been phenomenal and I have interpreted and followed. I am confident the route and the destination is planned and if it has reached you the reader, then it is on course and once it has shared its story and rested, will move on and gather pace.

The following sub-chapters 2.1 to 2.6 of 'My Story' have been taken from my first book, 'The Making of a Spiritual Medium'.

2.1 Childhood

Cardiff is the capital city of Wales in the UK. In the nineteenth century it had the busiest seaport in the world, because of the thriving coal and iron trades. On the eve of the First World War in 1913, coal exports reached their peak and the international price of coal was struck in the Coal Exchange building in the dockland area. It was here the world's first £1 million pound deal was signed. Eventually that £1 million cheque was framed, and as far as I am aware, still hangs in the Coal Exchange building.

To sustain this growth the surrounding docklands areas grew into cosmopolitan communities, with seafarers from all around the world making Cardiff their home, and the dockland area known as 'Tiger Bay' achieving worldwide fame.

It is a very different story now in Cardiff, as after the Second World War demand for coal slumped and international markets were lost as other countries developed their own steel industries. By the 1960s coal exports had virtually ceased. Cardiff has had to totally reinvent itself and has done so very successfully, attracting foreign investment and relying heavily on the service industries, especially tourism.

The Bay where I live is on the site of the old docks, spreading out into the docks community. Appealing apartments and houses are intermingled with a brilliant mix of restaurants, pubs, clubs, cinema, bowling, a casino, the exciting Millennium Arts Centre and fantastic places of historic interest including the Norwegian Church, which has a special place in my heart. This is all set around our wonderful harbour. A barrage has been put in place, as we have one of the world's greatest tidal ranges up to fourteen meters. At low tide our harbour would have been inaccessible for up to fourteen hours a day. The barrage eliminates the effects of the tide, and gives Cardiff the opportunity to once again capitalise on its greatest asset – its waterfront.

My mother's father was a Norwegian seaman. His name was Bjorn Kristian Kjonnings and he was a Chief Engineer. When his ship sailed into Cardiff Docks in 1920 it would have been a different docklands that greeted him. He met my mother's mum, Beatrice, when walking around Cardiff Castle. At that time he could hardly speak English. Beatrice married her Norwegian seaman and they had four daughters, but he died at the age of fifty-three. My mother was the third of their four girls. Her name is Berit, and she and her youngest sister Maureen both married local men, the older two sisters having married and moved away. My Aunty Maureen's husband was named Emrys, and together they had four children. My parents had two children, me and my sister Gail.

My name is Yvonne and I was born in 1953 in my grand-mother Beatty's house on a council estate in Tremorfa, which is an area next to Splott. In that house lived my grandmother, mother, father, sister and me, plus Maureen and Emrys, all in a three bedroomed house! In 1955 my mum and dad were given a new council house in Llanrumney, to the East of Cardiff. Maureen and Emrys stayed with my grand-mother, and raised their eventual family with her help.

My father and Uncle Emrys both worked in the Eastmoors Steelworks and our households were very close. My dad worked in the melting shop, and sometimes the skin on his back would be red and sore because of lime dust. I never heard him complain, and he worked all the hours he could to ensure we had a nice home.

In the early days of our moving he relied on public transport to take him back and forth to the steelworks in Splott. I know there were occasions when the transport wasn't running due to bad weather, and my dad would walk to work and back, even if there was thick snow. This was a round trip of about ten miles, with two very steep hills to climb. He worked Christmas days and Boxing days; he was no stranger to doublers, sixteen-hour shifts, so he could provide for us.

My mother had the best of everything. She loved clothes, and my father bought her a long fur coat. She wore high-heeled shoes, and I used to think she looked like a film star. My mum made all the clothes for us two girls and was a perfectionist, very conscious of our image to the outside world.

In the early days our mum was a housewife, later taking a part-time job as a waitress. I can clearly remember that two bedroomed house. We were a happy household, and my parents bought a German Shepherd dog we named Pal, and so we were a family of five. We were two streets away from a farm and my sister and I, along with neigh-bour's children, would go to the farm and look at the animals. Sometimes the farmer would let us help and that was magic. We always had Pal trailing behind us.

As small children, my sister and I were sent to Sunday school at the local Methodist Church. I loved the Bible stories and really believed all I was taught. God became a big part of my life. If I was anxious or frightened about anything, I would pray to God and do deals with him. I was particularly anxious about my father. My mother would often refer to him as 'your poor father' and point out to my sister and me all the hard work and sacrifices he made for our family. My mum made me feel so sorry for him.

My dad had a clever mind, and could have really achieved academically. He was born in 1927 and named Vivian, and as a boy he went to Moorland Road School in Splott. He won a place at a grammar school, but my grandmother reasoned her other three boys hadn't had this opportunity, so it wasn't right my dad should. His Headmaster from the School went to see my nan at home, but she was not for turning. My dad missed a wonderful opportunity, but he never resented it. My dad left school at fourteen and went to work on the railways. He started as a cleaner in the engine shed, but quickly became a locomotive fireman. In 1946 at the age of eighteen he volunteered for the Army, and was sent to Palestine with the 21st Lancers. He was in the army for six years, during which time he married my mother, and my sister Gail was born.

When he left the army his rank was a Corporal, and he was a Gunnery Instructor on Centurion Tanks. He loved his job but my mother didn't want the life of an army wife, and gave him an ultimatum. This is how he came to work in the steelworks.

My dad was a very passionate man; he loved my mum and us kids fiercely. He was very involved with the Union in the steelworks, and was a staunch believer in fighting for workers' rights. He would sit on industrial tribunals, and I used to listen to his tales of injustice against workers. He was a charismatic speaker, but had a fiery temper, and could look really frightening when in a rage. He loved animals and would take Pal for long walks in the countryside when he came home from his shift. If he was on the night shift my mother would say, 'your poor father has worked all night'. And my sister and I would have to be quiet around the house as my 'poor father' would be sleeping.

My first spiritual experience took place when I was about four. At night I would come out of my body. I don't remember how this happened or where I went, but I remember the coming back. I would have a man with me. I would tell him I didn't want to go back into my body; I wanted to go into someone else's body just to see what it was like. He would always answer, 'I have told you before, this is your body and this is where you belong, you cannot enter someone else's body'.

I remember when I would wake in the morning I would feel very guilty because I had been disloyal to my parents by wanting to be someone else for a while. I imagine it was this that stopped me confiding the experience.

My mum was born in 1929 and had the potential to be a medium. From a child she had spiritual experiences but was terrified of them. My sister and I grew up with the stories of how, when my mother was little, she would see faces on her eyelids when she closed her eyes at night. They were of no one she knew and would mouth words she couldn't understand. Sometimes the faces were distorted. She would be so frightened she wouldn't go to sleep.

My mum has been an asthmatic all her life and as a child was very frail, her episodes of seeing were called hallucinations by the doctor. Sometimes my mum would see faces when her eyes were open. They could be on the wall, in a corner, anywhere and she would scream. My poor Nan must have been frazzled with it. I can vividly remember sitting at the table with my mum and she would be motionless, just staring ahead. My sister and I would ask her to 'stop it' but she didn't seem able. My mum also had problems sleeping, and was horrified to experience sleep paralysis. She would wake up from sleep and be unable to move. She couldn't open her eyes or her mouth, and was unable to make a noise. This terrified her.

At one stage my mother was seeing a psychiatrist to help her with these problems. If only she could have gone to an experienced medium to help her understand what was happening to her, but there was no one to turn too, just the medical profession. My mum is elderly now and still sees the faces on her eyelids. She still sits staring into space, but is no longer afraid.

My mum was incredibly close to her mother and her sister Maureen, and I think it was quite a hardship for her to move away from them. When my father was in work, my mother would take my sister and me back and forth to Tremorfa on the bus, so we could visit with my Nan and the others. Very often we would sit, and the adults would talk about spiritual matters. My cousins, sister and me would be fascinated to hear of these happenings.

They talked of when our Nan's brother was in hospital, but he appeared at the house, knocking on the front door moments before they were given the news he had died. They said when our Gramp died, later that night he could be heard walking up the stairs in the house. Apparently my Nan's sister Maggie was into spiritual things, and could read tea leaves. They would also talk about neighbours, with my mother catching up on the local gossip. There was such a diversity of people, all working class, most struggling to provide for their families.

My parents would try to have one night out a week with my aunt and uncle, and we kids would be looked after by our Nana Beatty at her house. Very often the drink would cause arguments, and on their return my father would over react and my sister and I would be crying and frightened. In the morning my mother would say 'Your poor father, he is so upset about last night', and I would feel desperately sorry for my 'poor father'.

My mother did eventually settle in Llanrumney, as our new area was made up of young families with children, and mum made friends with most of the other mothers. Across the road lived Peggy and Arthur with their son Russell, and Peggy became my mother's lifelong friend, until Peggy's death some years ago.

My mum and dad grew up in the war years, and I think their generation had a need for security that perhaps made them cautious of life. My parents had negative opinions about most things outside of their environment. They are both forceful and controlling personalities, as well as being very loving, and over-protective of my sister and me. My dad is a strong Leo, my mother a fiery Aries, and my sister and I are both nurturing Cancerians.

My mother would control in an emotional way, which was how her own mother had been. If my dad was on night shift, sometimes my sister and I would play her up and be naughty when in bed at night. My mum would shout up to us 'If you don't behave I am going to run away'. Sometimes she would pretend she was leaving, and would make exaggerated walking noises, and then slam the front door. My sister and I would listen and then start to cry. My mum would say 'Right, I am giving you one more chance'. My mum was the leader of our little pack, and would normally get the better of my father. When my dad would leave for his shift I would pray to God to bring him home safely, and would always negotiate some deal or other, what I would do for God if he looked after my 'poor father'. Some days I would avoid walking on cracks on the pavement, another I might compulsively count certain things. I still do the counting thing to this day, and some-times it is worse than others. It can be really intrusive.

I used to worry about religion a lot, there seemed so many rules and regulations, and God was portrayed as a very judgmental person. If I met anyone who was really nice but wasn't a Christian, I would worry about them, thinking what would happen to them when they died. My prayers at night used to take for ever, the list of people to be included got longer and longer, and then I would compulsively worry I had forgotten someone and would run through a quick check list.

My mother used to use the Bible if there was any conflict. She would get the Bible out and ask my sister and me to swear on the Bible, this was a means of ensuring she had the truth from us. One time, cream had been taken from the fridge. My sister swore on the Bible it wasn't her. My parents were exempt from such matters, so that left me. I hadn't taken the cream, but I reasoned if I swore on the Bible I hadn't taken the cream, something bad must surely happen. Someone in our family was not being truthful, or perhaps I might have taken the cream and not remembered and so I did a quick negotiation in my mind with God and took the blame.

Having said all this I know I was a very sunny child, always talking, laughing and singing. The anxiety and worries were for me alone to know. I am positive I never verbally shared these worries with anyone else but I was also a very emotional child, and when I was taken to watch Bambi in the cinema I cried so much I was hyperventilating. Anything remotely sad would have me in floods of tears and I did not seem to have robust coping mechanisms.

However, we were a happy and loving little household, but with imperfections the same as any other household, although ours was to a lesser extent than a lot of others around us. My parents did their very best for us, and when my dad bought a car, I can remember lovely holidays. There would be our family in our car, and Maureen and Emrys with their four children in their car, and we would drive to Devon. For one week we would sleep in the cars, and the other week we would be in caravans. In that first week my mother and aunt would cook on primus stoves on the side of the road.

In our road were about forty houses. A few of these houses had large families, and the home life for some was not good. My parents would tell my sister and me about the 'goings on' in these households, and we would feel very sorry for the children involved.

I remember one time when my mother offered shoes I had grown out of to one of these families. The mother was really grateful and called one of her sons, who was in my class at school, and asked him to try the shoes on. He got them on with difficulty, as they were too small, and he was making a fuss about it. His mother hit him across the head because of this. My mum and I were so upset, and she never offered shoes to that lady again.

In another road near to ours, I had become friendly with a girl who always had a lot of money. I would go to the ice cream van with her, and she would buy both of us masses of stuff. She said her mother's boyfriend gave her the money.

One day she took me to her house. The smell inside was disgusting. I was aware it was very cold in the rooms, with no lino or rugs on the floors and piles of dirty washing everywhere. Upstairs in a bedroom was a baby with a napkin hanging down his legs, heavy with urine. He was covered in excrement that had seeped from his nappy. The smell was vile, and there was no-one in the house. The baby was on his own, and really distressed. My friend was not at all fazed by this, but went and got a bottle for the baby. She laid him down, so he could hold it himself.

I didn't know how to express the compassion I felt; it enveloped me like a blanket. From then on I wanted to do nice things for this girl all the time. I couldn't stop thinking about what I had seen and realised how very, very lucky I was. My friend and I would have been about nine years of age at this time.

I loved school, and excelled at drama and singing. There has always been something of an actress about me, and to this day I sing away when I am working. I was also good at English, and loved to write essays. My mother says I was a constant talker, and would even read out loud to myself.

Our lives had a rhythm, everything revolved around the home and our family in Tremorfa. Sometimes we would go to my dad's mum Emily who lived in Splott, and I loved it when I could stay with her for the day. Emily's husband William, my grandfather, died when I was a baby.
I always went to the local library near to where Nana Emily lived. The

building was really old with highly polished wood and it had a distinctive musty book smell. The hushed atmosphere would make you think there were wonderful secrets in all those books, and this appealed to my sense of drama. My dad's brother Frank and his wife Phyllis lived around the corner from my Nana Emily, and I am not sure how much they appreciated my love of music, for I would bash away at their piano, even though I couldn't play a note.

Life for me was very secure and happy, but living with two dominant parents meant I wasn't forming my own opinions, I was prone to feeling sorry for people, and was easily manipulated. The God thing was a worry because he was all seeing, and my religion made him seem so judgmental, and so life with all its rules and regulations was a big responsibility. I also had a vague sense of there being something else around me, but that something wasn't tangible and therefore unexplainable.

When I was eleven our wonderful dog Pal died, and the pain I felt was indescribable. We had been on holiday for two weeks, and Pal was put in his regular holiday boarding kennels. We were waiting for the van to appear in the street to bring him home to us. The van came, and the man got out, but Pal wasn't with him. I thought my world had ended.

We had taken a neighbour's daughter with us on holiday, and unbelievably her father had died while we were away. He was only in his thirties and seemed in perfect health when we left for the holiday. I can remember being with her and I wasn't able to stop crying. She told me her loss was far worse than mine, which of course it was. She was so calm and able to contain her emotions. I recognised this and admired her for the control she showed, whilst I had absolutely none. I think of her sometimes and realise how incredibly brave she was.

That year we also moved house. We were given a transfer to a three bedroomed council house in Tremorfa. My mother's asthma facilitated this for us, as it was recognised the air in Llanrumney was not good for her. She had asthma attacks and chest problems the whole of the time we lived there.

I was so sad to leave our little house, our friends and neighbours, and particularly upset to be leaving what was left of our life with Pal. Around that time I had a dream where Pal and I were standing on the top of a hill. I was walking away from him, but he was following me and I was telling him he couldn't come. However, he continued to follow me, and then I woke up. I hoped he was saying he would follow wherever I went.

Our new house was around the corner from my Nana and aunt's house, and it was great to be able to go in and out of there, and be with my cousins.

Moving home meant moving school, and as I already had friends in Splott Secondary Modern School, I was really happy about this. The school stood on Splott Road and was in an old Victorian building, with the boys kept separate from the girls. You attended a secondary modern school if you had failed the eleven plus, as this exam supposedly ascertained the type of schooling that was appropriate for you.

I loved that school, although there was a shortage of facilities. For instance, the toilets were in the playground, with the girls backing on to the boys toilets. The boys had knocked a hole through so the girls couldn't use certain toilets. At lunch time, if you had school dinners you would line up in the yard and be marched down the road to Eastmoors Hall. The dinners were cooked off the premises, and arrived in large steel containers. For field games, we would be marched to Splott Park. There was such a lot of poverty in that school, and various nationalities attended as pupils. Quite a few of the kids had prostitutes for mums, and there were a lot of absent fathers. Some of the home lives of different children were terrible.

I remember one incident where all the kids were lined up in the morning, waiting to be marched in to school for the day. There was total silence in the playground, and suddenly a male voice rang out, calling the name of one of the girls. The high stone walls that surrounded the school magnified his voice. We all looked, and there was a scruffily dressed man shouting to one of our school friends. Apparently this was her mother's boyfriend, and that morning our friend had taken his shoe laces for her shoes. He made her take off her shoes, undo the laces, and hand them to him in front of all of us. Not a word was said by anyone, the teachers didn't intervene. He swore at her whilst snatching the laces, and she had to walk back to her place with her shoes slapping against the soles of her feet.

I can remember looking at her sad, down-turned face and feeling such overwhelming emotion for her, but not knowing how to express this. You could see the other pupils and the teachers felt the same as I did. She was given her space but treated with kid gloves by all of us.

Another time, one of the boys was in the girls' playground showing off. A male teacher came to march him away and the boy obviously felt embarrassed. He was black, very popular, a bit of a clown, but known for having things bad at home. His clowning turned to aggression and he picked up a metal netball post and swung it at the teacher's head, knocking him to the ground. The teacher was rescued by his colleagues and the boy was marched away, and then we never saw him at school again.

One of the girls in our class lived with her mum and brothers and sisters. There was no dad at home. The mum was dying of cancer and all the kids faced the prospect of going into care. Something happened in a cookery lesson which made this girl flip. She hit the cookery teacher, and the teacher ran out to get the headmistress. The headmistress was then attacked. This girl was expelled from the school, but we all knew she was reacting to overwhelming feelings of grief, and none of us girls wanted her expelled.

Near to our new house was a mother, father and their two teenage daughters. The father had gone to prison for interfering with the daughters and the mother was having a relationship with a much younger man. When the father came out of prison he moved back in with his wife and daughters, and his wife continued the relationship with the younger man. I have seen that younger man jump out of the first floor window because the husband was entering the house.

This younger man used to dress in black leather and he had a motorbike. He used to sometimes pretend to be a policeman and would ride up to a busy junction in his leathers, stand the bike in a prominent position, and direct the traffic. He was prosecuted for this.

One of the daughters left home at fifteen and we never saw her again. The other daughter went on to have about five children by different men. Most of them eventually ended up in care. One of the babies was born blind, and we were told this was the result of the mother having an untreated venereal disease. Another of the babies died at about six weeks, as the mother had him in bed with her and rolled on to him. She was about twenty-stone in weight. One time at Christmas three of these kids were in the street on Christmas day. They were in their underwear and the eldest was only about five. My mum and a neighbour asked them where their mother and grandparents were, and were told there was no one home. They had been left alone from the day before. The house was cold and there was no sign of any Christmas presents or food. The neighbour took them in and fed them that morning.

Another time I remember seeing men going into the house with camera equipment. My mother said the mother and daughter were posing for pornographic pictures.

One of my good friends in school was of mixed race. Her mum was white and her father was black. She had quite a few brothers and sisters, and her father sexually abused nearly all of them. They lived in fear of him, and I remember my friend used to be withdrawn and so quiet at times. I didn't know then the extent of what was going on in her home life. I only found out later when her father was jailed for attempting to murder her sister.

My last school year was spent at Willows High School in Tremorfa, which was a replacement for the ancient Splott School. It was so exciting to be among the first pupils to use the new facility.

I didn't know anyone that wasn't working class, until one day a teacher at the school took my friend and me home to her house. She drove us there in a sporty car, and genuinely wanted to give us a nice experience. She was such a positive personality and we girls loved her. I can remember her showing us her husband's wardrobes. There were rows upon rows of shirts, all colour coded. Another wardrobe held all his suits, and I couldn't believe it. My friend and I were overwhelmed and didn't touch anything but just soaked it all in.

Our teacher's husband came home unexpectedly, and it was obvious he wasn't pleased to see us there. We had to leave immediately. He gave us a lift in his car, and dropped us off on the main road that runs through Cardiff, about two miles from our home.

We had to walk the rest of the way. That made me feel bad and I couldn't tell my parents where I had been and what the husband did, as my father would have gone mad. I could imagine him going to their home and grabbing the husband by the throat. My father was forever giving lifts to me, my sister and our friends so we would be safe, and this man hadn't given a thought to our safety.

At this time I got my first job, working on a Saturday for a delicatessen on Bute Street in the Docks. It was opposite a pub called the Custom

House, and all the prostitutes used to use this pub as a meeting place. I would look out of the big window in fascination.

The family I worked for were Greek and I really loved them. They were so kind to me. The smell in the shop was amazing, and I loved the different coloured olives and the fascinating cheeses. The herbs and spices were incredible, and the colour and smell of them was a new experience for me.

The customers in that shop were another source of fascination to me. They were all nationalities and would gossip away, sharing their highs and lows of life with us behind the counter. The owner of the shop was called Marigold and her mother was Hetty.

Hetty lived a couple of doors away from the shop and was so strict with me, and if the conversation with the customers was not suitable, she would order me to the stock room. She would caution me as to what was suitable and what was not, and would always threaten to tell my father if she thought I was interested in something inappropriate.

I loved that lady, she was rich in life experience and, although stern, had a real quirky side to her character, and she would often have me laughing out loud.

Walking down Bute Street you would see three-storey Victorian houses, and these houses would represent all nationalities. You would find a Jamaican house with a cafe at the front, cooking and serving Jamaican food, as well as offering accommodation. There was a Chinese house, again with a café at the front, and so it would go on. These houses catered to the seamen but, of course, with the decline of the docks, their business had practically gone.

I believe by this time I had stopped sensing that something else that seemed to be around me when I was younger. Religion was playing a lesser role in my life as well, and that was a real relief. Some times I would go to bed and forget to pray, and the next day nothing dreadful would happen, and so I got more and more relaxed about the whole thing. I was starting to think God wasn't as strict as I had been led to believe.

2.2 Stepping out

"On life's path we can encounter many difficulties and when we are hurting and in crisis we sometimes fight against the tide, wanting to take the easy road. However this easy road normally doesn't find us learning the lesson and so another situation comes about which might be different from the first but kind of has a synergy of connection and we then might start to wake up to the fact that the universe is somehow orchestrating events so that we learn a lesson". Abba Eban, orator, Israeli statesman and diplomat 2nd February 1915 - 17 November 2002.

I was now fifteen and about to leave school with my Certificate of Merit. Our school didn't offer us CSE exams, as that was for the Grammar School pupils. I was not equipped to do anything other than a menial job, but my parents had saved to send both my sister and me to Cleves Secretarial College, where we were taught shorthand, typing and bookkeeping. I took to the shorthand and typing with ease. That was a lovely period for me, and I will always be grateful to my parents for having the vision to equip the both of us for life. I know it was a great financial sacrifice to them, and they both had to work hard to accomplish it.

At college I was mixing with girls whose backgrounds were different from mine. In fact there were very few people from a council estate. Quite a few of the girls were from wealthy backgrounds, and I found it all fascinating. This was the time of a music revolution. Soul and motown hit the British music scene. We used to go to the Top Rank on a Saturday morning and dance to Diana Ross and the Supremes, Marvin Gaye, Otis Reading, Sonny and Cher, as well as groups such as The Beatles and Jerry and the Pacemakers.

All colours and nationalities would pack into that dance hall. There was no colour distinction among the young and, in fact, I think we white kids admired the black kids because a lot of the music our generation loved was from the black population.

My social circle began to widen and I was starting to take my first steps out into the world as a young adult. I had little judgement of what was appropriate or inappropriate behaviour by others, and I was used to human tragedy, as it was all around me. I didn't have any opinions of my own, I was quick to feel sorry for people and was easily manipulated emotionally, and here I was being let loose.

My year at college was up, I had finished my Saturday job and I was now sixteen years of age. My mother took me for a job interview in Mount Stuart Square, opposite the Coal Exchange in the Docks. It was with a firm of maritime solicitors called Lean and Lean. Roydon Dickinson Lean was the senior partner, and it was he who interviewed me, or rather he asked the questions and my mother answered.

I sat looking around his office, which had files piled everywhere. They were all on the floor and on shelves around the walls. There were also enormous leather-bound books with paper bookmarkers hanging out of them. I wondered how on Earth he would ever know where anything was. My mother did a superb job for me, and I was to start work within a few days.

I had fantastic training in that office. Everything had to be done just right, and learning all the new legal terminology was like an introduction to another language. Every morning I would be given dictation either by Mr Lean senior or his son, Mr John Lean junior. I would type away on a black Adler manual typewriter with my Tipp-ex erasure sheets near to hand. Those were the days when you would have a letterhead, carbon and white paper in the machine, so that you could make a copy for the file.

I was the office junior and was also responsible for answering the phone, making tea, going to the shops to get everyone's lunch, as well as doing the banking and post. When I was out of the office I found everything so interesting as it was in the thick of Tiger Bay and as well as being a commercial area, it was still a red-light district. Some of the things I saw were unbelievable.

At lunchtime the prostitutes would always be strolling around the square. They would try to blend in with the office workers but I could identify most of them because of seeing them outside the Custom House pub. They would try to make eye contact with the men. There was a large black lady called Sadie, and she would blow kisses at me if I looked at her and I knew she recognised me from the delicatessen. To me she seemed really frightening and I would keep my eyes to the ground when I saw her coming, but I couldn't resist a peep and she would always catch me looking.

My mother would make my father take me to work and pick me up whenever his shifts allowed, as my parents were worried about me being there. More than once I was propositioned by kerb crawlers as I walked along. I was advised by my mother to walk on the inside of the pavement, to deter anyone from grabbing me and bundling me into a car.

After a year of working at Lean and Lean I went to work for solicitors near the town centre and at various times worked in both the criminal and matrimonial departments. My sympathy always laid with the victim or the person who was hurting and these feelings I had always provoked a strong reaction within me but I never formed a real opinion of the guilty party. I think this might have been because of the environment I lived in, as my community had no alternative other than to be accepting of the bad behaviour of others, you somehow become conditioned. Working for solicitors was showing me how through using the mind you could dissect a situation piece by piece, creating a path that allowed you to follow the trail that led to what ever the situation was. In this way you could form an opinion of the situation, person etc. and work towards some kind of resolution. I began to see how the consequence of actions was dealt with in the legal world and this understanding was reinforced when, as a result of my shorthand skills, the new firm I worked for extended my role and I was sometimes asked to do the preliminary interviews with clients. I would take down their statements, and get them to fill in legal aid forms.

The things that went on behind closed doors were mind-blowing. Some of our female clients were living in really abusive situations. They would suffer all types of cruelty at the hands of their partners, and yet they continuously attempted reconciliation. It was always the children who suffered in these situations. Sometimes a separated or divorced mother might take a new man into her home and he would resent her children. One woman told me for about four years her eldest son was not allowed to sit at the dinner table with the rest of the family as the stepfather wouldn't eat with him. He said the boy made him feel sick. The mother accepted this, justifying her actions by reasoning she had to 'keep the peace'.

We had such a mix of clients in that office. I remember a really small man in his late twenties called Tiny. His wife had thrown him out of the family home because he was an alcoholic and was also addicted to barbiturates. Tiny would turn up in reception without an appointment and he would be passed to whoever was free, and so all the staff knew him. He was a real character.

One day he came in and a few of us were stood around him talking. He was saying he wanted to give up the drink and drugs and go home to his wife and children. We were all praising him and encouraging him in his way of thinking. A colleague called Chris asked him if he had any drugs on him, and Tiny confirmed he did. To emphasise how serious he was, Tiny told Chris she could have all his drugs, and he handed some tablets over to her. Chris kept saying to Tiny 'Are you sure you want to do this?' and he would answer 'I really, really do want to go home. I've had enough.'

When Tiny left the office he said he was going home to his wife and children and we were all waving him off, telling him to be strong. We stood around Chris and she was asking 'What should I do with them?' I said 'Flush them down the toilet Chris.' And she did. That was that, and we all went back to work feeling really happy.

About three hours later Tiny was back. He looked really awful. He was sweating profusely, his eyes were wild and he was talking fast, while licking his lips constantly. He asked to see Chris, and a whisper went around the offices. We all knew what he was there for, and couldn't believe the situation we were in.

The partners of the firm knew nothing of what had taken place earlier, and the reception was full of clients. Poor Chris had to go out and face Tiny. I was made to go with her, because it was my idea to flush the tablets down the toilets. The others were stood huddled together, watching from a safe distance. Chris told Tiny what she had done and he went ballistic. He was screaming at her, and we backed away from him but he kept coming forward. The receptionist dialled the police emergency number, and one of the senior partners came rushing out of his office. The whole place was in chaos.

Chris and I had to lock ourselves in the ladies toilet, and Tiny was kicking the door. Within a short while the police came and they had a hard job restraining Tiny. Eventually he was taken away. All of us involved in the incident were given a severe reprimand for our stupidity. A few weeks after this incident we heard Tiny and a couple of his friends had been burned alive when a derelict building they were sleeping in caught fire.

One of the senior partners specialised in crime. He would very often take me from the matrimonial department and send me on some task for him. He regularly sent me to the local Whitchurch Hospital, which specialised in mental health.

I had to take statements from patients who had drug problems and had committed various petty crimes to feed their habit. Some of the patients had irreversible brain damage through drug abuse, and I had to get used to being 'touched up' on a regular basis.

There was one patient called Gerald who would always be around when I visited. He continually changed his clothes. One minute he was dressed for the day, then he would disappear and return dressed for bed. On and on it went, and this was how he spent his day. He would trot back and forth strumming an imaginary guitar between changes. I was told he had gone on the hippy trail in the East and had taken bad acid. He was on a constant trip.

The firm also dealt with murder cases, and some of the information I was privy to was dreadful. I witnessed all kinds of human perversion, cruelty and tragedy. We dealt with one murder where an Asian couple had murdered their son's girlfriend and her young child. Their justification was the son had dishonoured them. They wanted an arranged marriage for him, but he would have none of it. When they were brought to trial and found guilty, the son hanged himself. Another time the body of a baby was found buried in a local park, and the mother was found and charged with infanticide.

There was also a pornography case, and I couldn't believe the sickening images I saw. They were of animals and children, and the guilty people were quite clearly shown in the photographs. They had made no attempt to hide themselves, thinking they were above the law and would never be caught.

In the lunch hour I would walk with some of my colleagues the short distance into the town centre. Very often when we left the building a midget man would be waiting for us. He was always dressed really smart. The moment he saw our little group he would hurl obscenities at us.

None of us knew him and had no idea why he singled us out, but he would follow us into town. He would shout 'Whores the lot of you, children of Satan, prostitutes that's what you are, nothing but dirty prostitutes'. We were mortified but would giggle to hide our embarrassment. We would manage to lose him and then more often than not we would bump into Thelma.

Thelma was a lady who at that time would have been in her forties. She was tall and slim, with frizzy, light brown hair. She wore longish, flowing, flowery dresses and had the mind of a child. She would dance around us and lift her clothes up, showing her underwear. Nearly the whole of Cardiff knew Thelma and she loved to be in town, weaving her way around the people. She would link arms with the men and spin them around.

We would sit in the gardens by the Museum with a sandwich and a drink, and Thelma would join us. She was so vulnerable, and we would tell her she wasn't to keep lifting her clothes up, and then off she would go, dancing in and out of the people.

About this time I had discovered drugs, as they were everywhere. I experimented with speed and LSD. The speed made me hyperactive and I would continually talk, had little appetite and sleep was very difficult. The LSD was powerful and gave a heightened sense of euphoria. I loved my work and once I realised the drugs were not compatible to working life, I only took them at restricted times.

I went to the Isle of Wight Pop Festival to see Jimi Hendrix, Melanie, The Doors, Jethro Tull, Supertramp, Leonard Cohen, Joan Baez and many others. I went regularly to live concerts, travelling all over the country to see such acts as The Rolling Stones, Queen and The Who. There are not many people or groups I haven't seen perform.

I have a deep love of music, and my favourite artist is the late singer Kirsty MacColl, but regrettably I never saw her perform live. I love the way she wrote and sang about life, and I think we can all relate to so many of her lyrics.

Throughout my childhood and into my adult life I was a victim of my emotions and my nurturing instinct was very dominant. I made decisions because I felt sorry for someone, or felt it would be rude to say no. I would react badly when my efforts were not acknowledged or if I felt in my times of need I did not get the same level of commitment back. I never used wisdom to sum up any situation and I would have an inner voice or intuition that would challenge my behaviour and decisions but invariably I ignored it because I was weak and always took the road of least resistance, the easy road. My view on life was totally unrealistic and yet I struggled to see life in any other way and my life choices were starting to cause me considerable pain.

Although I was learning about life, and despite taking drugs, I was still an innocent and still had bad judgement. I was now seventeen and this was when I met Billy. He was the singer in a local rock band. Billy was very thin and full of energy. He was the life and soul of the party, and he and I were instantly attracted. I hadn't really had a proper boy-friend up until this time, but we soon fell in love.

He told me stories of his childhood that immediately aroused my compassion. He had been brought up on a farm in West Wales and was the third of four children. His mother had died when he was five and his father had struggled to keep the farm and home going, as well as raise the children. There were times when Billy and his siblings had to go to a local children's home for short periods, as his father found it difficult to cope. I saw Billy as a person who needed to be loved and looked after, and I set about mothering him. Very quickly he asked me to marry him. I was thrilled and agreed.

I went in my lunch hour to a local department store and bought my own engagement ring. Billy wasn't able to pay for it as he had no money, and he couldn't accompany me as he had things to do. The ring was white gold with artificial stones. I thought it was wonderful.

I soon realised Billy's life was chaotic. For instance, he drove a car and I discovered he had no driving licence, tax or insurance, and he didn't seem able to hold down a job. He appeared to borrow money and never pay it back. He would go to the pub with no cigarettes or money, and then others would have to support his drinking and smoking. Although I was mortified at this, he was completely nonchalant.

I began having second thoughts about being with him, and when he talked of us getting married I was worried, and decided it was not for me. When I told him he was inconsolable, and threatened suicide. He said he couldn't live without me. He begged me to marry him and promised he would be different, and so reluctantly I agreed. I felt sorry for him, and didn't understand he was not my responsibility.

Although having these faults, Billy was multi-talented. He could repair any engine, spray any type of vehicle and was fantastic at DIY and gardening. He seemed able to turn his hand to anything and people really liked him, as he was quite charismatic.

My father lent him money to start his own gardening business, and he had loads of work, but half the time he would be missing. My father was a particularly responsible person with regards to money and obligation. He would recommend friends to use Billy's services, and would be disgusted when Billy would let the friends down as Billy was ducking and diving, usually in and out of the pub.

I was trapped. I had to go ahead with the marriage because Billy was now my responsibility. I had an inner voice that was struggling to be heard, and it was opposed to my decision, but I squashed it. I could not contemplate Billy taking his life; I could never live with those consequences, and I did have feelings of love for him. Whilst Billy was happy for us to live in rented accommodation, I wanted to buy our own house and so my parents loaned us the money for a deposit on a three bedroomed terrace house in Splott.

It was 1971 and I was eighteen and Billy was twenty-three. A few days before the wedding Billy and I went with my parents to the local social club. We played a game of bingo and I said a prayer to God to let me win, as we were desperate for money. I won a house by calling on number twelve, and we were getting married on the twelfth, and this felt really strange. What a coincidence. Inside my head I said 'thank you', in case this was divine intervention.

Before our marriage the gardening business was closed, and Billy went to work as Assistant Manager of a hardware store. I was still working at the solicitors', and when we settled down to married life I worked out a schedule of outgoings that included paying back my parents. It was incredibly hard juggling our finances and it seemed natural I would take responsibility for this.

At this time, just like my mum, I began experiencing sleep paralysis and I found this to be really distressing. I would start to wake from sleep but would be unable to move. I would try to open my eyes and cry out but was frozen and it seemed as though there was someone in the room with me and there would be a weight over my body, as though I was being pinned to my bed.

Also like my mum, at various times I would also see images when my eyes were closed. Also, I used to very often see an eye but mostly it wasn't open and then occasionally it would be partially open. I used to see colour that was fantastically vibrant.

I was also experiencing coincidences and other unexplained happenings that defied reality but I was so limited in my way of thinking I would push them aside as they did not fit into my belief structures.

Looking back I can see how the universe was trying to help me and what was of interest throughout this time was that physical, unexplained things were happening. For instance, at one time I had a call from a friend who was terribly distressed as she had had yet another blazing row with her husband and he had packed his bags and was gone. Even though it was inconvenient to me I said 'I will come now'. I went to grab my car keys and they were gone. They had vanished into thin air. I spent a good half an hour searching the house but to no avail.

Money was very scarce at this time but I scraped the money together for a taxi. When I arrived at my distressed friend's her husband had returned. She opened the door a fraction and whispered to me he was back and she would call me the next day. I had to walk home and I fumed all the way. When I got back to the house there were the keys hanging in their usual place.

My life was a mismatch of experiences and although I was living amongst human dysfunction and tragedy, I was an observer and having experienced no real pain myself, I was cushioned. I had developed dysfunctions of my own and without me knowing these took me down a path where I had to suffer in order to feel the pain, and through my marriage I was going to learn some painful lessons.

After four years of marriage I became pregnant, and our son Kristian was born in 1975. I had worked full-time up until two days before he was born. I couldn't believe this beautiful and perfect Pisces baby belonged to us. It was a wonderful experience for me to be a mother.

Shortly after this Billy was facing redundancy. Encouraged by me, he spoke to the company he worked for and asked if he could become a tenant at one of their shops. We were thrilled when he was offered the tenancy of a shop on the outskirts of Cardiff. I was so proud of him, and couldn't believe how much he had changed. The tenancy was put in our joint names, as we had to take out a loan against our property, but Billy kept me firmly away from the business, even though I felt I could have been an asset doing book-keeping. He was now firmly in control.

It was such a large shop in a busy area, and as well as being a hardware store it also had a grocery and newsagents section. It was really hard work, and nothing was automated in those days. Everyone mostly paid by cash, and the sales would be rung in to the till. I stressed to Billy he would have to be completely organised from day one and offered to help with the administration, but he wouldn't hear of it.

I was aware Billy employed youngsters, but was upset when he started paying them to open up for him early in the morning and organising the newspaper runs. This was because he would get home so late in the nights, very often drunk, and he was finding it difficult to get up in the mornings. I constantly worried whether Billy had tight systems in place. There were no mobile phones in those days, and it soon became apparent Billy was doing the usual ducking and diving. I could never get hold of him. I would phone the shop and youngsters would answer. They would never know where he was.

Kris saw very little of his father, and sometimes Billy would promise to be home early to see Kris before he went to bed. I would tell Kris his daddy would be home, and he would be so excited. Many is the time I have watched my son fall asleep on the settee, having tried to keep himself awake for this magical appearance that never happened.

It was around this time other strange things started to happen once more. I again had the feelings from my childhood, that vague sense of there being something else around me, but that something was not tangible and therefore unexplainable. I started to see objects move, but would doubt what I saw.

For instance, a picture might move back and forth, or a glass would move across the table. Lights would sometimes go on and off as if in code. They seemed to react to my having certain thoughts; it could be I was questioning what I had seen, and on and off they would go. If I were on my own in the room, the television would turn off and then come back on. If someone was in the room with me, it never happened. I also started to see colours regularly on my eyelids when I closed my eyes, and I would also see colours with my eyes open, say on the wall, the floor, ceiling that type of thing.

Although unhappy I didn't contemplate leaving Billy, because being a single parent was not really socially acceptable at that time. Everything appeared so complicated, and I didn't want the stigma of being a single mother. I had such high hopes for Kris and wanted him to have every opportunity to achieve.

In 1977 Kris was nearing two, and we were able to move to an area in Cardiff where the schooling was excellent, as well as being nearer the shop. I reasoned I should be content with my lot, although this was completely at odds with my inner voice, that intuition which was still struggling to emerge.

I didn't feel secure as I had so many questions. For instance, were the young boys opening up at the proper time? How would Billy ever know? It seemed to me the only time he would know would be if a customer complained. Also, were all sales going in the till? On and on the questions would beat in my head, but if I voiced them to Billy, that would be an excuse for him to march out and go to the pub, as he said I was nagging.

I knew I had to get control of my life and so I found Kris a part-time place in a nursery, and got myself part-time work at a firm of solicitors. I was to establish a matrimonial department for them. This was a fantastic opportunity, and I was so happy about it. The solicitor I worked for was on the duty rota at Central Police Station.

One day he was called to represent a man who was to be charged with murdering a local woman. The man was charged and refused bail, and so was on remand in Cardiff Prison. He kept demanding his solicitor visit him, and I would be sent in the solicitor's place. This client had a thick northern accent, and he was in his twenties. He had come out of the army the year before and had wandered around the country.

He quite liked the idea of a young woman visiting him, and one day the prison sent word he wanted to confess to the crime he'd been charged with, but he would only confess to me. I went with my shorthand pad and pencil at the ready. I spent around an hour with him, and what he told me was sickening. Apparently he arrived in Cardiff by train and had no particular reason for visiting the City. He was wandering aimlessly from place to place. He said he was head-shot; feeling totally depressed and was unable to stay with his family.

He found his way to a pub near to the city centre. In the pub he met a young woman who was also homeless. They started asking around the pub if anyone would give them a bed for the night. One of the regulars at the pub was a lonely alcoholic lady. She was a tragic figure, and her life experiences had sent her on a spiral of self-destruction, and she was drinking to dull the pain.

This awful man described to me in detail how he killed this lady who had offered him and his new companion a bed, and sex was part of his motive. I knew he enjoyed telling me this, and I struggled to stay professional, scribbling furiously away on my shorthand pad.

I rushed back to the office to type the statement, and passed it on to the solicitor. He asked me to go back to the prison with him to get the statement signed, but this time I refused. I didn't want to be near such evil.

One of the clients was a man in his forties called Alan. He was a long distance lorry driver. He lived with his wife and child in a house they had bought on mortgage. Alan was a real workaholic, and took his role as provider for the family seriously. He was in a state of shock when his wife told him she wanted a divorce. She alleged the hours he worked were unreasonable, and said she was left to bring up their child virtually single handed. Alan was so distressed about the situation. His wife refused to discuss it with him, and he poured out his anguish to me. He kept repeating he had done nothing wrong, except work long hours to bring in the money.

While the divorce proceedings were going along, Alan came to me in the office and told me he had discovered his wife was having an affair. He had been given an anonymous tip-off about his wife and her relationship with a good friend of the family. Alan sat crying. He felt so injured and couldn't comprehend his wife had lied and schemed.

Apparently, acting on this tip-off, Alan pretended he was working away but in fact had stayed in the area, and was watching his house. He had followed his wife when she left the house, and she went to the friend's home. Alan sat outside for about an hour. Through the window he saw his wife and friend leave the lounge and they obviously walked up the stairs to the front bedroom. The curtains in the front bedroom were then closed and the light went off. Alan left the scene as he had seen enough. He now knew the truth.

He stayed with me in my office for about an hour, and I used every ounce of energy I had to get him stable. He was in such grief and shock, and I was worried. I made him coffee and eventually he pulled himself together.

He hugged me and said he felt better, and told me I wasn't to worry as he would be fine. Two days later he was found in the cab of his lorry. He had gassed himself. I felt bereft and kept going over our meeting, torturing myself. I was one of the last people to have seen him alive. This incident had a profound effect on me for quite a while.

Meanwhile, I started to go out and about on my own, getting a life again. Kris was safe, as he was with my parents at those times. One night I met a young man who was studying civil engineering in Cardiff University, and I began seeing him behind Billy's back and, although this relationship was short-lived, I felt very guilty. I had a fabulous time with my student and this made me all the more discontent at home.

At this time a tragedy happened. Billy's father died suddenly. A few days after his death Billy and I were in our house and we were arguing. A photograph of his father was on top of our television. It came off the television and went through the air to the other side of the room where we were stood, landing at our feet. Billy immediately said 'That's my father, he doesn't want us to argue', and we both sat like a pair of frightened kids. In my mind I thought 'Now there's intelligence with these happenings'.

When my son was around two and a half years of age, my sister asked if I would go out with her that evening. I didn't really want to go, but she persuaded me. I couldn't get hold of my husband to tell him but went ahead and took my son to my parents and then met up with my sister in Cardiff town centre. Walking along the street my sister and I were discussing where to go but couldn't make up our minds. Over the road was a pub called The Philharmonic. We had never been in there before, and at my suggestion we decided to pay a visit.

We bought our drinks, sat at a table, and my sister said to me, 'Yvonne, don't look now because you will never guess who's just walked in'. When I looked, there was my husband stood at the bar with his arms around a young girl, and she was very pregnant. It was unbelievable and I was in total shock, I could not fathom how this life changing coincidence had happened. It was so confusing to see him stood there. I had never heard him mention this pub before, and didn't even know he came to town to drink. I always assumed he drank at a pub near the shop, but could never ask him, as he always denied he did any such thing. I told my sister I wanted to leave without him seeing us. We did this and I went straight home.

I sat in the lounge in a darkened room waiting for Billy to appear. He came in at about one in the morning and jumped out of his skin when he saw me sitting there in the dark. He said 'What the hell are you doing?' and I said 'I have been to the Philharmonic and saw you'. Billy immediately dissolved into tears, and he sobbed and admitted his guilt. He said it was an accident; he didn't love the girl and didn't want the baby, but didn't know what to do. I told him I was leaving and taking Kris with me, and he immediately said he would take his car, drive on the motorway and kill himself. I remember saying to him 'If you do that, please make a good job of it as I will not be sitting at your bedside, and make sure you don't take anyone else with you'.

In my head I thought back to when I'd tried to break off my engagement to him, and he had kept me with him by threatening the same thing. I had an inner knowing that I'd come a long way from that time. I also recognised I didn't love Billy, and had not loved him for a long time.

I was surprised such a massive coincidence had occurred, and how this chain of events had revealed the truth about Billy. Sleeping in the bed on my own that night, I had my eyes closed and saw part of an eye on my eyelids. I tried to bring this eye in to focus, but it kept disappearing. Eventually I fell asleep.

I later found out my husband and the young lady, who was obviously his girlfriend, had never been in that pub before. He was devastated I had caught him out and was initially insistent that I had him under surveillance. He honestly believed he could lead a double life and get away with it, he was that certain of my gullibility.

Even then I did not appreciate how the universe had orchestrated this event and how much effort must had gone into influencing all concerned to meet at a central point, but it is a fact that because of this huge coincidence, at the age of twenty four and after six years of marriage I became a single mother to my wonderful son. We carried on our journey together and things settled down and we had a good life, with plenty of crazy, unexplained things continuing to happen.

Billy was distraught I'd found him out. He couldn't pull himself together, and would beg and plead for me to stay. I told him I wanted the house sold and my name taken off the shop. He came out fighting, and said he had nothing all his life, he had worked really hard and was not about to have me take it all away. One minute he was nasty, the next he was crying and pleading. He was manipulating me emotionally and I began to feel sorry for him, and also felt guilty that I had been seeing someone without him knowing.

These feelings led me to agree to sign over the house and business to him, in exchange for the sum of £3,000. I knew all about the divorce laws and what I was entitled to, but I agreed this sum out of compassion and guilt. I was in fact entitled to double that amount, but by accepting the lesser sum it meant Billy could keep the house and business. It never occurred to me Billy wasn't interested in how Kris and I would manage. It was all about him and how he would manage.

I bought a run down and neglected two bedroomed-terraced house in Roath, Cardiff, which cost me about £6,000. I had difficulty getting a mortgage, as in those days single mothers were not looked on as viable, but through my legal contacts I achieved this. Kris and I were out of the old house within twelve weeks of everything happening.

2.3 Taking the easy road

The reality of day-to-day living in my new circumstances began to sink in. I had agreed Billy could have reasonable access to Kris, and he agreed to pay maintenance to Kris and me at the rate of £7 per week each. With my legal work and the maintenance we would just about manage.

At this time I had a visit in work from a lady called Debbie. I was told she was in reception with a baby in her arms, but I didn't know who she was. When she was shown into my office I recognised her as the pregnant girl Billy had been with. I was flabbergasted. I asked her what she wanted, and she said she didn't really know, but she and her baby were on their way to a hostel. She knew where I worked and felt compelled to come to me. I asked her why she wasn't going to live with Billy in his house, and she said he told her the house was now mine. Apparently her parents had told her to choose between them and Billy. She could go home to them with the baby if she would finish with him, but she was in love with him and so refused. I couldn't believe what I was hearing, and again all those feelings of compassion and nurture came to the fore, this time for Debbie and her baby. I still had the keys to Billy's house, and I asked my boss if I could leave work early, to which he agreed. I took

Debbie and the baby to a local shop to buy provisions, and then I drove them to Billy's house. I let them in, made them comfortable and phoned Billy. When he knew what I had done he was outraged, and said he would never forgive me.

My divorce from Billy took place in 1978. Over the next few months Billy would pick Kris up on a Sunday and they would have a really good time. The only down side was very often Billy wouldn't have the maintenance money.

I would have to argue with him in front of Kris, and it used to spoil the occasion. I quickly realised I couldn't regard Billy's money as disposable income, and so looked for something to supplement my earnings.

A good friend of mine called June was working at party plan selling pottery, and so I joined her and became an agent working some evenings and weekends. It was a good thing I did because shortly afterwards Billy didn't turn up on his regular Sunday visit. There was no phone call from him, or any other attempt at communication. Kris had his little bag packed to go swimming, and he was devastated. He was three years of age and was making all sorts of excuses for his father. He said things like 'Perhaps daddy has forgotten our address,' and 'Perhaps daddy is ill'. Kris was never to see his father again. I found out through friends Billy had taken off to Spain. He had split from Debbie, sold the house to a friend of his, and handed the tenancy of the shop back to the company.

We never received another penny in maintenance, even though eventually I was told Billy was back in the UK, and was living once again in West Wales. I would never have attempted to collect the money due from him, reasoning if he couldn't give it with a good heart, then we didn't want it. Kris repeatedly asked had I heard from Billy, was there a letter from him or perhaps a telephone call? His behaviour became quite aggressive at times, and I knew my poor son was hurting, and I was hurting for him.

During the next three years our lives were happy. I was working two jobs, and was fortunate enough to have my parents as unpaid baby sitters. Kris was a joy. He was such a loving child. He was a very practical and hands-on little person, and from two years of age he used to bath himself and wash his own hair. When my friends Mary and Tony's little boy Nathan came to stay, Kris would also bath Nathan and wash his hair and then go on to dry and dress both of them.

At that age Kris could even make a cup of tea. If you gave Kris a tool kit and an old alarm clock, he would be in his element. I used to give him wood and he would cut and hammer, experimenting with joints. He was six when he changed his first plug. My mother gave him the job to do for her, and I couldn't believe he'd done it.

In February 1981, on Kris's sixth birthday, a party was in full swing in the house, and there was a knock on the door. Kris answered, and there stood a taxi man with a box of toys. He told Kris they were from his father. The excitement was high as Kris and his friends unpacked the box, and I watched my son's reaction closely. He seemed fine and really pleased with the presents. When everybody went he sat on my lap, sucking his thumb and said 'If Billy sends presents again, will you take them to the children's home?' and I said 'Why Kris?' and he said 'Because he didn't bring them himself'. I couldn't grasp a six-years-old child could think on such a deep level, and looking at my son I felt humbled. How had Billy and I ever produced a child such as this?

Later that evening Kris and I were tidying up. One of the presents Billy had sent was a fishing rod. A hook from the rod was on the floor, and as I picked it up the hook went through my thumb. There was a barb on the end, and there was no way I could get the hook out. Kris and I went to the local casualty department. As we were standing at the counter, a blonde lady came up to me and said 'Are you Yvonne?' and I told her I was. She said 'I am Debbie's mother. She is over there, and has just pointed you out to me. I want to ask you a question that's been on my mind for a long time. Did my daughter break up your marriage?' and I told her 'No', and I said she was not to worry about that. I went and spoke with Debbie and saw her child, but had a really strange feeling. That inner voice was there again, and I began to think of the possibility that this sequence of events was no coincidence.

During the next year Kris and I moved house twice, firstly to a larger house directly across the road from us, and then to a three bedroomed house very close to my parents. I was proud of what we were achieving on our own. Our homes had always been happy and there were always other people's kids there. Sometimes Kris would have up to four children sleeping over. I had a good circle of friends and they would always come to me in a crisis. I always seemed to know what they should do, and was very quick to help and, in fact, would give over and above what was required of me. I am a very positive person and could infuse my friends with my positive way of looking at things.

I was also dating various people, but most of them I kept away from my son. I had let one boyfriend get close, but had quickly realised that again I had poor judgement, and broke off my relationship with him. That inner voice was at last getting through to me.

I had left my job at the solicitor's because my salary was quite low, and I was also feeling weary of the emotional nature of the job. I found an excellent position working as a PA to the Managing Director of a marketing company, as well as doing the party plan. Between the two jobs I was earning really good money, it was 1982 and Kris was seven.

It was winter time and the snow was thick. I was walking to work with great difficulty and a man driving a large four-by-four vehicle stopped and offered me a lift. I recognised him from around the area. I was grateful to accept and he introduced himself as Michel. Michel was a first generation Italian. He came to Cardiff when he was two-years of age, along with his elder brother Paolo and their mum and dad. He was a real ladies' man, and immediately made a play for me. He looked up my telephone number in the directory and began calling me on the telephone and I was terribly flattered, but after a couple of days of his attention, and as a result of his asking me out, I asked him if he was married.

He replied, 'Yes I am, but what has that got to do with you coming for a drink with me?' I was so disappointed and also quite offended, and my tone relayed this to him. He then left me alone.

About six months later I bumped into him. He immediately asked me out again, and when I reminded him he was a married man he said, 'Well that is where you're wrong. My wife has left me for another man and I could really do with someone to talk to'. He told me he was in a bad way emotionally. My instinct was he was distasteful to me, despite a physical attraction, but he said he was hurting and so I felt sorry for him. I met him and we had a nice couple of hours together, and I told him I thought his difficulties were karma, 'what goes around comes around'. He had been very willing to meet with me while married, and his wife had gone a step further. He wouldn't accept this, and said his actions with me were a symptom of their failing marriage, but he hadn't realised why the marriage was failing until it was too late. He talked a good story, but my inner voice was now working and I was having none of it.

When I left I wished him well, but made it clear I wouldn't be seeing him again. He called me over the next week, but I was quite non-communicative. One day I arrived home and there he was on my doorstep. I was really irritated by this, but his eyes filled with tears, and he said he just needed to talk. This set the pattern for the next few weeks. Sometimes I would be quite rude to him and tell him I was busy, but I felt so guilty when he walked away. He would look so miserable.

One time he asked me out, but I refused his offer and I told him I was meeting my friend June. She and I regularly went to a wine bar. We were in the bar having a drink and in walked Michel. He came straight over to me. I asked him what he was doing there and he said 'I only came to buy you both a drink, can't I even do that?' He bought us a drink, but I let him know he was intruding. He was so pushy, and I wasn't comfortable with it. When Michel called at the house Kris would sometimes be there, and he was lovely with Kris. This was something in his favour.

Two awful events happened at this time. We were given devastating news. My mother's youngest sister Maureen had cancer. She had been unwell for a while, and when she eventually had an exploratory operation, it was discovered she had bowel cancer. Her bowel was removed and she had a colostomy bag. She was only forty-eight. While Maureen was in hospital recovering from the operation, my grand-mother Beatty died. She had heart failure. We were all inconsolable. My mother was distraught and poor Maureen had to be told. I remember rushing to my Nana's house when I heard she had collapsed, and seeing her lying on the floor. My cousins and my mum were there, and it was awful. When my Nan was taken to the funeral home, I went to do her makeup, as she always liked to look nice. I felt no fear, and had an inner knowing I could talk to her and she would hear.

Maureen came home to a very different house than the one she had left. My Nan had always been there, and it must have been so traumatic for her. She was desperately ill. My poor mother was falling to pieces and couldn't cope with the loss of her mum, and her sister's obvious decline. The months went by and Maureen was struggling to survive. I had a thought in my mind that wouldn't go away. Something kept telling me Maureen would die on Kris's birthday.

In 1983 we celebrated Kris's eighth birthday at home, and my mother was with us when Emrys called to say Maureen had taken a turn for the worse. My mum and I rushed to the house. Maureen was clawing the air, fighting for breath. There was oxygen on hand, but now it had no effect. I sat in a chair and tried to reach her with my mind. I was saying 'Please Maureen stop fighting, let go, let go'. I was also speaking to my Nan in my mind, asking her to come for Maureen. I didn't know if any of this would do any good, but it felt right to do it.

All the family were with Maureen when she took her last breath. She was such a fantastic and loving lady and her husband and four children were distraught. It was such a relief she'd gone and would have no more suffering but I was stunned it had happened on Kris's birthday, just as I'd thought.

I went home crying and exhausted. In the night I was woken by my aunt's voice very softly calling my name, 'Von, Von'. I shouted 'Where are you?', but no answer came back. On my eyelids were beautiful colours of purple, and then changing to lime green, and then back to purple.

After my aunt's death I became ill. When I was fifteen my appendix had burst, and as a result of poison escaping into my system, I suffered with cysts on the ovaries. I had two previous operations to remove cysts, and I recognised the symptoms. It was so upsetting to be told by the specialist that I had to be admitted to hospital immediately. This would place a real burden on my parents. My sister would help out, but they would have Kris full-time. My mother was still very distressed over her mother and sister's death, and Michel came to the rescue. He insisted he could make life easier. He said he would liaise with my mother and help out. Telling Kris what was happening was less traumatic, as I was able to assure him Michel would bring him to see me constantly. Michel also gave Kris the incentive of visits to the park on the way home from the hospital. My mother was grateful for this help, and so now my attitude towards Michel changed. I had become indebted to him.

Michel was as good as his word, and displayed a real caring side to his nature. Kris was in and out of the hospital, always happy and laughing, telling me where Michel had taken him. When my parents visited, they would express their gratitude that Michel was such a help.

When I came home from hospital Michel presented me with tickets for a one-week holiday for the two of us in France. It was all paid for, and my parents had already agreed they would take care of Kris. I felt uneasy about that, but it was done. I could not turn him down, after all it was a generous gesture, and he had paid for the holiday in advance. I had only ever been to Jersey, and so visiting France was lovely, but I wouldn't have chosen to go. My wonderful son had been away from me too long, and I would have preferred to be with him, or taken him with us. Also my parents deserved a break, and so I carried quite a bit of guilt to France.

Michel and I came back from the holiday a proper couple. That inner voice was still shouting but I reluctantly ignored it. I had been treated like a princess by Michel, but he had also made me feel responsible for him. He had the opportunity to pour out all his unhappiness, and he took full advantage. He told me he loved me, and wanted to be with me. He wanted us to live together and I agreed. There was no going back, I was in too deep. He was manipulating me by playing on my emotions, and I had started to feel sorry for him, and the mothering instinct was rearing its ugly head.

After our holiday, I went for a night out with my sister. We met up with a few other people, and coincidently one of them was Michel's boss's wife. The wife asked me who was looking after Kris, and I said Michel. She asked why he was looking after Kris, and I told her we had been seeing one another for a while. She abruptly stood up, said something to her friend, and both of them left. I was astonished. What had I done? Her departure was so rude. My sister and I could not understand. I went home and told Michel and he didn't make much of a comment.

The next day I got a call from his boss. Apparently Michel and the boss's wife had been having an affair, and his wife didn't know about my relationship with Michel. The boss said his wife blurted this out to him on her return home from the previous night. She told him Michel had stopped seeing her a few months before, and she couldn't understand why but, after meeting me, she had her answer. Michel's boss was devastated and out for Michel's blood, and I was equally devastated. The boss and his wife split up shortly after.

I told Michel I never wanted to speak to him again. He cried, begged and pleaded, but I would have none of it. Unbeknown to me he begged my sister to meet him. She did, and he really sold himself to her. He told her when his wife left him he had been in a terrible state, and the boss's wife had consoled him, and in a moment of weakness he had given in to temptation. He said as soon as he started going out with me he had stopped seeing her, but she was like a stalker and he was frightened of her, and so hadn't told her about seeing me.

I was in a terrible state because of what had happened. I let myself be persuaded Michel had acted out of character, even though my inner voice was trying to caution me. It seemed such a huge thing to keep him out of our lives, when all of us had already bonded. I can make no excuses for my weakness, and looking back I shudder with distaste at the person I was then. Michel kept working in the same place and had no problem seeing his boss, the man he had betrayed, every day.

Michel was living alone in the home he had once shared with his wife. She was pressing him for her share of the property, and so he decided to sell it. We were going to pool our money together and buy a larger house for the three of us. He got a buyer for the house very quickly, and he and his wife decided who would have what furniture. He was to replace some of my furniture with his furniture, and that way both of us would feel at home whilst temporarily living in my home. The sale went through, and we had a busy time sorting through his belongings. When he was firmly moved in, he dropped a bombshell. He had no money! Apparently his outgoings had been more than his income and he was heavily in debt. He had to pay off a load of debt, leaving him with no money. I couldn't believe it.

Kris was so excited Michel had moved in, and I felt I couldn't ask Michel to leave, and once again circumstances in my life seemed very complicated, and my character was so weak. I couldn't bear to take the hard road and finish our relationship as I should have done.

I still wanted to move house and Michel wanted us to buy a place together. If this was to happen I insisted Michel had to agree to have the value of the new house apportioned, to take into account the money I would be investing. He didn't want to do this, and we rowed bitterly. That inner voice was struggling to be heard again, and I was half listening. I reasoned if I protected Kris and me financially, then it would be all right to stay with Michel. He was so attentive and loving and Kris was really happy, and I was so very weak.

Meanwhile unbeknown to me Michel had been applying for jobs in different parts of the country. Working alongside his boss was becoming increasingly difficult as, although Michel had no problem with the situation, the boss understandably wanted him out. Michel was a Facilities Manager and was good at his job. It didn't take him long to get an offer from a company in Bristol. Once he had the offer he sat me down and told me of the opportunity. He wanted us to move near to Bristol and had details of property for sale in the Chepstow area, which is near to the Severn Bridge that links Wales and England. Chepstow is on the Welsh side and Bristol is on the English side of the bridge. Chepstow is approximately thirty miles from Cardiff. It would mean I would have to leave my jobs, as the hours would not fit around our family life, but the idea was compelling as it would be a fresh start for all of us.

We moved within the year, and I had my way with the apportionment of the property. I owned sixty percent, and Michel owned forty percent. This apportionment would carry over to every house we lived in. If the relationship fell apart Kris and I wouldn't lose out financially. Michel was really unhappy about this.

Our new home in Chepstow was lovely and the facilities in the area were wonderful. Kris loved his new school and was thriving. I found work as a sales executive, selling and merchandising designer sunglasses for a London based fashion house. Our family and friends in Cardiff were only half an hour car journey away and so we saw everyone weekly.

We lived in that house for five years, and mostly they were happy times. We had acquired a rescue dog, a black Labrador called Lucky, and we all adored her. A couple of years before we had also acquired a cat we called Blue, and Lucky and Blue kept us all laughing, as they constantly vied with each other for attention.

Eventually we decided to move, and began to look for what we thought of as our dream home. We had been searching and searching for the right house, and eventually saw a likely prospect. It was a beautiful detached house, in a lovely setting, and in the same area as we were already living, but it needed so much work. Michel fell in love with it, but I told him it was too much for us to take on. He argued and cajoled. He said he could do all the work himself. I reminded him he detested DIY, and said I thought it would cause problems between us, but he persuaded me, against my better judgement. He said, 'I promise you I will do all the work myself, and I will not complain'. So that was it, the legal wheels were put in motion for us to buy the house.

Before the move I had a birthday, and Michel was to take me out for a special meal. I was so excited and when I got home from work, set about getting myself ready. When Michel came in he had a face like thunder. 'What's wrong?' I asked, 'Nothing's wrong, why should there be?' he said, 'Because you have a face like thunder' I replied. 'If you are going to start,

I am out of here' he said, and that was it. He walked out and took off in his car. I waited and waited, but he didn't come home that night. It was unbelievable; once again I was in a state of confusion, with the inner voice struggling for dominance.

The next day he came home with a present and a card for me. He said he was sorry about the night before, but the stress of the move was getting to him. I was so hurt, but didn't have the strength to argue with him. I felt so uneasy with that inner voice tugging at me constantly.

We moved to the new house in September 1989, and it was in a worse state than we first thought. The place was filthy. We had to take all the carpets up, and the curtains came down, because of the smell in the house. We set about cleaning, stripping walls, preparing paintwork and we employed an electrician and a plasterer. We were both continuing to work full time, and so we were tired. Kris and I would have music on whilst working away in the evenings and on weekends, but Michel was in a foul mood. He would complain we were making a noise, and say he didn't want us doing any of the painting as we would make a mess. He was making life quite unpleasant.

After a month Michel asked if I would mind if he played tennis on the Saturday, he said he thought he deserved a break. I agreed and said for him to enjoy himself. He left Saturday morning at about eight, and said he would be back after lunch, around two. He arrived home about ten at night and said 'Sorry I'm late' and I said 'Sorry isn't good enough'. He said 'Oh f--- off then' and I said 'No, you f--- off', and he did. He went upstairs, emptied all his belongings into black bags, loaded up his car without a word to me, and drove off. I was stood in a house that had no carpets or curtains, the electrics weren't finished, and it was cold. I was in shock and sobbed and sobbed. Luckily Kris was with my parents.

Over the next few days I didn't tell anyone Michel had left. I kept thinking he would come back. I hadn't heard from him, and didn't want to start ringing around looking for him. It was so humiliating. Kris kept asking for him, and I would say he had gone away with work. I had to put on a brave face.

After about two weeks I was starting to admit defeat and began to worry about the mortgage payments. Would he pay his share, and how would I manage? I called in an estate agent, with the idea of putting the house on the market, but was shocked to hear it had gone down in value because of its unfinished state, even though a lot of work had already been done.

This presented a big problem for me. I was working out our finances, and realised if the house was sold I couldn't afford to stay in the area. Kris was now in high school and I wanted him to stay where he was. If I wasn't careful I would have a repeat performance of what happened when Billy and I had split up, and Kris and I would find ourselves back where we had started.

By now, Kris was aware something was wrong, and so I had to tell him Michel had left. I couldn't believe his reaction. He cried and cried, and made himself ill. I had to have the doctor to the house, as his throat was so swollen. He had tonsillitis and just laid on the settee in an unfinished room, wrapped in blankets in utter misery. I had to swallow my pride and ring Michel at work. He answered the phone and when he knew it was me, his manner was completely hostile. I told him we needed to talk, and he said he would call around that evening. I then had to tell my parents what had happened, and they came and took Kris home with them.

Michel called to the house, and he was so aggressive. He told me he was sick of me and said nothing he ever did was good enough. There were lots and lots of allegations made by him, and I couldn't relate to what he was saying. We seemed to be living in two different worlds. Who was this person he was talking about? I asked him if he was coming back, and he said 'no'. I found myself begging him, and telling him I would do anything he wanted to make things better. He said he would think about it. I asked him where he was staying, and he said the name of a friend of his from the tennis club. Michel didn't realise, but I knew this person through the legal world, and he was a solicitor.

We agreed Michel would call me the next day with his decision. Two days passed and I didn't hear from him. Plucking up courage I rang his friend's number and asked to speak to Michel. 'Sorry but he's out at the moment' his friend said, and I asked him to tell Michel I had called. A few hours later Michel turned up at the house with his belongings.

From the moment Michel moved back, my inner voice was active and gave me no peace. Once again, when I was in bed and my eyes were closed, I saw an eye on my eyelids. This time it was clearer and the eye was half open. Christmas was approaching and I sat Michel down and said to him 'I know you're having an affair'. He looked shocked. 'Don't be so ridiculous' was his reply. I was so calm and certain, but I couldn't tell you how or why. I said to him 'If you have any feelings for me, you will tell me the truth', but he continued to deny my allegations. I told him 'I will catch you out', and he replied I was 'losing it'.

Christmas Eve we were meeting up with my family for a meal in a local pub. When it was Michel's turn to buy drinks, although there was a bar in the room where we were sat, he went to the downstairs bar. This was where the telephone was. I saw my father get up and walk down the stairs. He came back up, and I heard him tell my mother Michel was on the phone. A little later Michel returned with the drinks and I just watched him.

I had long-term friends who were Shirley and her husband Tony, and Kim and her husband Chris. I had worked with Shirley years before and Kim was Shirley's daughter. Tony and Shirley lived in Tintern, which is an area very close to Chepstow. Christmas morning the four of them came around to our house for a drink. When the first drinks were poured Michel said he was going out to buy more mixers. I told him there was plenty and he needn't worry. A little later Michel said he felt like smoking a cigar, and was off to the shop to buy some. Tony said 'It's Christmas day Michel. I think you should stay with your family'. Michel told Tony to mind his own business, and reached across to pick up his car keys. Tony clasped Michel's wrist and said 'Put the keys down'. I was stunned; it was as though there was an unspoken communication between all of us. I had honestly not voiced my feelings or suspicions to anyone. Michel backed off, and by the time our four guests were leaving, other guests were arriving for lunch, and it was as though the crisis was over. Michel became the perfect host.

The next day was Boxing Day and we spent this with Michel's family in Cardiff. When we left them we went for a walk with the dog. I said to Michel, 'I think you should come clean and tell me what's going on'. He refused. I told him, 'I promise you I will find out the truth, but it will be much better coming from you'. He did not deny there was anything going on but unkindly said 'Prove it'. I kept up the pretext of happy families until the celebrations were over but once they were over I knew what I had to do. My inner voice was telling me to look in Michel's car. Kris was to sleep at my parents' the night after Boxing Day, and Michel was taking him. I hid Michel's car keys so he had to take my car.

Immediately he was gone I went to his car. In the boot I found a card with the name Pam on the envelope. On the front of the card was a latticed window with the profiles of two lovers outlined in the window. The inscription said 'To Pam with much love M'. There was a present wrapped in Christmas paper. I opened it and found a little box with a powder puff on the top, and a bottle of cheap perfume inside. Despite feeling sick inside, I had to laugh at his choice of present. Pam was obviously no high-maintenance lady.

Michel came back to find me sitting on the sofa with the card and present to Pam next to me. 'I am allowed to have friends', was his cold reaction. I told him 'Get your things and get out'. He said he wouldn't go, and I told him he had no choice. I rang Shirley and she came straight around and sat with me while Michel collected his things. He left the house with a real attitude, and showed not one ounce of remorse. I took his betrayal very badly and his behaviour fuelled feelings of inferiority in me.

The next day I called my parents and told them what had happened. I had to tell Kris what had happened as he sensed something was wrong. I reassured him we would be fine and asked him not to worry. My father brought him home later and told me Kris had been crying in the car. My father asked Kris what was wrong, and my wonderful eleven-year-old son told him 'I'm all right Bamp, I'm not crying for me I'm crying for my mother'.

Over the next few weeks I set about taking control of my life. I rang Michel's tennis friend and told him I knew he had given Michel an alibi, and I wanted him to know I knew. I told him I believed in karma and wished for him what he deserved, and I would leave it up to the universe to decide what that was.

I again had the house valued and this time, although I would still be losing money, I decided I had no other option. The estate agent couldn't put the house on the market without Michel's agreeing. Pam lived in Cardiff and I roughly knew the area she lived in and so Shirley and I drove there to see if we could see his car. As we turned on to the estate, there was Michel coming towards us. What a coincidence, it was incredible, the hairs on my arms stood up. I felt I had been led to him. The estate was like a rabbit warren, with quite a few different means of entry and exit. What were the chances of that happening, and the timing, it was stunning. Michel saw us and stopped his car. I got Shirley to go and speak to him. She was gone for ages, and when she came back she told me Michel was in a terrible state. He couldn't stop crying and was begging her to speak to me. He wanted to come back. That was a complete turn around. I couldn't take it in.

Shirley and I drove to a shopping area for coffee, and we were sat in the window of the café and Michel walked past. He locked eyes with me and gave me an imploring look. I looked away. He stayed staring at me, and tears started running down his face. I was sickened and told Shirley he hadn't shed a tear when Kris and I were hurt, but now he hurt he was crying, and he was crying for himself.

Michel refused to put the house on the market, and the message he gave me was 'We can work things out'. Even though he was staying with Pam he would phone and beg me to take him back. He then started to appear at the door, and would ask if he could do anything for me. Sometimes I would call the dog and say she needed walking, other times I might tell him the rubbish needed to go out. He would do any chores I asked.

Two months went by and I became ill, the old symptoms of ovarian cysts appeared. I couldn't believe my luck. How would I manage with Kris, the animals, hospital and money? I told Michel if he really wanted to try again he had to tell Pam in front of me he wanted to be with me. In the end he telephoned her from our house, and I listened on the extension. Kris didn't want him back, and said he couldn't forgive him for hurting me. I persuaded him that for now it was the best course of action.

Michel moved back into the house, and two days later Pam rang me. She wanted to talk, and I knew now was my opportunity to find out the truth. It emerged Pam and Michel had a relationship all through his marriage. She said when Michel's marriage broke down she was elated, and thought Michel would be with her. She then stopped hearing from him. Apparently Michel and Pam met up again three years after he and I had moved in to the first home we had bought together. She confirmed the night of my birthday, when Michel had stormed out, he was with her. They had stayed at a hotel together and she said this was because she didn't want Michel taking me out. So there it was, I wanted to know the truth and I had it. I could make no more excuses for any decision I made in the future. I now knew what he was. I felt absolutely worthless.

The day Pam rang I had an appointment at the hospital. I was told by the consultant I needed a complete hysterectomy, and I was booked to have the procedure in two weeks' time. My life had turned into a hell. I would lie awake going over everything in my mind, constantly thinking what to do for the best. I believed my present poor health was as a result of the stress I was under, and I vowed to never go there again. I knew it was my own fault, I had been given plenty of warning as to Michel's real character, and I hadn't listened.

Michel was being the model partner and father, but Kris and I were cautious. My first priority was to my son, but he was coping really well. He and I had turned a corner, and our emotions were no longer raw. It was like as though a spell had been lifted, and we had the upper hand in the situation. I became absolutely calculating. I did myself a checklist of for and against staying with Michel, and I sat with Kim and went over the list. I valued her input more than anyone else's. We both agreed my main concern was Kris and his schooling, and to achieve my aims I needed Michel's income. There was a side to Michel that was fantastic, and when that side was dominant he made life so easy.

I sat with Michel and recounted to him everything Pam had told me. He cried the whole time. I told Michel I would work with him to rebuild our relationship, but the rules had changed. I said I needed constant reassurance from him, as I no longer trusted him, and if I wanted proof of anything he told me, then proof I had to have. He would have agreed to anything he was so desperate to stay.

A couple of days after the talk with Michel, my childhood friend Mary told me Pam worked part-time in her sister's pub, and her sister told Mary that Michel was often in the pub and was regarded as Pam's partner. This all seemed unbelievable and I started shouting and laying down the law, but still I didn't walk away.

2.4 Suffer it and grow

Time went by, I had my hysterectomy and Michel was a brilliant nurse. When I was back to full health I went back to work and our lives continued. Kris sat his GCSE school exams and achieved good passes in all the subjects he sat. This meant we could now move out of the area, as we were no longer tied to schooling. Kris could continue his education in a college in Cardiff. We had both decided we wanted to return to our roots and leave all the bad memories behind. Kris and I would discuss this when we were alone, and Michel was not a consideration.

One day I was visiting with Kim and Chris at their lovely home in Cyncoed in Cardiff. We took the dogs for a walk and on the walk we saw a beautiful house that was for sale. It obviously needed to have work done to it, but it was opposite open fields and woods and it really was perfect for us. I loved it and immediately took Kris to see it. He loved the house as well. I told Michel that Kris and I wanted to move from Chepstow and had seen a house we wanted to buy in Cardiff. Michel said it sounded a great idea, and then I dropped the bombshell that we had not discussed Michel coming with us.

Michel was devastated at this and cried bitterly. He pleaded with Kris and me to include him in our plans, and was very forceful in persuading us he had changed. After lengthy discussions between the three of us we agreed we would stay together as a family. Kris gave me the deciding vote, saying he would go along with what ever I wanted, as Michel no longer had an effect on him. We put our house up for sale and began negotiations to buy the new house. We immediately got a buyer for our house. It was in my mind I could still back out of our agreement with Michel and get away from him.

I recognised I was quite cowardly and would always give in to Michel's distress but I half thought if I made the decision at the last moment, then there would be little time for emotions. Perhaps that way I could make the break. I am sure Michel sensed my thoughts, as he was just wonderful during this time. He would become very emotional about the past, crying and saying he nearly lost me and Kris, and he would never forgive himself for his behaviour.

Once again the dreaded nurturing feeling overcame me, and I felt sorry for him. I was starting to recognise my pattern of behaviour. I could only come out fighting in response to a hurt, but once the hurt was over there would be no fight in me. My character had a huge flaw in it and I recognised this and was sickened by it, but instead of leaving him I prayed.

I didn't know who or what I was praying to, as I had long ago relinquished religion, but I gave a plea to the universe. 'If there is anyone there, please help me. If Michel ever betrays me again, please let me be in a position, both emotionally and financially, to stand on my own two feet, so I can leave him behind'.

We moved from our old house into a rented flat in Cardiff. This was a temporary arrangement as we were paying a builder to do the necessary work to the new house. I was not going the DIY route again. Walls had to come down, arches were created, and outhouses turned into a utility room. A new kitchen and bathroom was installed, as well as fitted wardrobes in all bedrooms. Everywhere was decorated. Fitted carpets and made to measure curtains completed the transformation. It was a dream home. I was so proud. Kris loved it, for him it was paradise. There was so much room and the views were fantastic, as the house was elevated.

Shortly after moving to our new home, my childhood friend Beverly and her husband Howard visited. They mentioned they were buying a parcel-delivery franchise but needed a partner to match their investment and be responsible for marketing the business. I felt this was a timely opportunity for me. I had money I could call on, and there had been a thread of marketing all through my working career. Michel was not happy for me to do this but I saw the possibility of achieving financial freedom for Kris and I, should we ever need it.

This might be part of the answer to my prayer regarding Michel and his future behaviour. The first indication there was a problem between my friend and her husband came when we had just opened the business and she said to me, 'If a woman called Mandy rings asking for Howard, please will you tell me about it?'. 'Why?' I asked. 'Well she has been stalking him,' was the reply. Oh dear, there goes that inner voice.

The transport industry is really no place for a woman, except in the office. The front end of the business involves long hours and manual labour. The workforce is predominantly male, and you need their respect and co-operation to make things work. This was Howard's domain. I was quite happy in the back office, which was my domain. Beverly would be in and out of the office, and constantly checking up on Howard over the radio system when he would be out delivering goods. From the beginning, during his time out of the office, Howard would be ducking and diving. I found myself in the middle of a domestic dispute, and I was involved because his disappearing would have an impact on the business. If he was working a particular area and you couldn't give him instructions for delivery and collections, then it created a problem and service levels would drop.

Beverly eventually confided the area Howard had allocated for himself to work was the area Mandy lived. When Howard's mobile bill came, there were pages upon pages of a number not known to me, but identified by Beverly as Mandy's. So there it was, Beverly had her proof Howard was probably playing away, but where did that leave me? Beverly said she would sort it, but all that happened was increased ducking and diving by Howard, and more surveillance by Beverly.

I was in the office one day and a man entered and introduced himself as Eddie, Mandy's husband. He showed me documentation from Companies House stating Mandy and Howard had recently formed a limited company, and were operating a parcel-delivery franchise. Eddie said he was alerted when he discovered his wife had forged his signature to re-mortgage their home. She had used this money to buy the franchise she and Howard were operating.

The penny then dropped, everything was sliding in to place. I thought of the form Howard had devised for me to fill in when I went on a sales call. The form required in-depth detail, listing all the visited company's details, their parcel movement, who was servicing them, the rates they were paying and the rate I was quoting.

Howard was passing this information to Mandy, I was doing all the leg work and Mandy could then walk in and compete against my quote. He was also delivering and collecting goods on behalf of his other company, but utilising our vehicles and other resources. Our business was subsidising his other business overheads. I had difficulty understanding the logic of this but it was a fact, and it defied logic.

What a fool I was. Over and over again people played me, and I was sick to my stomach. Mandy's husband left and I telephoned Beverly. She came to the office, and I told her what had happened. She didn't show much of a reaction to my news. I explained I couldn't work with her husband, as you needed trust for a partnership. I asked her to get Howard to give me my money back and I could leave them to it. 'Leave it to me', she said.

The next day I went to work, Howard was there and told me none of what I'd been told was true. I told him I'd seen the proof. He said Mandy's husband had forged documentation. I said 'So if I go to Companies House and do a search, I won't find what he showed me?' He said 'Well all I have done is offer a friend help, but the business is nothing to do with me'. I was getting nowhere.

I was desperately trying to listen to my inner voice and felt compelled, when I had the opportunity, to call the franchise head office, even though I knew once I had done this there was no going back. As franchisees Howard and I were bound by rules and regulations. I spoke to the Operations Director, and was stunned to be told they knew what Howard was doing and, in fact, were looking for a replacement franchisee. They were on the verge of taking the business away from us. They had received complaints about the service levels in our area and also had an anonymous tip-off about Howard being a director of the other business, which was in violation of our Franchise Agreement.

The Operations Director visited me that evening. He told me I could take over the franchise. If I didn't want that, then I would lose the money I had invested. I agreed to go it alone, and felt really strong in my decision.

Howard and Beverly were bitter about losing their money, and neither wanted to take responsibility for what had happened. Howard refused to admit his guilt, and Beverly was aiding and abetting him. I hardened my heart to them and got on with running the business.

As I have explained, this was no business for a woman, and I struggled to familiarise myself with the running of the front end of the operation. I would be in work for quarter to six every morning, and not leave until about eight in the evening. Some of the men in my employ were Howard supporters, and did their utmost to sabotage my efforts. I had to let them go, and re-employ almost a new workforce.

I was becoming really hard when I needed to be. It was 1991 and Kris was sixteen and could look after himself; he proved a real asset at home. Michel was very supportive, and eventually started to open the business for me, and would then go on to his own job in Bristol. This enabled me to arrive at eight-thirty. Whilst there Michel would supervise the unloading of the parcels to be delivered, make up runs for the drivers and issue instructions for their day. I would organise and run the office, be out and about selling, do the accounts and have overall responsibility for the whole operation.

The more the business grew, the greater the problems became. There would be more money in, but increased overheads going out and, of course, at this time the country was in recession. Customers were demanding we cut their rates more and more, as other companies competing for their business were offering the same service for less money. Running the business exposed parts of my nature I didn't know was there, and they weren't always attractive. Cash flow was a problem, and I was constantly telling half-truths to the suppliers. I had to wear a mask and act positive in front of the staff and customers, always giving an image of control. If anyone in the business stepped out of line I could be deadly, and customers who didn't pay their bills on time had to run for cover.

I was dealt a crippling blow when the franchisor of our operation sold the franchise to a haulage company for £1. The haulier used our delivery network to prop up his ailing business, and within three months he went bankrupt. All the franchisees were owed large sums of money, and I was owed £35,000. The business world was no place for the faint hearted or anyone with a conscience, but still I plotted to survive yet another obstacle. My perseverance paid off, as I became an independent as opposed to a franchisee, having found a network that needed a South Wales partner.

At this time I started to wake at about three every morning. With my eyes closed I would see on my eyelids a square like a television, and in the square would be different, vivid scenes that had a three-d effect. One night there was a kitchen with a lady busying herself. She turned to me and waved. This really shocked me, as I had been quite content being an observer of these scenes, but the lady conveyed to me she could see me as I could see her. Another time there was a farmer with cows around him, he also turned, and he doffed his cap at me. The square got bigger and bigger as the nights went on and eventually after a few months it was like a cinema screen, and always with different scenes being enacted.

One night the screen didn't appear. Instead on my eyelids, letters were tumbling. They came from the left, right, bottom and top. If I turned my eyes to the left or right for a closer look, they would disappear. I could only retain them by looking straight ahead, and they would be in my peripheral vision. Another night numbers came, and then another time faces. These faces were particularly fascinating and were both male and female, different ages and nationalities. Some would be face on, others sideways. They might be smiling or straight faced. I didn't know what to think but I was enjoying the show. I was getting better and better at seeing what was to my left and right, top and bottom, whilst continuing to look straight ahead.

Finally, one night on my eyelids, up in the far right hand corner, was a square. The square was really small but I knew there was something in it, as I could see movement. I strained to see what was in the square. Turning my eyes to the right was useless, as the square would disappear. I could only retain the square by staring straight ahead and it would stay in my peripheral vision.

The next night, and some nights after that, the same square would appear, always up in the far top, right-hand corner. Eventually I could see a little face inside the square. It was a little fat face all scrunched up, with the mouth puckered, and the eyes going back and forth. It was fascinating and I strained to see it. I could only retain it for a while and then it would be gone.

Eventually I was no longer woken up at three in the morning. I would say the whole process had taken about four months. Afterwards, I would get visualisation on the eyelids at random times, and the colours would come often, as did the eye, which seemed to be opening wider.

Even though Michel was supportive of me, I still had this inner voice worrying me. There was something not right. I was so busy I didn't have time to monitor where Michel was, but reasoned he could not be up to his old tricks as he was as busy as me.

One day I was rushing through the warehouse and I fell over. I hit the concrete floor face first and was knocked unconscious for a few seconds. I went to the hospital for emergency treatment, as my head was cut and my nose had a piece missing out of the bridge. You could see through a hole in my nose to the inside. I was x-rayed but didn't have any fractures, but my nose was a problem. It couldn't be stitched as there wasn't enough flesh to bring it together. My face was swelling, and my eyes were blackening. Dressing was put over my nose, and I was given an appointment to return once the swelling had gone down. I was told I would need plastic surgery.

I went home and was in a terrible state. I hurt all over, and my emotions bubbled up and I couldn't stop crying. I was in torment. I had this intrusive inner voice that wouldn't give me any peace. I was frightened of life, and frightened to listen to this voice; I felt real self-loathing and couldn't bear any more pain. To calm myself I ran a bath. I lay back in the bath and in front of me was a near-empty jar of coco butter on the windowsill. The jar had a plunger, and as I looked the plunger went down and the coco butter trickled out. I was so amazed I stood to have a better look, and as I did so I sensed my dead grandmother, Beatrice, with me. I could even smell her, and she wrapped her arms around me. The dreadful emotional and physical hurt rose from my body, and went out through the top of my head. I lay back in the hot water and felt a loving, comforting sensation that wasn't of this world. It was an exquisite feeling.

When the water cooled I came out of the bath, dried myself, scooped up the coco butter and, on automatic pilot, spread it over my head and face, including my nose. I got in to bed and slept the sleep of the dead. In the morning, although still bruised and swollen, the hole in my nose had closed. I couldn't comprehend what had happened. It was so spectacular I couldn't take it in.

This was such a stressful time and, even though I had now had a hysterectomy, I still had health problems. Over the years I had five abdominal operations, and I was now suffering with lesions. I needed to go into hospital but it was impossible with our present situation. Again the universe provided a solution. The company Michel worked for closed. He did try to secure another position but it proved difficult. I did some re-organising of the staff and he came on to the payroll of my business and I went into hospital. I was in hospital for ten days and Michel was amazing. He would come from work straight to the hospital to see me in the evenings, even though I would tell him not to. He assured me everything was fine in work and at home, and he seemed so laid back and happy.

I started to feel closeness with him missing for a long time. I was regaining trust. Since finding out the truth about him, he and I had lived together virtually like brother and sister. There would be the occasional physical contact, usually after a drink, but now I began to think we could put the spark back in our relationship. I felt love for him as he was being so kind. While in the hospital I told him how I felt, and said I wanted to put the business in our joint names in recognition of this trust. He was very emotional about this. I was wearing rose tinted glasses and saw a future where we were strong and together. I could see success in everything we did and I was so happy.

I left hospital on a Sunday with steel staples running from hip to hip. I was told to take things easy and not to drive. I woke around five on the Monday morning. Michel was lying next to me, and I felt overwhelming love for him.

I wanted to wake him and tell him how I felt, to say I thought we were blessed to have our family, home, and a business we could share together. I also wanted to say I would come in to work with him, to be near him.

A thought came into my head saying 'No, don't do that'. In my dreamy state I was completely taken aback, and thought I could sense my Nana Beatty. I lay listening, but heard nothing. Was that thought voice real? On my eyelids were the vivid colours, especially purple. The alarm clock rang and Michel got up. 'You're awake early' he said. I acknowledged him, but didn't attempt to say anything else. I felt as though I was being influenced by some power. When Michel left I eventually went back to sleep. I woke with a definite voice I identified as my Nan's, in my head saying, 'Now you can get up and go to him'.

Driving was difficult because of the operation, and when I arrived at the business it was eight o'clock. The last of the drivers was just pulling away. Michel was only just on his own, and the office staff was not due in for another hour. When I went inside he went mad. There was no happiness to see me, just anger. 'What are you doing here, go home. You should be in bed' he said. The hairs on the back of my neck stood on end, and there was that inner voice speaking to me, and now I was hearing it loud and clear. What was going on? 'Well I am here now so I might as well have a cup of tea', I said. He replied 'Well the phantom phone caller rings this time every day, and when I answer the phone goes down. I will make you tea and you can answer'.

My stomach turned, and when the telephone rang I picked up the receiver, but I remained silent. No one spoke on the other end, and eventually the phone went down. This happened three times, and Michel was pacing up and down, telling me to go home. I wouldn't let him near the telephone. I answered it when it rang for the fourth time and, although I remained silent a woman's voice said 'Michel is that you, can you speak now?' and I said 'No love this is Michel's partner, will I do?', and she put the telephone down.

I stood and looked at him. I was engulfed by the most awful negative thoughts and emotions, but there was no way to express them. I didn't want to shout or have any kind of a scene, but I felt very, very ill.

At that moment Nicola, who worked in the office, came in. Michel had to pull himself together, as he was crying. Nicola could see something was going on, and she put her arms around me and told me it was wonderful to have me back. She and I had become great friends during the three years she had worked for me. I went into my office and called Michel in.

'Who is she?' I asked, and he immediately responded 'The woman from the estate agents my brother is using to sell his house'. Michel's brother Paolo was now on his own, as his wife had died and they had no children. As a result of his wife's death and his own failing health, Paolo was selling their house and looking for a flat to buy.

Michel told me the woman's name was Angie, and he gave me her telephone number and I called her. A colleague answered the phone, and from her attitude I could see Angie's colleague was aware of the situation. Angie didn't want to speak to me, but I told her colleague I would call to the office in person, as Angie could not escape me. When she eventually came to the telephone I said 'I would like to meet you and suggest you leave for the Post House Hotel now, as I am on my way'. She refused and said 'I can't just meet you, I am in work', and I said 'I'm sure you can think of an excuse to leave, you seem efficient in lying'. She tried to take control of the situation, saying she had done nothing wrong, but I was very forceful and told her if she didn't agree to meet me it would go badly for her.

Michel let all this happen. He made no attempt to protect this woman, and I think he thought she could persuade me of their innocent relationship. I left the office and drove to The Post House Hotel. I had no intention of causing a scene, but I hadn't known what was going on, and therefore felt powerless. I now wanted to empower myself.

The woman was stood in the car park, drawing heavily on a cigarette. She was stood near the entrance to the hotel, and when I approached her she was furious. She started talking fast but I continued walking, and as I walked past her I said 'Coffee lounge, now. This is my show'. And she had to follow behind me, her high-heeled shoes clip-clopping all the way.

I sat down in the coffee lounge and she joined me, and I had a good look at her. I said 'I wanted to see what you looked like, and to tell you our rubbish at home is collected on a Thursday. I will give Michel until Thursday to get out. He is rubbish and you are welcome to him'. She said 'Oh, don't be ridiculous, I never slept with him you know'. I said 'He suffers from premature ejaculation, and even if you had, you wouldn't have got a lot out of it', and we sat weighing each other up.

I asked her how it felt to be in possession of my rubbish, and she said she didn't want him. I asked her if she was married and she said 'Yes', did she have kids? 'Yes', did her husband know how she spent her time? 'No'. Where did she live, and she said 'I'm not telling you'. I told her, 'Give me twenty-four hours and I'll have that information, and I'll let you know I have it'. She was really worried and said 'What are you going to do?' and I told her 'How does it feel not to know? Well, hold that feeling because I've held it for a long time, and you helped in that'.

I got up to leave, and she said 'Is that it?' and I told her 'He has done this before; he is a serial adulterer who is emotionally immature. I'm not interested in the why, what or where, the fact he has done it again is enough and I don't want to fight you because he is my leftovers, and you are welcome to him'.

It was obvious I had shocked her. I never once raised my voice, and I was proud of myself. In fact, when I got in my car I was laughing, thinking of what Michel's reaction would be if he knew what I had said to her. I recognised I had a really nasty side to my character, but I couldn't be sorry at that moment as I felt a little bit of self respect start to emerge.

The laughter didn't last long, as then the pain set in, both emotionally and physically. However, I couldn't dissolve as I had given Angie a deadline of twenty-four hours, and I was determined to come up with the goods. I would not ask Michel for her address, as he would be frightened of providing me with that information, in case I told her husband. I had no intention of doing so, but didn't want Michel or Angie to know that.

I had a friend who worked in another local estate agency, and I rang her. She didn't know Angie, but knew people who owned a shop next to where Angie worked. Give me a few minutes she said. She then rang me back and gave me Angie's full name and home telephone number. I rang the house. A man answered and I said 'Hello, you don't know me, but I am a friend of Angie's. I want to drop some makeup at your house as I'm in the area, can you give me the address please'. And he proceeded to give me the address. He then said 'Angie is here, would you like to speak to her?' She came to the telephone and I said 'Hi Angie, got you in two'.

I went home and crawled into bed. I closed my eyes and there were beautiful colours on my eyelids, amazing purples and lime greens. I went to sleep watching these colours swirl and peak, back and forth, back and forth. Michel came home that evening, and had his brother with him. I knew his brother was there to smooth things over. Like Michel, Paolo had the gift of the gab and he thought he could win any woman over. I came down the stairs smiling and said, 'Hello, do you want a coffee?' and I made sure I kept smiling.

I made coffee for the three of us, and when we were seated I said 'How is the property search going Paolo?', and he said 'I'll have to find somewhere soon, as those stairs are a real problem for me'. I replied, 'Now don't worry, Michel is in close contact with your estate agents, and I am sure between the two of them they will get things sorted'.

I told them both to enjoy their coffee, and as I walked from the room my parting shot was 'Michel, back bedroom please, and I want you out by Thursday, on rubbish day'. It felt so good to do that. I felt like rubbish and I really wanted him to feel like rubbish as well.

Michel was so much like his brother, as his brother also had an eye for the ladies, and Paolo's wife had suffered because of it. In fact, within two weeks of her death, Paolo started courting her sister and he told me 'I married the wrong sister'. Six weeks after making that declaration, Paolo was in hospital with prostrate problems. He had an operation that wasn't successful, and it left him with an indwelling catheter attached to his private parts. I like to think his wife influenced this event, or at the very least was laughing about it, and it was surely another example of karma 'what goes around comes around'. I was revolted by him.

I went back to work the next day, and Nicola and I had a good talk. She was in a dreadful position, but put herself aside and told me exactly what had been going on. During my absence Angie had constantly been on the telephone to Michel. He would leave for long lunch hours, sometimes a whole afternoon, and he asked Nicola not to tell me these things. She had to take on extra tasks to make up for Michel's lack of commitment. Poor Nicola, I put my arms around her and cuddled her. She was such an emotionally delicate person, and was just coming to terms with problems in her past. She was quite distrustful of men because of her experiences and this was the last thing she needed. Michel knew this and he was also aware he needed to be a good role model for Nicola. It was something he and I had discussed previously.

I couldn't take in how unprofessional, disloyal and immature Michel was. He was a liar and a cheat, and completely manipulative. What was wrong with me that I could take this person as my partner? I had to look at myself very closely. I had to acknowledge there was no one else to blame for the life I had led and the predicament I was in, but I knew I was changing and I was so glad of that.

So here I was with a stomach full of metal clips, but I was unable to rest. I knew I had to look after myself, but it was important to get things sorted. That evening Michel and I sat and talked. I emphasised he had to leave the house by Thursday; I no longer considered him my partner. He couldn't stop crying and begged me to give him another chance. He kept saying I had got everything wrong, and he was innocent. I felt the stirring of compassion for him. The more he talked, the more I lost my hard edge.

There was no way I would consider living with him, but I told him if he wanted to stay working in the business I would consider it, but it would depend on his behaviour. I said I was no longer willing to give him a 50% share in the business, but would consider a lesser percentage if he proved himself in the workplace. I stressed I would put up with no nonsense, and expected him to be professional in work, and respectful to me at all times. I in turn would give him the same respect. He sat and listened with tears running down his face. He said 'You don't have to do this; it doesn't have to be this way'. And I said 'A simple yes or no to my proposal will suffice'. I was hardening myself. This old fiddle was sick of being played.

I stayed at home and in bed for the next two days. Thursday came and I expected Michel to leave. He came home looking very unsure of himself, making no move to go. Kris knew exactly what was going on and he wanted Michel gone. He was now eighteen, and was disgusted with Michel. He called him Percy Perfect because of his pernickety ways around the house, and said his double standards were sickening. It was obvious Michel wasn't going to leave without pressure, so I told him he couldn't stay the night, and I asked him for his keys. He packed an overnight bag and before he left said to me 'If you need me I am at my brother's. Was I supposed to call for him in a crisis? He was the crisis!

I went to work on Friday and Michel was sitting in the office wearing dark glasses. I was furious to see the drivers around him, patting his shoulder and offering support. As the drivers passed to get to their vehicles, they could barely conceal their feelings towards me. I was dismayed to realise Michel was crying, and obviously telling them he had been mistreated by me. He was enlisting the troops, gathering them to his side.

Later in the day I heard him talking on the telephone. He didn't realise I was there but was saying 'After all I've done for her, all the hard work I have put in, and she treats me like this'. He was also crying again. I looked on the caller display and realised he was talking to one of our regular female customers. This was the straw that broke the camel's back. My reputation among the staff and customers would be in tatters if he continued this behaviour. I felt so weak physically and should have been home recuperating but instead, here I was fire-fighting. However, he underestimated me because my hard side had lots of practice over the last few years. This side of me was now honed to perfection, and I had the potential to be lethal given the right set of circumstances, and these circumstances were just right.

That night I asked a locksmith to meet me at the work premises. I had him change all the locks. I also had him go to the house and change the house locks. My sister helped me collect every article of Michel's from the house, and we drove with his belongings to his brother's. I had Michel's wages, with a month's holiday pay and his P45 in an envelope, along with a sarcastic reference highlighting his weakness and betrayal. My sister and I emptied the car and when she knocked on the front door, Michel opened it. She pointed to his belongings in the front garden, and then handed him the envelope saying 'This is for you'. I went to the cash dispenser at our bank at five to twelve that night and drew out the maximum amount of money allowed for that day, once it was gone twelve I again drew out the maximum amount of money allowed. The next morning I was in the Bank as soon as they opened and I cleaned out any money left in our joint account.

I realised I should have severed all ties with Michel when I again found out what he was up to. I shouldn't have used a half-measure, which was giving way to my repeated pattern of weakness. I went to bed that night and was desolate. I couldn't stop crying. I felt so wounded, and wondered if I had physically harmed myself with all the stress and work while recovering from major surgery.

I was woken from sleep with a telephone on my eyelids. There was a cross over the telephone and inside my head the words 'Suffer it and grow' came. I was being told to stop weeping and wailing and looking to others for support. I had to go it alone and suffer the pain, in order to grow. In my head I said I understood, but asked for help with sleeping in the nights, as I was lying awake, and it was a torture. Every night after I had asked for help, I slept soundly. Every morning when I woke up I would say 'Thank you'.

The next couple of months were a haze. There was nothing but work and problems. I had to tell the staff my personal business, as they had a distorted view of the truth. I needed to enlist their help in keeping the business efficient and in profit. I promoted one of the drivers to Operations Manager, and he took over the front end of the business.

Shortly after Michel left I had a visit from my old neighbour Jo from Chepstow and she said to me 'At last you've got rid of the b------ have you?' I was shocked to hear her say this, and asked her why, and she said 'When you lived opposite us Michel used to come home in the lunch hours to walk Lucky. He started knocking at my door and, of course, Graham would be in work. The first time I called him in and made coffee. He flirted with me and I was so uncomfortable. The next time he called I told him I was busy and couldn't ask him in. He then started telephoning me, and eventually said he had fallen in love with me.' I was amazed and said 'Oh Jo why didn't you tell me?' and she said 'I couldn't Yve, I felt so awful about it. I did tell Graham though, I had to. Graham spoke to Michel and told him to stay away from me. Didn't you ever wonder why we had stopped socialising with you as a couple?'

I thought about her questions and admitted I had. I put a brave face on things while she was there but when she left I gave way to tears. My humiliation was complete.

2.5 No going back

I went to a solicitor to discuss my financial situation. He sent a letter to Michel to begin negotiations. Once things were stabilised I planned a holiday for Kris and me. My parents decided to join us, and we flew to Florida for two weeks. My mother's eldest sister May lived in Jacksonville with her husband Fred. We planned to visit her, and also visit with some of her children.

The holiday was brilliant and seeing our American family was lovely, and I forgot all the problems back home. The sense of freedom was heady, and a fabulous memory I have is driving along the sands at Coco Beach, with the Beach Boys blasting 'Surfing USA', and Kris and I singing and laughing. Another wonderful memory is being with my cousin Linda and her family at their ranch in Middleburg. They have a black creek running near their property, and a large tree had a rope tied to its branches. We would swing on that rope and drop in to the creek. The weather was lovely, and our screams echoed along the water. Kris also had a day surfing with his cousin Sean and Sean's mates. Returning home to the UK we were laden with luggage, as we had taken full advantage of the many shops.

Within two minutes of being in the house the telephone rang, and it was Michel. He wanted to know if we had a good holiday and said, 'Welcome home'. I was brought down to Earth with a bang. Back at work the telephones were ringing, but not for business. Customers were cancelling our services. They all told the same story. They had been approached by a sales representative from a national carrier, and given a cheaper quote. This sales person knew the profile of our customer's freight and what I was charging them, and had cheaper quotes already prepared.

The recession had hit business hard, and no one could refuse the opportunity to save money. I lost forty per cent of my customer base within a week. It looked as though the business was finished, as I couldn't sustain those losses and didn't have the energy to fight back. Someone had given my customer base to the opposition. Welcome home indeed!

I thought back to my plea to the universe, when we were moving house. I had prayed 'If there is anyone there, please help me. If Michel ever betrays me again, please let me be in an emotional and financial position to stand on my own two feet, so that I can leave him behind'. It seemed my plea was to be ignored, but I was willing to take responsibility for my actions. I knew I hadn't listened to that inner voice but, instead, had let my emotions rule me. It was unrealistic to expect the universe to save me.

Without the business I faced financial ruin, and there was more to come. In the post I had a letter from my solicitor telling me Michel was asking for the apportionment of the property, which was put in place when we bought our first property together, to be over-ruled. He also wanted a share of the business. I again put out a plea to the universe. 'Please help me. I'm frightened of life. I don't know who is listening to me, but I know you are there, and I am sorry I've ignored you, but I'm ready to listen to you now'. I now had decisions to make regarding the business. I worked on financial projections, but the reality was, I needed a miracle.

Before I went to America I had been approached by an acquaintance of Michel's to quote for volume parcel freight. The friend was Lesley and he owned a household catalogue company. I rang Lesley and told him he needed to approach another company for the parcel work, as I was closing the business. He asked me why, and I told him. He then asked if I would drive over to see him, and this I did.

When I got to his offices, he was sat in the boardroom with the Finance and Sales Directors. I sat with them, and they asked a few questions. Lesley then made me the most amazing offer. He said I could move my business to his premises and I would pay no rent, electricity or rates. I could even have the use of his warehouse-men and equipment. He took me to a section of his large warehouse where offices sat empty, and he marked out an area in the warehouse that I could consider mine. I asked Lesley 'Why are you doing this?', and he replied 'Because I can'.

I agreed to his offer, and when I was driving from the meeting, I knew I had been given a miracle, and it was influenced by some higher power. Despite repeatedly not listening to my inner voice, my plea to the universe was being answered, and it seems I was being dealt with leniently.

In bed that night I dreamt I was at a fast flowing, wide river and I could not get across, although I knew I had to. There was a man stood on the other side of the river, and he was familiar to me. He was calling for me to cross, and I was shaking my head. He pointed his hand at the water near me, and with a splash a sturdy stone appeared. He kept beckoning. Dubiously I stepped on to this stone, and again he was beckoning me. When I shook my head he raised his hand, pointed at the water and with a splash another stone appeared. I was gaining confidence and this continued until I was halfway across. Again he pointed at the water, I saw a splash but I couldn't see a stone.

He held his two hands towards me and had the most beautiful look on his face. I knew he was compelling me to have faith; he wouldn't let me sink. I turned and looked from where I had come, the stones that had led me had disappeared, there was no way back, I couldn't go back. He said 'If I give you the stones will you take the steps?', and I said 'Yes'. He said 'Sometimes you won't see the stones, will you still take the steps?' I looked around me and could see no other way out of my situation. I couldn't stay standing on a stone in the middle of a fast flowing river, frightened to take the next step and I couldn't go back.

He looked so good and loving, I had no choice, and I said 'Yes'. I remember taking that step into the unknown but didn't retain the rest of the dream. I woke and it was a new day, suddenly I had faith. I was looking forward to organising the move for the business, and the hard work ahead was not daunting to me.

The move of business premises went smoothly, and at last I could focus without overwhelming pressure. I was slowly rebuilding the business and my life. Michel was doing everything in his power to secure half the equity of the house, but this was 1993 and the housing market had crashed. Interest rates had rocketed, and there wasn't a lot of equity left in our house. He was also asking for money from the business. Even though he was fighting with me, he would still ring and cry and beg me to forgive him. I again spoke to the universe. 'Please help me secure our home so Kris and I can stay living there.' And I had an inner knowing things would work out. Yes, I had faith!

In work one day, a person came in to my mind who I hadn't spoken with for at least a year. This was a business acquaintance and, on an impulse, I dialled his number. We exchanged pleasantries and he said 'I was so sorry to hear of Michel's brother's death'. I asked 'When did he die?' He replied, 'Last week, and the funeral is tomorrow.' The death had not been in the local paper, and had I not made this call I probably wouldn't have found out. I knew I was influenced to make that call, and my heart was pounding. Michel was the main beneficiary of his brother's will. His financial status would change substantially and he would have no reason now not to pay towards the mortgage on our house, as well as other bills. This was another of those life-changing coincidences. Silently, in my head, I said 'Thank you'.

I was sorry Michel's brother had died, but for my own purposes I had to let Michel know I knew. I rang him, he answered and I gave him my condolences. He was shocked and said 'How did you find out?' The tone of his voice was hostile; one day he had been begging, and now he was hostile. The reason for that was not hard to work out.

I rang my solicitor and told him the new development. He asked me 'What do you want to do?' and I said, 'I don't want any of Michel's money, but I want you to secure the house for Kris and me'. And so it was. Michel relinquished his share of the house, and the mortgage and title was signed over to me. He also stopped asking for any share of the business. I was free. The universe had answered, and when I looked at the sequence of events that had influenced and guided me, I was in awe. That night lying in bed I was treated to a light show. On my eyelids the colours tumbled from left right, bottom and top. They were psychedelic colours. I loved it and went to sleep smiling.

Shortly after this Michel left the UK and went to live in Italy, as his mother had moved back there after the death of her husband. He rang me the night before he left and he told me he was sorry for all that had happened and he wished me well. His words had a devastating effect on me. I was like a balloon that gets pricked by a pin. All the air left my body and I couldn't speak. The pain I felt was excruciating and everything seemed so utterly pointless. I couldn't cope with Michel's kindness, and the walls I had built came tumbling down.

Michel was shocked at my distress and kept saying 'I am sorry, I am sorry', over and over again. When I pulled myself together I was able to answer 'Its okay Michel, I couldn't have learned from a better b------ than you'.

2.6 Life is about the journey and not the destination

As I have said previously, I long ago started the process of relinquishing structured religion, which was quite a brave and difficult thing to do and involved a process of taking little steps and comforting myself me or those I loved were not being struck down for my abdication.

I truly loved the Bible and all the little stories it contained and I also agreed that the Ten Commandments was a good structure for civilised behaviour but having stepped outside of my environment when I entered the work place I was meeting people of different religions and cultures and also people with different ways of acting and thinking, and I liked the majority of the people I met. They seemed to have their own commandments, which were reflected in their way of living which, although in a different format to the Ten Commandments, equalled the same thing.

I started to believe as long as I tried to be a good person then it was OK to let go of the rules and regulations of religion that didn't sit right with me. I didn't want to think anyone of a different religion would end up in a different place to me when they died, or someone who was a good person but acted or thought in a different way to me would be barred from wherever it was I was going, and so I was glad to let my belief system regarding religion go.

However, even though I could not accept the divide between the different religious beliefs I still believed there was an overall Creator and I knew this Creator was a power greater than me. I started to speak in my mind and say 'I don't know who you are or what you are but I need help. I am frightened of life because I don't seem to know how to live wisely. I am sorry I have ignored you when you have been trying to get my attention but I want to listen'.

I was continually speaking in my mind and asking for help and guidance. I would often think of someone and they would call me, or when the phone would ring I would know who was calling and I was still having amazing spiritual experiences and my confidence started to grow that I could be different if only I could find the strength to change but in the meantime whilst I was struggling to find that strength, life continued to be very, very hard.

When I was very stressed I was also having weird experiences with my hearing, sometimes I would hear what sounded like a room full of people all talking or mumbling and I would strain to hear what was being said but could never make it out. It seemed to me as though I was tuning into a different frequency. At other times I would get a high pitched noise, like a modem type of noise, the sort of noise you would get when a fax machine or a computer was dialling out to get an internet connection. I eventually complained to my doctor about this and I was sent for a hearing test at the local hospital but they found there was nothing wrong with my hearing. My doctor attributed these symptoms to stress.

Very slowly I started to get stronger. My decision making process was altering and I no longer reacted impulsively. I would stand back and observe, letting my mind tick over. I allowed my inner voice to guide me and I did not feel bad about making a judgement and sometimes saying 'no'.

I was constantly being told via dreams and other means life was about the journey and not the destination and at last I was beginning to understand this. I had learnt many lessons to get me to the stage of using my intuition and my mind instead of my emotions and I started to curb my desire to make a square peg fit into a round hole. I know emotions are an essential part of human life and can be awoken in us at any time. However, if you act on emotions they can get you into all sorts of problems and I really had had enough of these unnecessary problems.

When I finally accepted there was probably a spirit worker from a higher power working with me, I would continue to ask for help and guidance but would also ask for help in achieving what ever it was I had come to Earth to do, or to experience. I found the courage to challenge my many belief systems and take down the rigid structures that had formed my concept of reality and which had held me back so much.

I had started reading everything I could on the subject of spirituality and one day I found an old spiritual book. In the book it explained when a Medium is in training to work with spirit workers, the trainee is brought out of deep sleep to a passive level and with the trainees eyes closed the workers project visualisation, which can be seen by the trainee as if the images are on their eyelids. The visualisation is to expand the vision, and peripheral vision of the third eye. It started with colour on the eyelids and then progressed to images. It mentioned the square with the little fat face in. This would occur at the end of the expansion. This was part of the making of a spiritual medium. I couldn't believe what I was reading. This was the first time I had found any reference to the things that were happening to me. In my mind I said 'I want to work with you, show me how. I want to be a spiritual medium'.

Even though my life was still in a mess I really did have an inner knowing I would be helped to navigate my way out of my difficulties if I was prepared to put the effort in and listen.

Then one night I woke up and thought I was having some kind of a fit. My body was bouncing from side to side. I was actually coming off the bed, and hitting my left side, then bouncing back to my right, then my left and so on. I went in to panic mode. I became aware of a man standing on the right side of me. He spoke to me mind to mind, he said 'It's okay, you have woken up too soon'. Immediately he said that, I stopped panicking. I felt like a plane coming in to land, but the landing was bumpy. Slowly the bouncing became less violent, and then it gradually stopped. I looked, and the man had gone.

Life was certainly getting very interesting and I was very open to the possibility that my spirit had somehow been visiting another realm.

My sister was also interested in spiritual things and a series of happenings and coincidences had taken her down the healing path. She joined an accredited healing group as a trainee healer but the facilities they were using were really inadequate. My son and I lived in a beautiful and spacious house but as I was working long hours and he was in University we were hardly ever there. With my sons blessing I lent the healing group our home to hold a weekly healing clinic.

Shortly after the healing clinic started, one night I got home from work and felt really weird about entering the sitting room. The hairs on the back of my neck were stood on end. I pushed open the door without entering the room, and everything seemed fine. I walked in and standing in the far corner was a man. He was dressed in a 1920's type of baggy suite, and was excessively thin. He looked as though he had consumption. I would put his age at about fifty two. I stood frozen and looked at him, and he looked back at me, with a placid expression on his face. I began to realise he was not absolutely solid. There was something about him that didn't seem right. I didn't feel threatened by him, just uncertain of his presence. He made no move and so I said 'If you've come for the healing, you have the wrong day'. His facial expression changed and he gave me a tolerant look, and the thought came in to my mind, 'You know I'm not here for that'.

Memories came flooding in; he was the man who was with me when I was four and came out of my body. He was also the man in my dream, helping me to cross the river, and he was the man at my right side when I thought I was having a fit in my bed and he was telling me not to panic and saying I'd woken up too soon. I asked him 'Who are you? What's your name?' and he smiled. That smile conveyed to me his name wasn't important. In typical human fashion I said 'If you won't tell me your name I'll call you HQ, as I know you are instructing me'. Slowly he faded and I was left looking at the blank wall.

Even though I was unnerved about this man appearing in my home I couldn't stop thinking about what had happened and had no real alternative other than to accept this man was a spirit person from some other dimension and he was working with me.

It was a bit like living in a parallel universe. On the one hand I had all this unbelievable esoteric stuff happening and on the other hand I had all the normal, Earthly things going on and I had no option but to just get on with life, putting the mysteries aside. I had moved from

Lesley's business premises when I was strong enough to stand on my own two feet, but the transport business was hugely problematic I was so worn down with work, and felt on the verge of collapse under the pressure. I employed fifteen people in the business, and the staff knew I had a sympathetic nature, and quite often they took advantage of this. I was constantly fire fighting. Any problems the staff had, they quickly became my problems, and I was always doing over and above what could normally be expected, and I was suffering because of this.

Also circumstances had conspired to draw me in to administer the healing clinic at my house. It had become really successful, with lots of people coming with all sorts of problems, and some good results being achieved. Because it was at my home people would automatically ring me with any queries or requests and if there were any problems with the healers attending the healers would also ring me and then I would be the one trying to sort out replacement healers.

On the night before one particular healing clinic, two healers rang and said they could not attend the clinic the next day. I had a particularly busy day ahead of me in work the next day and I felt very stressed and so I spoke in my mind to the person I now called HQ and said 'I know the clinic will be really busy tomorrow and I really do not have the time to find replacements. How do you expect me to cope with this? I can't just pull healers' out of nowhere, so it's over to you. You had better get it sorted'. I lay in bed thinking and thinking and admitted I was buckling under the strain.

I knew the business was important, as it funded not only Kris and the healing clinic, but also me. I needed help with the business as I was not coping and I was also lonely. I asked HQ to send me a man who would be like a soul mate to me. I asked for someone who would help me on all levels.

Thursday morning came and I was in work for six and was already encountering problems, as two people hadn't turned up. At every available moment I was speaking to HQ in my head. I told him there was no way I was going home that night unless he got things sorted. I knew if there were only two healers' working, there would be a backlog of people when I got home. I was just too weary to be bothered.

I had no lunch hour that day, and by two in the afternoon felt my head was exploding. I needed to get out for ten minutes. I drove my car aimlessly, not knowing where I was going. I found myself in the shopping area of a place called Aberdare. I stopped the car and looked around me, and noticed I was opposite a new age shop. I got out of the car and approached the shop. I opened the door and went to the counter. There was a sign advertising healing. A very attractive, older lady appeared from behind a curtain and I said 'Who is the healer?' and she said 'I am'. I said 'Look this may seem weird, but there is a healing clinic every Thursday evening at my home in Cardiff. There will be a lot of people there tonight, and two of the healer's can't make it. Would you consider coming?' She immediately said 'Yes, write your details down and tell me what time to be there'.

I left the shop feeling overawed at this power that could influence events so easily, and I also felt incredibly humble. Driving back to work I said to HQ, 'I want to thank you for working with me, and I want you to know my faith is building, and I have total belief and trust in you'.

Three days later I met a man who I believed was my soul mate, sent to me by HQ in answer to my plea. He was connected to one of my customers. I was asked by this customer to partner this man at a dinner party. I was too shy to do this, but the next day the man rang me. He invited me to dinner at his house, which coincidentally was directly around the corner from my home. I went and had a lovely time.

He was a fifty years of age, retired man. He had run a very successful business in Australia and had come back to live in Cardiff, which was the place of his birth. He was renting the house near me whilst looking for a permanent place to buy. He was very laid back, and was like an old hippy, but he was an extremely astute businessman. He would discuss my financial problems with me, and understood that the recession had a devastating affect on businesses, particularly those in the service industry. He was also interested in the healing and so we had a lot of things in common. We settled into a very comfortable relationship and it was so fantastic for me to feel supported. We both kept our own homes but did make non-specific plans for a future together.

About a year after this meeting I started having a feeling of unease regarding the house that Kris and I lived in. I began having thoughts of moving which were completely unrelated to anything that was going on in my new relationship. I said to HQ 'I think you are influencing me to sell the house. I'll put it in the hands of an estate agent but, I know if I've got it wrong and you don't want me to sell, then no one will want to buy it'.

The agent came, and I was in the kitchen making tea while she was looking around the house. She came in to the kitchen and said to me 'Do you have a big black dog?' and I explained we did have a dog but she had died recently, much to our distress. The lady was really embarrassed and she said she realised it was the spirit of a dog she was seeing, but she didn't usually share these experiences with anyone. I laughed and told her the house was used for spiritual healing, and I was well used to spiritual happenings. She told me she saw our beautiful dog sitting on the settee, looking out of the lounge window. Our dog always sat there and loved to see what was happening in the road. I felt this was confirmation from HQ regarding selling the house. It was a spiritual link.

A few days later the agent rang me. She told me she had sent a photographer to take photos of the outside of the house. She asked if anyone had been home when the photos had been taken and I told her 'No, Kris and I are out early every day'. She said there were people visible in my bedroom window, and the central figure was a lady holding what looked like a scroll in her hand. She promised to post the photo to me so I could see for myself. When the photo came I couldn't believe it. She was right. There were people clearly visible in my bedroom window, and there was the lady with a scroll-like object in her hand. I was later told by an experienced medium the lady was holding plans in her hand. I realised HQ

was responding to my asking about putting the house on the market. He was telling me I wasn't to worry, as there were plans in-hand.

Meanwhile I had suffered a real catastrophe in work. I was used to customers ceasing trading and taking money owed to me with them but one particular customer who owed a large sum of money to me went bankrupt. I immediately reduced staff levels, putting even more pressure on my role within the company, and I also set about finding smaller premises. I had to do everything to reduce the overheads. I found smaller premises, but before we could move in, the landlord had to put certain things right in order to comply with Health and Safety.

I was so stretched in work that I took the landlords word for it the premises would be ready at a certain date. A week before the date I rang him and he told me everything was done and we could go ahead and move in. It is a mammoth operation moving business premises and there is a lot of arranging to do with services such as moving tele-phones etc. I did all of this without checking the new premises were ready as I chose to believe the landlord.

On a Wednesday evening me and the staff worked late into the night, loading two forty foot trailers with all the goods from the offices and the goods to be delivered to customers the next day. When we arrived in convoy to the new premises it was unbelievable, nothing had been touched and the responsibility was mine whether or not I was pre-pared to compromise Health and Safety and also saddle myself with a landlord who was not trustworthy. I had the option of moving in to these unsuitable premises, or I could turn back to the just vacated premises. Of course, the other frightening option was that I could stop the business. I found a quiet corner so I could quiet my emotions, use my mind to process the situation and listen to my inner voice.

It felt a very spiritual moment and I knew I could not turn back, just as the stepping stones at the fast flowing river in my dream had shown me, there was no going back, and I knew I could not compromise on my responsibility to my staff. I spoke to HQ in my mind and said, 'just as you told me in the dream when I was crossing the river, I believe you are giving me a step without showing me the stone and I don't know where I will land. I don't see how I can stop as people are relying on me, how will they manage, and what about me? I won't be able to pay my mortgage and what about the clinic? Also I'll owe people money, what about them?'

The list of problems seemed endless, but I had the sense HQ was holding out his hands to me, showing me if I couldn't see the stone, I could still take the step. It was the ultimate test of my faith in him and, just as the dream had shown me, I knew I could not go back; there was no going back. Without saying anything of my decision to the others we parked the trailers at the old premises and all went home.

I sat in my lounge and was in shock. I was asking HQ 'What am I going to do?' Loaded on the two trailers were all the goods to be delivered the next day and I couldn't let people down. Into my mind came thoughts of two men who operated the same business as me, but in Newport, which is a town next to Cardiff.

I rang them and told them my situation. I said 'If I give you my customer base you could take over my business, but you have to take my staff as well', and they jumped at the opportunity.

I made arrangements for them to collect the goods that night, and I also rang around the staff telling them of my decision to close, but offering them the opportunity of employment with the new company in Newport. So that was it, overnight the business had gone. The next day was Thursday. I was at home to greet the healers, and explain what I'd done. We waited for patients to arrive, and not one turned up. That was really amazing because the clinic had been so busy. We sat in the lounge and everyone agreed, the clinic at my home was closed. We wrote to the patients telling them, and giving an alternative venue for them to receive healing.

What an absolute amazing turn-around in my life. I had to busy myself sorting out my finances and stabilising myself for the future but everything just slotted into place as if by magic, and it was magical that there was this power that could guide you if you were willing and able to listen. Here I was at the age of forty two knowing there was a new path but waiting for it to show itself to me.

Although our house was still for sale there was little interest in it, and I was happy to let things drift along. However, my new man was getting itchy feet and he decided it was time for an adventure and he decided he was going to live on a boat in Spain. He asked me to go with him. He painted a wonderful picture of us living an idyllic life. I discussed this with my son and, although he was still living at home he was ready to move out, as he was 21 years of age.

It was agreed he would come back and forth to me for holidays, and when he finished his electronic engineering degree he might even come and live there. By this time my partner had moved from his rented accommodation and he had bought a house, which he then put up for sale.

I spoke to HQ and said 'If this move to Spain is in the plan, then it will happen. If it is not in the plan, then it won't. I am happy for you to influence events'. And it was true, for the first time in my life I knew it was about the journey and not the destination.

My partner got a buyer for his house straight away while mine just sat there, and so he went on ahead to set things up for us in Spain. After a few weeks of being away he started calling me saying he was anxious for me to join him. There was nothing I could do as my house hadn't sold, and that was that. He told me repeatedly he was missing me and he complained had he realised he would be in Spain for such a long period of time without me he would never have left Cardiff.

Then a miracle happened, I got an offer on the house. The offer was not as good as I had hoped for, and I discussed it with my partner. I told him I was willing to let the house go so we could start our adventure together. He didn't act particularly enthusiastic at my news. This was confusing to me, as I assumed he would be thrilled at this turn of events. When he rang the next day he was more responsive, and I rang the agent and accepted the offer.

Over the next few days my partner would ring, but he was quite cool. The note of desperation had left his voice. I sensed some kind of battle was taking place within him. Meanwhile, a surveyor came to the house and did a full structural survey on behalf of the buyer. However, every time my partner would ring he would blow hot and cold. One afternoon the estate agent rang and said my buyer wanted a further reduction on the house, as the survey had shown some areas of concern. I said to tell the buyer I was not interested and to forget the sale.

The agent told me not to be hasty as they might go ahead at the agreed price, but there was no need for me to sell the house at a lower price now as I realised my partner had revealed a side of him that wasn't attractive to me.

I was no longer the old Yvonne navigating her way through life using her emotions, and if he had commitment issues or any other issues it wasn't up to me to heal him. I no longer wanted to take the easy road as I recognised in time this led to pain.

I was gutted, as I truly did love him but not enough to make another mistake. I had thought he was my soul mate and that evening I cried to HQ saying, 'Why did you let me think he was for me?' I went to bed in my lonely house and as I snuggled under the blankets I heard a loud crash coming from the direction of the downstairs hallway. Someone must have broken in, there was no other explanation. I couldn't understand why the burglar alarm hadn't gone off and then thought perhaps I hadn't activated it. I picked up the telephone and dialled the emergency police number. I told them I was in the house on my own and I thought there was an intruder. They said they would be there immediately.

I opened my curtains and looked out the front window. I saw four police cars pull on to my drive. Police jumped out and they ran around the sides and back of the house. I opened my bedroom window and a policeman asked me to open the front door. I told him I was frightened to come down the stairs and threw my keys to him. I heard him open the front door and my burglar alarm started to beep. I ran down the stairs to turn it off.

In the hallway I had decorative artificial ivy trailing down the wall, which was as light as a feather. The ivy was off the wall and lay diagonally across the hallway, as though staged. The policeman stood looking at me and said 'What's this then?' I had no explanation and thought 'He must think I'm crazy, or perhaps attention seeking'. If the ivy had fallen off the wall, it would have landed in a heap and, as it was so light it certainly wouldn't make the crash I heard. 'There must be someone in the house' I said, and so the policemen looked around. 'There's no one here love, and in any case you had the alarm on. If there was anyone walking around downstairs the alarm would have detected them' I was told.

I apologised for wasting their time and they told me I was to call them again if I was worried. They left and I reactivated the alarm and went back to bed thinking, 'What on Earth was that all about?' HQ was silent, and eventually I went to sleep. The next day I rang an experienced medium and told her what was going on in my life and the incident with the ivy that had occurred the night before. I asked her opinion on what she thought it had meant. She told me 'You have received symbolic communication from spirit. They have used the artificial ivy to tell you it wasn't the real thing with this man, he was a plant but I bet he helped you immensely didn't he?', and I had to admit he had but I needed to clarify things and said 'You mean, I am being told he was sent to me, but not as my soul mate?' 'Yes, exactly', she said, 'He was a plant and not the real thing at all.'

What an absolutely breath stopping moment, so many things clicked into place. I was able to go back and visit in my mind all the unexplained happenings and put a symbolic interpretation on them. I realised I was being spoken to in a universal language made up of symbols and the medium explained we get these symbols in our sleep state via dreams as well as our waking time. I discovered this language, once I had found the key, was something I could quite easily interpret and I was completely and utterly overawed at this.

A few months after this, in early December 1996, the estate agent rang and made an appointment for people to view the house. Just before their arrival I ran up the stairs, and a photograph of the house that hung in the landing had moved. It was completely off centre. I said to HQ 'I'm moving, aren't I?' it was another symbolic communication and true to form the people loved the house and asked if I could be out by Christmas. They were cash buyers and I had twenty days to pack and leave.

A couple of nights later I went to bed and, although it was bitterly cold, I started to feel excessively hot. Eventually I got out of bed and opened the curtains and windows to let in the cold air. In the sky were bright, coloured lights.

They looked like search lights, and they were over my house. I almost had the impression it was some kind of aircraft or spacecraft above me, but only the lights were visible. I would say there were around twenty beams in all. I leaned out of the window to get a better look. The house was on a bend, and coming from the right I saw a silver car, possibly an old Mercedes. There was a woman with long blond hair driving. She was staring intently at my house and I thought 'She's going to crash if she doesn't look at the road'.

The car seemed to glide around the bend, and disappeared out of sight. Within moments the car was coming back, but this time from the left. I realised what I'd thought was long blond hair was in fact a white hood, and on closer inspection the face seemed sexless, neither male nor female. Again this person didn't look at the road but was focused on my house.

The car drove out of my vision and, within moments, was coming back from the right again. I watched this person stare at my house, with the car gliding around the bend and the face turning as the car turned, so the house never left their vision. When the car disappeared I waited expectantly for it to reappear, but it didn't. I looked up at the lights and they were gone and I felt freezing cold. I knew I had been influenced to witness these things, but what did it mean? I tried to work it out. Symbolically a car is a person, as the body is just a vehicle, and a Mercedes would be regarded as one of the best. As the car was an old car could that mean an old spirit/soul? Was that what the sexless being driving the car was representative of, the spirit/soul? I like to think it is representative of the spiritual power that was focused on me, and guiding me.

2.7 A Journey of the Mind

"Curiosity has its own reason for existing. One cannot help but be in awe when he contemplates the mysteries of eternity, of life, of the marvellous structure of reality. It is enough if one tries merely to comprehend a little of this mystery every day." Albert Einstein.

Since that time my life has sorted itself out and the years have gone by and I have gone on a journey of discovery and have continued to have these amazing experiences. In the early days of my development I would analyse the universal language that was coming my way and think it was leading me here or there, wherever it was I wanted to be. I now realise you have to throw many things such as right and wrong, wisdom etc. into the mix and be brave enough to take a step without knowing where it will land and the hard road turns out to be the road of least resistance.

I check my motives and try to recognise if any frailties such as jealousy, spite etc. are influencing my actions in any situation or dealings with others, and I work hard at not having any preconceived ideas about my destination. I try to remain emotionally and mentally balanced, as I am really happy to focus on the journey.

I have noticed when I get it wrong the universe always let me know, and sometimes these lessons can be painful and I quickly try to right what ever it is I have done wrong. It seems when you know better, karma is quick to respond and that by acknowledging and working with this power you are also acknowledging cause and effect.

I am a very grounded person and cannot accept anything that seems fanciful and fluffy. I had a need to know about this power that was working with me, and the mechanism that allowed these less than ordinary experiences to happen.

I was full of questions such as 'Why are we here, who or what is God and who or what is spirit, where do we go when we die and why are there so many different religions worshipping a God who seems to have differing rules and regulations, what is it all about and how does it all work?' On and on the questions went.

I began to look at the World with a real curiosity and thirst for knowledge and I was constantly asking for help and guidance to get me to see the bigger picture and I seemed to be led to what I needed to know so I could form an opinion on what I was learning. Although I wasn't being given all the answers, I was being given the opportunity to interpret the symbols, explore the wonders of the world, consider my experiences, stop, listen and use my wisdom and intuition to express an opinion and change my way of being, so I could resonate in harmony with the whole of the universe to which I was connected.

People, books and information would come my way as though by magic and all would bring a message or impart knowledge that answered questions. Many symbolic happenings and dreams would also provide me with valuable information.

I read about ancient monuments and civilisations, historical writings, religion, symbolism, astrology and the astrological ages, in particular Pisces and Aquarius, and I was fascinated at what I was learning about the science that was out there working in the intangible field of consciousness. I would continue to speak in my mind to this unseen power that was working with me and ask specific questions and a response would always come in one form or another.

At one stage I was having dreams where I was seeing atoms floating about. I didn't know what an atom was until I saw one on the television and then I realised what it was I was seeing in the dreams.

I decided to go to the library and find out about atoms but when I sat with the books I realised I did not have the education to enable me to understand what was written and so I asked in my mind to tell me about the atom but in a layman's terms. Sure enough a friend I had not seen for quite a while called at my house and brought with him a book and one of the chapters in the book said 'The atom made simple'. Slowly my mind began to expand and I was discovering huge contradictions in my old belief systems and the prejudices, fears and rigid structures that had affected the way I saw the world and held me back. This, together with knowing there was a power that was greater than me, was there for the good and everyone could tap into and communicate with, changed my whole way of being.

I was fascinated to learn we have probably lost from the historical records entire civilisations that in some ways were as sophisticated as we are. It appears some of the early civilisations such as the Olmec and the Maya do not provide us with a gradual evolutionary model of how their civilisations evolved. They just seem to have come out of nowhere, as though the evolutionary phase of those civilisations took place elsewhere.

This then led to me considering space travel and life on other planets. There are probably other planets out there with intelligent life forms and these life forms have probably visited Earth. There is certainly evidence of this when you consider ancient cave drawings and such like representing what appears to be space men and flying machines. Is this where the sophisticated Olmec and Mayan people came from, other planets that are out there in our universe? Also, who is out there now in the universe, at this moment in time, communicating their presence, their knowledge of us and demonstrating their superior intelligence by apparently using what could be laser technology to beam images on to such things as ice, sand and crops, representing advanced mathematics, ancient symbolism and complex geometries that is reported to be increasing in intensity and content?

When you consider the esoteric fingerprints here on Earth, there always seems to be people imparting knowledge which was out of place for the time, but helped to move humanity forward. I think who ever is out there in the universe and is communicating with us at this moment might help us to move humanity forward.

There are many things I am now able to have an opinion on rather than accepting with blind faith. For example, I believe in evolution as you can clearly see the physical body or solid casing of all living things evolves to keep pace with a changing environment. Evolution effectively explains the development of living species, the process of natural selection and other things. Charles Darwin gave us his wonderful theory of evolution that concentrates on the physical, but there is a missing element here, as there has to be something that drives/animates the physical body or solid casing. I think that element is the spirit/consciousness and this is the link to creation. Every living thing has duality, a physical body/casing animated by a spirit.

Our universe and world is so intricate that quite clearly it has to have been planned and designed by an intelligent Creator. If you look at the DNA molecule, which contains information and is present in all living things, you will find it is like a computer programme but written in its own special language. It is quite obvious it is only a mind that can develop language. It is the same with the universal language, the symbolic representation that, again, it seems quite obvious as it is a language it could only have been designed by a mind.

In the 21st century man has made huge technological advances and yet, as clever as we are our technology is faulty, as we have concentrated on the cause, what the technology we have created is supposed to do, rather than the effect.

We have very little remedy or antidote for what we have created and as a result our environment, Mother Earth and the universe is suffering, and that means we must suffer too.

The Creator of our world has put far more thought into the creation it has designed and provides an antidote for everything, even though it might take time and research for us to find it. The intelligence of that creative designer surpasses anything we humans are capable of.

I think the big bang is probably the answer to how this Creator created our universe and world, and quantum physics can most likely eventually tell us how this was achieved. With quantum physics we now understand that what is primary is energy and matter is a special kind of energy – it's organised energy. And what organises energy is the mind. The mind and consciousness comes first. Max Planck, the father of quantum physics said 'I regard consciousness as fundamental. I regard matter as a derivative of consciousness'. I consider it likely the Creator focused and projected its mind to organise the energy and achieve the big bang and if that is so then it has to be for a purpose.

I am of the opinion we existed before we came here on Earth and we continue to exist when we die. I have this opinion not just because of documented evidence but also because of what I have experienced. I have been out of my body and know I exist separate from it, I have duality. I also think we come here in the physical body to learn lessons and we come with loads of human frailties mixed in with the good stuff, and we also come with free will and when we come here the mind is locked, so what has gone before and the reason we have come here is not known to us.

That portion of the mind which is not accessible to us must exist elsewhere in another dimension or parallel universe. Science is already working with this theory and to me it makes perfect sense, and that inaccessible portion of the mind is probably what is referred to in spiritual circles as 'our higher self'.

My research has led me to think it is probable that two or more worlds exist, composed of different forms of matter but occupying the same space. We probably go back to one of these other worlds when we die. Does what we have learnt and experienced in this life merge with that part of us that exists in that other dimension or parallel universe when we die? I think so.

I think these other worlds are worlds of thought and feeling and whatever anyone is thinking and feeling is transparent and this is probably what is meant when people say the spirit world is a world of love. As there would be no physical body just thought and feeling, you would see hate, spite, jealousy etc as these things would be transparent and therefore would need to be overcome and there would be no hiding them.

I am confident there is communication from world to world and we in this world receive help from those in the spirit world and beyond, all of whom work for the Creator, to help us achieve what ever it is we have come here to achieve via the universal language of symbols, dreams, coincidence etc.

I think 'they' are all around us, occupying what we perceive as empty space and they influence this world in which we live in a really big way, which includes messing about with time and altering or orchestrating events. I also think the planetary influence on our environment and us

90

humans is significant and is another way of orchestrating people and events. In addition I consider all influence from this Creator is for the good and evil is something that can exist within the individual and we can all be devils, it is an aspect of the personality and is expressed through free will when in the physical body, and it is not a separate entity existing outside of the physical body.

The Creator of all this is obviously a power of immense intellect and has given us pieces of a jigsaw we can put together via clues, markers and signposts that talk to us in a cryptic and subtle universal language of symbolic happenings, symbols and dreams to help us go forward and make sense of life, and the historical and esoteric fingerprints that are all around us, are calling to us. However the Creator's words are at the mercy of the interpretation of man and can, and historically have been, used as a form of control and manipulation.

So as you can see I have theories and opinions on many things, all of which I can support by research, science, experience etc., but I am no longer rigid in my belief structures. I am very willing to remain fluid about my theories and opinions but I am concentrating on the journey and as the journey evolves and unfolds so hopefully will my ability to evolve and unfold with it.

The more I have changed and grown as a person, the more tuned-in I have become to others, and many people have been drawn to me and have shared their unexplained happenings with me, and I realised I had coherent theories about the things they were experiencing and I could give them explanations and possibilities that made sense of these happenings, I had already walked that path and now I was retracing my footsteps to walk with them. In this way I was helping people, and their way of thinking would invariably start to alter as they began to see life in a different way.

It was a natural progression for me to create a programme and offer courses in spiritual and psychic development, and so for the last twelve years I have worked in the spiritual arena. I see people on a one to one basis for spiritual counselling and guidance/life coaching, and for many years I had a weekly column in a local newspaper where people wrote to me for answers to their dreams and unexplained happenings. I have regularly been on local radio analysing dreams, answering questions and suchlike.

A few times a year I am invited to speak on national radio and I am regularly invited as a guest speaker for adult psychology classes at different locations around my hometown of Cardiff, giving the students an alternative perspective on the mind. I am also invited as guest speaker at various events and I am always happy to run workshops and courses for interested groups of people. I have also written and self published two books about the spiritual journey and the universal language

I get to meet all types of people from all walks of life who have had experiences and unexplained happenings they do not understand. I have worked with them to provide them with answers and possibilities, and I have watched them change as they begin to perceive life differently. In this way I have been doing market research and my findings are that something huge is going on as contact is being made from the Creator, via its agents, spirit workers and other means, to people living here on Earth in a big way. This contact is positive, as it can help and guide us on our path through what can be a very difficult life. This contact is getting stronger and stronger and more frequent and at the moment people singularly are waking up to this fact.

But this Age of Aquarius is not just about the individual it is also about the whole and so I should introduce a note of caution at this point. I think the book you are reading might accelerate and raise the consciousness of you the reader, and the more people that read it, the faster and greater the impact will be on the whole. This heightened awareness brings with it a responsibility so be warned, as once you know better you are more accountable.

My work introduces a gradual drip feed of information that has firm foundations that challenge belief systems that are built on sand, and the techniques I have developed help to still the internal chatter necessary to focus the mind.

The more our belief systems are challenged, the more the barriers of the mind will come down, and the mind will expand and become faster. Any irrational prejudice, intolerance, fear and misplaced beliefs that fire the emotions and restrict the free flow of the mind are banished, and this has a positive effect on impulsive and/or learnt behaviour, which in turn has a beneficial effect on our actions, and benefits the whole. When you then introduce to the mix the universal language of dreams and symbolic happenings so communication with an unseen force is possible, and the individual can test for them self, then the impact is significant. It is probable as you read this book many strange things will happen as the mind

92

expands and your thoughts become unknotted but don't be afraid, it is to be expected and it will reinforce the validity of what you are reading.

This journey of the mind can seem a solitary road and so, as you the reader begin to retrace my steps in the following pages, if you need help when the going gets tough and when you are weary, know you are not alone as we are all connected. This journey of the mind cannot be rushed and I am happy for you to set the pace. Sometimes you might need to go back a small distance if there is something that obstructs; it might be you will need to sit and contemplate the path you are travelling, asking for help to move forward. A little at a time is good, but it is no use taking shortcuts as to get the full benefit of the journey you need to experience it all. Perseverance is the key and is a price worth paying for the benefit you will receive, so please keep reading, and keep journeying onwards.

By reading this far you have proved yourself to be a true seeker of the meaning of life. I applaud you for joining with me in my quest in trying to figure out how it all works, and when you reach the end of the book, if your findings agree with my findings then recommend this book to others so that it travels further and further, unknotting minds as it goes. As many minds reach higher and higher, all of us together will help to raise consciousness, and together we can bring about change.

3

The plan for our lives

I think if there was no Creator and if we humans were simply here by chance as many believe then there would be no purpose in life. But what if there is a purpose for our life on Earth? There is evidence of a Creator all around us and it seems to me there is a plan for the Earth and also our life on Earth and there is much more to our existence than just living from one day to the next. Because of my experiences and the experiences of others I think we are, in fact, spiritual beings in physical bodies living life on Earth in order that we can learn lessons, grow in wisdom and expand our empathy and compassion. Our human frailties coupled with free will seem to be the precise tools we need in order to achieve this growth. However, we must be aware that once the spirit is placed at conception, we are at the mercy of not just our own free will but the free will of others, as well as at the mercy of random chance/accidents etc.

In order to be that purposeful person and before we are born it makes sense a lot of thought and preparation must go into our planned existence to help us achieve whatever it is we have come here for. This probably takes place in conference with spirits who are more evolved than us and when the plan is completed then consideration would be given to our earthly life and what ingredients are needed to make us that unique person capable of realizing our aims.

• Our date of birth would be chosen, as the planets are an energy influence, and as you will learn later, energy contains information. This would help to give us our character traits.

• Our parents would be chosen for the genes we inherit which will determine our colour, stature, facial features etc. and also for the environment and culture which we are born into.

• Finally we have to throw into the mix soul growth, arguably achieved in previous lives, which is probably why one person may be full of empathy and compassion whilst another may not care.

It is usual we have to live a large portion of our lives before we are able to look back and make sense of the reason why our mix had to be as it was. We might also recognise the universe was somehow orchestrating events at key moments but that often we ignored this as our free will kicked in. However, it is at those times we learn the most painful lessons which in the long run can lead to gain, which is probably where the 'no pain no gain' philosophy comes from.

However it is much easier to look back over a life of another once completed and if you look at famous people in history who have helped humanity move forward, and could be considered as Masters, you can see how just the right mix of ingredients came together, and how the universe seemed to lend a hand, which helped them achieve their notoriety. Martin Luther King Junior is a perfect example.

3.1 Martin Luther King Junior

Born under the influence of Capricorn on the 15th January 1929, Martin's grandfather began the family's long tenure as pastors of the Ebenezer Baptist Church in Atlanta, and Martin's father served after him and from 1960 until his death Martin acted as co-pastor. Martin attended segregated public schools in Georgia and then attended Morehouse College, a distinguished Negro institution of Atlanta from which both his father and grandfather had graduated, and from there he progressed to higher education.

In 1954, Martin was Pastor of the Dexter Avenue Baptist Church in Alabama. Always a strong worker for civil rights for members of his race, Martin was, by this time, a member of the Executive Committee of the National Association for the Advancement of Coloured People. With all the knowledge and experience he had attained he was ready to take his place as a leader when the first great Negro non-violent demonstration in the United States occurred. This event was the famous bus boycott involving the lovely black lady Rosa Parks, when she was asked to give up her seat to a white man and refused. The boycott lasted 382 days. On December 21 1956, after the Supreme Court of the United States had declared unconstitutional the laws requiring segregation on buses, Negroes and whites rode the buses as equals and Martin emerged as an outstanding and respected Negro leader.

Martin went on to campaign in an official capacity for the civil rights movement and travelled great distances to appear wherever there was injustice, protest, and action. He went on to lead a massive protest in Birmingham, Alabama, that caught the attention of the entire world, providing what he called a 'coalition of conscience', and inspiring his *"Letter from a Birmingham Jail"*, a manifesto of the Negro revolution.

He also planned the drives in Alabama for the registration of Negroes as voters; he directed the peaceful march on Washington, D.C., of 250,000 people to whom he delivered his address, "l Have a Dream". He conferred with President John F. Kennedy and campaigned for President Lyndon B. Johnson. He became not only the symbolic leader of American blacks but also a world figure. At the age of thirty-five, Martin Luther King, Jr., was the youngest man to have received the Nobel Peace Prize. When notified of his selection, he announced he would turn over the prize money of $54,123 to the furtherance of the civil rights movement.

On the evening of April 4, 1968, while standing on the balcony of his motel room in Memphis, Tennessee, where he was to lead a protest march in sympathy with striking garbage workers of that city, he was assassinated.

The above was taken from:
http://nobelprize.org/nobel_prizes/peace/laureates/1964/king-bio.html

The example used of Martin Luther King to demonstrate how we might be part of a plan hopefully shows how:

• Our date of birth would be chosen – Martin was born under the sign of Capricorn and if you know any Capricorns then you should recognise those born under its influence have the ability to work hard, particularly in business affairs. They are ambitious types with a great sense of responsibility and will complete any project once started. They are usually strongly dominant and are particularly good at ruling and directing. Powerful and intellectual personalities, the Capricorn person has a great sense of responsibility and social consciousness.

• Our parents would be chosen for the genes we inherit and the environment we are born into - Martin was born into a black religious family, of which his grandfather and father were well educated Preachers, a rare occurrence in those times. Naturally they would have wanted the children of their family to also be educated. He would have learnt how to address an audience and preach to the masses at his father and grandfather's knee. His family would have been privy to the inner most secrets of those around them and undoubtedly would have riled against the injustice that being black brought to their lives. There was probably many a discussion around the dinner table of which Martin would have been an avid listener. Martin would have been influenced by all of this and he followed in their footsteps and by a mix of education, passion for the underdog and charisma, and having learnt from the most vibrant and soulful preaching in the world, so it was he was able to captivate many audiences with his passionate views on civil rights.

• Finally we have to throw into the mix soul growth arguably achieved in previous lives - The black history that had seen people survive the horrors of capture, the terrible middle passage and years of slavery and the resulting racial segregation obviously stirred feelings of injustice, empathy and compassion in Martin that pushed him further than others who might somehow have been more accepting of their lot. He had the strength and passion, and had developed all the right tools to help right this terrible wrong, and take humanity and human consciousness forward. He displayed the qualities identified with advanced soul growth obtained through repeated reincarnations and was probably chosen to come to Earth and do what he did.

Also to consider is the fact that when Martin led the first great Negro non-violent demonstration for the famous bus boycott in 1955/1956, the television, which was invented in the early 1920's, had just been completed and released for consumer use. Thus the whole world could see America was racially segregated and this eventually helped influence a shamed America to bring in racial change. The timing of this was stunning and it would seem the universe was somehow orchestrating events so Martin's cause had a worldwide stage.

4

The plan for the Earth and the universe

Harold Burr, Emeritus Professor of Anatomy at Yale Medical School says that a complex magnetic field not only establishes the pattern of the brain at birth but continues to regulate and control it through our lives.

• Since the Earth's creation the astrological ages, which are time periods in astrology, have symbolically paralleled major changes in the Earth's development and the Earth's inhabitants' development. Each age is led by the Zodiacal sign of the constellation in which the Sun actually appears at the vernal equinox in the northern hemisphere.

I think if we apply the theory of a plan to the Earth and the universe we don't have to look too far for pieces of the jigsaw and clues as to the plans components, which to me seem like signposts on a road pointing towards the ultimate destination. The problem is the plan is so huge and incorporates so many jigsaw pieces and signposts that it is difficult to see the whole. Playing a key role in the overall plan is the astrological ages.

Our knowledge of the astrological ages has been handed down to us by our ancient ancestors. Their understanding of the cosmos has left us an inheritance we have not fully claimed as we have yet to understand the value of it and the role it plays in the overall plan for the universe. Our ancestors have given us a framework that allows us to join both the spiritual and commonplace history of mankind. From their esoteric and cryptic wisdom we can see the structure of the larger cycles at work in the heavens.

A search of the Internet tells us:

The astrological ages have a pattern of formation in correlation to the state of human consciousness and its ensuing civilisation. They are based on the astrological circle of the Zodiac and in the same way our personal horoscope reveals our inner self, and the continuing planetary cycles in relation to our chart indicate the actual process of growth, so do these long-term, cosmic cycles reveal the collective spiritual state of mankind.

98

One of the most important cosmic cycles is the 25,800 (approximate) period known as the Great Year, also known as a Platonic year or Equinoctial cycle, and it is made up of several astronomical factors. Like the 360-day year, the 25,800-year cycle of the Great Year is divisible into seasons, months, weeks, days and hours. The division into twelve months corresponds to the movement of the Sun through the twelve signs of the celestial Zodiac. Each Great Month lasts approximately 2,160 years, while each of its 360 days measures 72 years of our time or, approximately, the three score years and ten of man's allotted life span.

In each month of the common year the Sun appears to be in a different constellation of the celestial Zodiac as the Earth completes her annual 360-day cycle. Likewise, the Sun, due to the 'precession of the equinoxes', appears to remain in each sign of the Zodiac for around 2,160 years, or one 'month' of the Great Year. Because the Earth is spinning it develops a bulge at the centre and in addition the Earth tilts in relation to the plane of the solar system. The pull of the sun, moon, planets and other forces causes the Earth's axis to wobble. As a result of the particular direction of the Earth's wobble (in relation to its path around the Sun), the order of precessional alignment to the Zodiac (Pisces, Aquarius, Capricorn, etc) is in reverse order to the more familiar sequence of monthly alignments (Capricorn, Aquarius, Pisces, etc). This is where the term 'precession of the equinoxes' derives. The above was taken from:
http://en.wikipedia.org/wiki/Astrology

It seems to me Harold Burr has given us important scientific proof as to how we humans and other things in our environment respond to the influence of the cosmos. When I was researching this I woke up one morning and was asking questions in my mind about the planets and this complex magnetic field that Harold Burr tells us about. I was asking 'How does it work?' I went for a walk to help my thought process and when I looked up at the sky there was thick cloud everywhere but every now and then there were perfect round circles, holes, in the cloud. Through these holes beams of light were streaming and my surroundings and me were covered in sunshine. I thought 'OK I get it'.

Part of my research had led to me learning that light is ultimately energy and energy contains information. Light is part of the electro-magnetic spectrums whose energies continually surround and penetrate all living beings. Light is fundamental to life. Life on Earth is bound to rhythms of light caused by the movement of our planet. Light is a means of communication and these unseen beams of light penetrate everything!

A couple of years prior to this experience I had a dream I had written down and I remembered it and thought it might connect with this part of my research regarding the planets and the complex magnetic field. I found what I had written and it was quite vague but I had recorded that I was shown a symbolic electronic panel with lots of coloured squares in it. I knew each of these squares represented different aspects of the human personality, but that was all I had recorded.

Connecting it with the holes and the beams of light, I think it might mean that when a person is born, according to where the planets are in the heavens at their time of birth, these planets will light up these symbolic coloured squares/ magnetic field to a greater or lesser extent and could be likened to the manufacturers default setting of electrical/ electronic equipment.

There could be some coloured squares lit very brightly, and these aspects of the personality they represented might be dominant in that person. There could be other coloured squares hardly lit, and then these aspects of the personality might be undeveloped, and so on, and so on. I think planetary influence, nurture, environment, life experience etc. would then fire these squares. If we have bright squares that represent negative traits, imagine the effort we have to make with self-development in order to dim that aspect of our personality. In times of great stress and such like, we probably revert back to our default setting and we see ourselves react in the same old way.

I think this theory matches with the colour that can be seen in the aura. I also think this is what those in spirit probably see when they look at us, our coloured lights, and in this way they know what we are thinking and feeling. This is possibly how they see one another in their parallel universe, no body just coloured lights of varying brightness which have different meanings.

Putting all of this together, and if it is right, it seems to me it is a fantastically clever way for the Creator to help us with our mental and emotional growth both collectively and individually and if that is so, this growth has to be planned and there is obviously a planner. There must be a reason for us to develop and I would say this Earth is like some kind of training place.

Roger Coghill, in his book *The Healing Energies of Light*, pages 84-85, explains:

'When light enters the eye some 20% of it carries on past the retina and reaches parts of the brain, especially the hypothalamus, the pituitary gland and the pineal gland. So light can regulate the majority of our life processes, including hormone production, stress response, the autonomic nervous system and the limbic system that is the seat of our emotions. Light can also affect our metabolism and even our reproductive functions.'

I meditate using light and I find it really useful if I need help with a situation or am having problems or difficulties with a person. I visualise myself as being full of light, as though I am a fluorescent tube. I then send light from my heart to the heart of the situation or the heart of the person. I invariably find everything connected to that situation or person will then be smooth, with no difficulties or unpleasantness. I know many people who use this technique successfully, especially healers.

In the Christian Bible there are many passages referring to light and it tells us Jesus healed many sick people, because the light of God shone so brightly in him. I think symbolically this means light is part of God's mechanism that regulates our world and it carries beneficial and healing rays and when we think on that lighter level then we can bring those beneficial and healing rays to ourselves and we can also project them outwards.

In Chapter 7.1 you will see Matthew Manning visualises light when he is healing.

4.1 Age of Pisces

"The appearance of Christ coincided with the beginning of a new aeon, the age of the Fishes. A synchronicity exists between the life of Christ and the objective astronomical event, the entrance of the spring equinox into the sign of Pisces".

The psychologist Carl Jung from his book *Aion*.

It seems to be generally agreed the Piscean Age began at around 1-100 BC therefore at the current time we might be just entering the Age of Aquarius.

Pisces was Jesus' age and Jesus was a Master or an agent of the Creator, brought here to teach us something and help to move humanity on. Symbolically he was a fisher of men, reeling in people from the sea of life to teach them how to swim and be on top of life. He called Fishermen as his disciples and they too became fishers of men. Looking back I would say it is apparent Jesus has had a great influence on our world over the last two thousand years. As all Masters/agents are, he was undoubtedly chosen to do this specific job of work as he had all the ingredients need-ed, and he must have prepared for many lives for his incarnation as a world leader.

Just as Moses is said to have ushered in the Age of Aries, Jesus was born in the transitory period, as the Piscean Age was coming and the Aries Age was leaving. Jesus' teaching inspired Christianity. The symbolism surrounding the birth of Jesus illustrates the relationship between the sign of the Fish and that of its polarity, Virgo, and Jesus' mother was a virgin (Virgo) and she had a virgin womb as Jesus was her first-born child.

In the time when Jesus was born the masses would have been illiterate, as only the people with money could afford an education. Therefore if somebody wanted to communicate with others other than face-to-face they would have to draw a picture image as a symbolic message. There are many references in the Bible to Jesus performing miracles but I think most of them can be given a symbolic explanation. There is the story of Jesus feeding the multitude with two fishes (Pisces) and five loaves of bread (Virgo, the Virgin holding the shafts of wheat as the emblem of this sign) and symbolically he and his disciples were feeding their souls because the multitude were starved of spiritual nourishment.

Jesus is also known as the sacrificial 'Lamb of God' and 'Lamb' signifies the sign of Aries and Jesus, as sacrificial 'Lamb', therefore, closed the Age of Aries. Jesus is said to have walked on water and calmed the sea, sym-bolising he was on top of life, and he taught others to 'calm the sea of their emotions' and also get on top of life. He was also said to have turned water into wine, symbolising that he enriched life. Jesus was tempted in the wilderness by the devil. The wilderness symbolises the material world and the devil symbolises our lower, selfish side.

During the Age of Pisces the truth of our duality, that we are both body and spirit, was revealed. The sign itself shows the linking of the two fishes, as our spirit and body are linked. The evolutionary work of this age with Jesus' help has been the lifting of our lower physical nature to that of embracing spirituality. Jesus showed us the truth of who and what we are, a spiritual being living a life in a physical body to learn lessons and grow in mental and emotional maturity. Even with the death of Jesus' physical body he did not die but his spirit was resurrected, just as no living thing dies. It doesn't matter who or what we are, we all go through the same process and life continues in one or the other of the parallel universes.

To me it seems obvious from reading the bible that as well as being an amazing teacher, Jesus was also a medium and a healer.

4.2 Age of Aquarius

Jesus states he and his followers, at the last Passover, are to go into "the house of the man with the water pitcher." They are to follow him to the upper room and there prepare for a feast which he will share with them. Luke 22:10.

I think symbolically the man with the water pitcher signifies the Age of Aquarius and the upper room refers to a higher state of consciousness and the sharing of food refers to spiritual nourishment that is received from Jesus and shared with his followers.

Aquarius is an air sign and is the age of technological and social advancement while Leo, its polarity, is involved with the same influences but carries out its role in a highly personalised manner. Leo is concerned with the preservation of the one, while Aquarius is preoccupied with the needs and interrelationships of the many. Therefore this age will see people who are advancing for purely personal reasons being influenced to share their advancement for the good of all.

Aquarius pertains to the mental realms and as the influence of the Aquarian Age has been coming in we have seen the advent of all things to do with waves of the air, such as telephone, electricity, radio, aeroplane, television, Internet, and space exploration, and all are related to Aquarius. Modern belief in spiritual and psychic abilities have also come to the fore and leading the way were mediums with fantastic abilities who were capable of trance, transfiguration, direct voice, materialisation mediumship achieved via ectoplasm, etc. but unfortunately most of these gifts have died out now, they were just to help usher in the Aquarian Age and show us what was possible.

We are now mostly left with clairsentient abilities and working with the mind via telepathy, which incorporates mediumship and psychic abilities.

The Aquarian sign is often depicted as a young man/woman with an urn of water placed upon his/her shoulders, but notice the word WOMAN includes the word MAN. This age will bring out the feminine and intuitive side of all of us and telepathy, which is achieved via waves of the air, will be an accepted form of communication.

4.2.1 Things of the air

So as you have read, it would seem we are now somewhere in the 160-year transitory period which will see Pisces completely leaving and Aquarius settling fully in, and as Aquarius is an air sign it has brought with it all things of the air, such as:

Telephone 1875. After experimenting with various acoustical devices Alexander Graham Bell produced the first intelligible telephonic transmission with a message to his assistant, Thomas Watson, on 5th June 1875. When he heard that Elisha Gray was working on a similar device, Bell patented his telephone on 3rd March 1876. The following year he formed the Bell Telephone Company. The telephone was an instant success. Within three years there were 30,000 telephones in use around the world. Gray later claimed the invention of the telephone but lost the long legal battle in the Supreme Court.
http://www.spartacus.schoolnet.co.uk/USAbellAG.htm

Electric Light 1879. The modern world is an electrified world. The light bulb, in particular, profoundly changed human existence by illuminating the night and making it hospitable to a wide range of human activity. The electric light, one of the everyday conveniences that most affects our lives, was invented in 1879 by Thomas Alva Edison. He put together what he knew about electricity with what he knew about gaslights and invented a whole electrical system. http://www.ideafinder.com/history/inventors.

Radio 1896. Marconi began his research on radio waves while at home in Bologna, inspired by the possibilities he saw in the work of early pioneers such as Heinrich Hertz, Augusto Righi and Oliver Lodge. He brought his vision and his enthusiasm to England in 1896, in search of support and commercial application, and in the same year applied for a patent for a system of wireless telegraphy. Having demonstrated his system to the Navy, Army and representatives of the Post Office in trials on Salisbury Plain, Marconi arranged a demonstration to accompany a public lecture on telegraphy by William Preece, chief engineer to the General Post Office.

This was held in Toynbee Hall, the educational and charitable institution in London's East End, in December 1896. Preece operated the transmitter and whenever he created an electric spark, a bell rang on a box Marconi took to any part of the lecture room. There was no visible connection between the two. The demonstration caused a sensation and made Marconi a celebrity.
http://www.mhs.ox.ac.uk/marconi/exhibition/marconiarrives.htm

Aeroplane 1903. Orville Wright (1871-1948) and Wilbur Wright (1867-1912) requested a patent application for a "flying machine" nine months before their successful flight in December 1903, which Orville Wright recorded in his diary. As part of the Wright Brothers' systematic practice of photographing every prototype and test of their various flying machines, they had persuaded an attendant from a nearby life-saving station to snap Orville Wright in full flight. The craft soared to an altitude of 10 feet, travelled 120 feet, and landed 12 seconds after takeoff. After making two longer flights that day, Orville and Wilbur Wright sent this telegram to their father, instructing him to "inform press."
http://inventors.about.com/library/inventors/blairplane.htm

Television 1924. John Logie Baird was a Scottish engineer, most famous for being the first person to demonstrate a working television. His first crude apparatus was made of odds and ends but by 1924 he managed to transmit a flickering image across a few feet. On 26 January 1926 he gave the world's first demonstration of true television before fifty scientists in an attic room in central London. In 1927 his television was demonstrated over 438 miles of telephone line between London and Glasgow, and he formed the Baird Television Development Company. (BTDC). In 1928 the BTDC achieved the first transatlantic television transmission between London and New York and the first

transmission to a ship in mid-Atlantic. He also gave the first demonstration of both colour and stereoscopic television.
http://www.bbc.co.uk/history/historic_figures/baird_logie.shtml

Internet 1961. No one person invented the Internet as we know it today. However, certain major figures contributed major breakthroughs. Leonard Kleinrock was the first to publish a paper about the idea of packet switching, which is essential to the Internet. He did so in 1961. Packet switching is the idea that packets of data can be "routed" from one place to another based on address information carried in the data, much like the address on a letter. Packet switching replaces the older concept of "circuit switching," in which an actual electrical circuit is established all the way from the source to the destination. Circuit switching was the idea behind traditional telephone exchanges.
http://www.boutell.com/newfaq/history/inventednet.html

4.2.2

The coming of the Age of Aquarius has brought with it people with rare and exceptional mediumship gifts, to reinforce to us that we are body and spirit and whilst the body might die, the spirit survives and communication between worlds is possible. These exceptional mediums have done a great service to our world and the legacy they have left for science is perhaps as yet not appreciated, but I am sure that eventually it will be understood and all the pieces of the puzzle will come together as science progresses. The following spiritual pioneers are used by way of an example of this:

Helen Duncan - Materialisation Medium
Helen Duncan was born in 1897 and was a poorly educated Scot – she was also one of the most remarkable women Britain has ever seen. Her calling was to be a physical medium, a person who, under the right conditions, was able to exude from the body's orifices a mysterious substance called ectoplasm, which can be moulded into solid forms by people long since dead, allowing them to communicate with their loved ones on Earth once again.

Helen's gift was such that it could have radically altered society's view of the afterlife. Instead, it saw the medium imprisoned and, in the end, caused her death.

In 1944 she spent nine months in Holloway Prison, North London, after being the first and only person to be convicted this century under the 1735 Witchcraft Act. As a result of her trial, this antiquated set of laws were abolished and replaced in 1951 by the Fraudulent Mediums' Act.

The case infuriated Britain's then Prime Minister, Winston Churchill. Angered that a Georgian law had been resurrected, he labelled the proceedings 'obsolete tomfoolery'.

Yet many Spiritualists believe the British Government ordered Mrs Duncan's arrest not because she was allegedly fraudulent but for national security reasons. At a séance she gave in Portsmouth, a materialised form revealed information about the sinking of HMS Barham. The sinking was only later confirmed officially as fact, the Ministry of Defence had felt it was not in the public interest to announce the disaster sooner.

Shortly after, police broke up another Duncan séance in the same town and three months later the Allies latest perceived threat to the war effort found herself incarcerated at His Majesty's pleasure.

In 1956 police stormed another of her séances, this time in Nottingham. Ectoplasm was reportedly present which, it is believed, shot back into her body causing severe shock. Six weeks later she died, officially from diabetes and heart failure, unofficially as a result of detectives' blundering heavy handedness. Spiritualism had gained its first martyr.
The above was taken from *Medium On Trial*, Manfred Cassirer.

4.2.3 Alec Harris - Materialisation Medium

Born in 1897, Alec Harris's remarkable materialisation and direct-voice mediumship astounded all those who had the privilege to witness it; and the world is fortunate that his wife, Louie, recorded the details of her husband's great work in a fascinating book entitled *They Walked Among Us*. The strength and power of Alec's physical mediumship were universally acclaimed. One astonished sitter who attended a séance in Alec's home in the Whitchurch area of Cardiff, which is the capital city of Wales in the UK, remarked, 'The materialised people came out of the cabinet sometimes two or three at a time. On that amazing night, about twenty fully materialised forms greeted us and spoke with us, quite naturally. After a while you forgot you were conversing with so-called "dead" people'.

In the mid 20th-Century, the editor of Psychic News, Maurice Barbanell said of Alec's mediumship that 'the spirit forms not only show themselves in good red light, but they also hold sustained conversations, after having walked about ten feet from the cabinet'. But in the early days of his spiritual awakening, Alec Harris at first refused to accept the idea that he might possess such an incredibly rare mediumistic gift.

His family were Welsh Christians of the 'dyed-in-the-wool' kind. Born and bred in Treherbert, in the Rhondda Valley in South Wales, where Christianity was most certainly the order of the day, Alec wanted nothing to do with 'meddling' with the dead, or with the religion of Spiritualism. But then his sister, Connie, died and subsequently returned to the astonished members of her family when Alec attended a séance conducted by the remarkable Scottish physical medium Helen Duncan. His sister's spirit-return encouraged him to sit for the development of his own spiritual gifts, and he became one of the finest materialisation mediums to emerge from Great Britain in the 20th-Century.

Strangely enough, Alec Harris's sister Connie later made another successful spirit return in a materialised form, but this time through her own brother's remarkable physical mediumship. During the production of materialised spirit forms, Alec's spirit guides usually took him into a deep-trance, and the sitters were able to clearly see him sitting on his chair (bound hand and foot) inside the 'cabinet' - and the whole room was bathed in good red light while the materialised people walked around the room and spoke with their loved ones. At one memorable séance which was attended by Sir Alexander Cannon, Sir Alex spoke to two spirit forms who were Tibetans, and these conversations were held in their native tongue, which was unknown to Alec Harris or any of the other persons present at the séance. And a certain Prof. T J Haarhoff, who was a professor of classics, conversed with a materialised spirit who spoke to him in ancient Greek.

These events signal quite clearly the genuineness of Mr Harris's mediumship. Like other physical mediums before him, Alec was treated abominably by hostile sceptics who simply could not admit the possibility that what they were seeing with their own eyes was genuine phenomena, and he was hurt in a seance in South Africa when a journalist grabbed an ectoplasmic spirit-form, while other members of the press set off flashlights without permission. Alec Harris died in 1974 and will be long remembered for the amazing phenomena that was produced through his remarkable mediumship.

The above was taken from
www.lineone.net/enlightenment/alec_harris.htm

4.2.4 Leslie Flint - Direct Voice Medium

'I am a medium, I have the rare gift known as the independent direct voice. I do not speak in trance, I need no trumpet or other paraphernalia. The voices of the dead speak directly to their friends or relatives and are located in space a little above my head and slightly to one side of me. They are objective voices which my sitters can record on their own tape-recorders to play later in the privacy of their homes. Sometimes those who speak from beyond the grave achieve only a whisper, hoarse and strained, at other times they speak clearly and fluently in voices recognisably their own during life, and even after thirty-five years of my mediumship I do not fully understand what are the conditions which cause the phenomena to vary in this way.'

Leslie Flint came into this world in 1911 and left it in 1994. While here he became the finely tuned instrument transmitting thousands of messages from the world he now inhabits. No intellectual, but a plain speaking man, Leslie was born into poverty and raised amid family disarray. Yet through dogged determination and single-mindedness, he became one of the most celebrated independent direct voice mediums of the twentieth century. Through his remarkable gifts, he brought consolation and hope to the bereaved and understanding and inspiration to thousands, as well as shedding light on many strange corners of history.

With the advent of Mickey, his much-loved Cockney alter-ego in the world beyond, there began decades of service as a direct voice medium. Leslie gave sittings to those of every rank and degree, every profession, enabling the bereaved to learn of the great truth of human survival beyond physical death. His mediumship was also a channel for famous men and women whose spirit communications were on an elevated and inspiring plane, often throwing fascinating new light on the accepted annals of history.

Sceptics attended sittings, but left convinced. Others tested Leslie's genuineness in every way. Truly, he could comment 'I am the most tested medium this country has ever produced'. People travelled from all over the world to sit with him. Leslie also demonstrated abroad, particularly in the United States, where he was in great demand.

The final chapter of his life came with his retirement to Hove, where he enjoyed years of peace and happiness before passing on at the age of eighty-three.

Leslie acknowledged he 'had no education to speak of", yet words of the highest wisdom and most profound knowledge, often in a variety of languages, emerged at sittings. He was an upright, simple man, with little financial ambition or perception, but his service to mankind was of inestimable worth.

While much of the world sinks further into a morass of materialism, commercialism and tribalism, it is now more important than ever that mankind learns to appreciate the spirit world's reality, of survival of the soul, of the vital importance of good deeds and good thoughts to prepare the way ahead, and that, whatever our colour or creed, we are all spiritual beings expressed in physical terms.

The above was taken from *Voices In The Dark* – Leslie Flint – Foreword by Aubrey Rose CBE, Leslie Flint Education Trust,

5

The esoteric fingerprints here on Earth

I have found it particularly fascinating to read about the mysteries and unexplained things that are here on Earth and can challenge our concept of life and the advancement of man. These esoteric finger-prints include historical writing, structures and religion, and are another piece of the puzzle for us to work on and try to put together. Graham Hancock, Author, puts it so well:

"The way that history is taught in schools and universities, you find an enormous focus on the last 5,000 years since the supposed introduction of writing, and the development of the first big cities in the ancient world. It's almost as though everything that happened to humanity before 5000 years ago is somehow irrelevant and everything that went before us is necessarily much more primitive and backward. Evidence is mounting that we may have lost from the record entire civilizations and once it becomes broadly accepted it's going to force a very major change in the way that we look at our past. If great civilizations, which perhaps in some ways were as sophisticated as we are, have come and gone and been forgotten then it's not a huge jump to realize that could happen to us too. Plato, who was a very credible figure, speaks of a lost civilization that was swallowed up in a single day and a night 9,000 or so years before his time, and he was talking about Atlantis. Also, there is evidence of more than one lost civilization and there are a number of obvious categories of evidence. One concerns physical monuments, structures that have survived and another concerns myths and tradi-tions and the religious scriptures of ancient cultures".
Graham Hancock from his book *Fingerprints of the Gods*.

The following eight sub-chapters are just a few short examples of the esoteric fingerprints here on Earth that I have taken from Graham Hancock's book *Fingerprints of the Gods* but have condensed for ease of reading.

5.1 The Mystery of the Maps

In 1929, a group of historians found a map drawn on a gazelle skin. Research showed it was a genuine document drawn in 1513 by Piri Reis, a famous admiral of the Turkish fleet in the sixteenth century whose passion was cartography. He had privileged access to the Imperial Library of Constantinople and admits in a series of notes on the map, that he compiled and copied the data from a large number of source maps, some of which dated back to the fourth century BC or earlier.

The Lt Professor Charles H. Hapgood of Keene College, New Hampshire requested evaluation from Lt Colonel Harold Z Ohlymer, USAF of unusual features of the Piri Reis World Map, as the lower part of the map seemed to portray the Princess Martha Coast of Queen Maud Land Antarctica and the Palmer Peninsula. Colonel replied that the geographical detail shown in the lower part of the map agreed very remarkably with the results of the seismic profile made across the top of the icecap by the Swedish-British Antarctic Expedition of 1949. He said 'This indicated the coastline had been mapped before it was covered by the icecap. We have no idea how the data on this map can be reconciled with the supposed state of geographical knowledge in 1515.'

If the Queen Maud Land was mapped before it was covered by ice, the original cartography (study and construction) must have been done an extraordinary long time ago. It is well-known that the first civilization, according to the traditional history, developed in the mid-east around year 3000 BC. Who was here 4000 years BC, being able to do things that only NOW are possible with the modern technologies?

There are other ancient maps which challenge traditional history, such as a world map drawn by Oronteus Finaeus in 1531, which had been copied and compiled from several earlier sources. This appeared to document the surprising proposition that Antarctica was visited and perhaps settled by men when it was largely if not entirely non-glacial. This takes civilisation back to a time contemporary with the end of the last Ice Age about 11,000 years ago in the northern hemisphere and makes us question whether there is a lost civilisation.

The sixteenth century's most famous cartographer was Gerard Kremer, otherwise known as Mercator. He included the Oronteus Finaeus map in his Atlas of 1569 but there were also identifiable parts of the then undiscovered southern continent and so he must have had at his disposal source maps other than those used by Oronteus Finaeus.

Philippe Buache was an eighteenth century French geographer who was also able to publish a map of Antarctica long before the southern continent was officially discovered. The extraordinary feature of his map is that it seems to have been based on source maps made earlier, perhaps thousands of years earlier, than those used by Oronteus Finaeus and Mercator. What Buache gives us is an eerily precise representation of Antarctica as it must have looked when there was no ice on it at all.

So now we see that there were human beings capable of accurately mapping landmasses all those years ago. The combined effect of the Piri Reis, Oronteus Finaeus, Mercator and Buache maps give the impression that Antarctica may have been continuously surveyed over a period of several thousand years as the ice-cap gradually spread outwards from the interior, increasing its grip with every passing millennium but not engulfing all the coasts of the southern continent until around 4000bc.

5.2 The Nazca Lines

The Nazca plateau is a barren place in Southern Peru that has 200 square miles of uninterrupted tableland. When winds blow they don't have any effect at ground level and the pebbles on the ground absorb and retain the suns heat, throwing up a protective field of warm air. In addition the soil contains enough gypsum to glue small stones to the subsurface. Once things are drawn here they tend to stay drawn. There's only about an hour of drizzle every ten years, making the area one of the driest in the world. Therefore if you were an artist and wanted to express something grand and important to be visible forever these flatlands could be the answer to your prayers. Scattered apparently random are literally hundreds of different figures. Some depict animals and birds but far more take the form of geometrical devices in the form of trapezoids, rectangles, triangles and straight lines. Viewed at ground level they are little more than grazes on the surface. Viewed from above these latter resemble to the modern eye a jumble of runways and gave rise to thoughts of a landing strip for alien spacecraft.

Experts have dated pottery embedded in the lines ranging from 350 BC to AD600 but they tell us nothing about the lines themselves, although the most recent are at least 1400 years old but they could be far more ancient than that as the artefacts from which such dates are derived could have been brought to Nazca by later people. No one knows their purpose just as no one really knows their age. It's clear that the animals and birds antedate the geometry of the 'runways', because many of the trapezoids, rectangles and straight lines bisect (and thus partly obliterate) the more complex figures. It is believed the artwork has been produced in two phases, with the earlier of the two phases being more advanced. The execution of the zoomorphic figures calls for far higher levels of skills and technology than the etching of the straight lines.

Dr Phillis Pitluga, an astronomer with the Adler Planetarium in Chicago made an intensive computer aided study of stellar alignments at Nazca and she has concluded that the famous spider figure was devised as a terrestrial diagram of the giant constellation of Orion, and that the arrow-straight lines linked to the figure appear to have been set out to track through the ages the changing declinations of the three stars of Orion's Belt. Also the Nazca spider is identical to one of the rarest spiders in the world found only in the Amazon Rainforest. Does this mean the artists came from the Amazon and, if so, how did they travel? How were they able to duplicate minute details of the spiders' anatomy (the reproductive organ positioned on the end of its extended right leg) normally visible only under a microscope?

The whale and the monkey are as out of place in this environment as the spider. A curious figure of a man, his right arm raised as though in greeting, heavy boots on his feet and round eyes staring is also out of place. Other drawings of the human form are equally peculiar; their heads enclosed in halos of radiance, they do indeed look like visitors from another planet. The hummingbird is 165 feet long, the spider 150 feet long and the condor stretches 400 feet from beak to tail feathers, as does the pelican. A lizard, whose tail is now divided by the Pan-American Highway, is 617 feet in length.

How could they have been so perfectly made when, without aircraft, their creators could not have checked the progress of their work by viewing it in the proper perspective? None of the designs is small enough to be seen from ground level where they appear only as ruts in the desert. They show their true form only when seen from an altitude of several hundred feet.

5.3 The Inca trail to the past

The last custodians of the ancient religious heritage of Peru were the Incas whose treasures were ransacked during the thirty terrible years that followed the Spanish conquest in 1532. However a number of early Spanish travellers made sincere efforts to document Inca traditions before they were entirely forgotten. Some of these traditions speak of a great civilisation that was believed to have existed in Peru many thousands of years earlier. Powerful memories were preserved of this civilization, said to have been founded by the Viracochas (named after a God), the same mysterious beings credited with the making of the Nazca lines. Connecting the far flung corners of the Inca Empire was a vast and sophisticated road system, two parallel north-south highways, one running for 3600 kilometres along the coast and the other for a similar distance through the Andes. Both these great thoroughfares were paved and connected by frequent links with an interesting range of design and engineering features such as suspension bridges and tunnels cut through solid rock. They were clearly the work of an evolved, disciplined and ambitious society.

The Incas worshiped the Sun God whom they knew as Inti, and they also worshipped Viracocha, which means foam of the sea. They built a magnificent temple for Viracocha at Cuzco and evidence suggests that he had been worshipped by all the civilisations that had ever existed in the long history of Peru. Accounts of Viracocha likened his appearance to that of Saint Thomas, depicted as a lean, bearded white man, past middle age, wearing sandals and dressed in long, flowing robes. Whoever he was, therefore, he could not have been an American Indian as they are relatively dark-skinned people with sparse facial hair. Viracocha's bushy beard and pale complexion made him sound like a Caucasian.

Through all the ancient legends of the peoples of the Andes stalked a tall, bearded, pale-skinned figure wrapped in a cloak of secrecy. He was known by many different names in many different places but he was always recognizably the same figure. Viracocha, foam of the sea, who came in a time of chaos to set the world to rights. The same basic story was shared in many variants by all the peoples of the Andes region. It began with a vivid description of a terrifying period when the Earth had been inundated by a great flood and plunged into darkness by the disappearance of the sun. Society had fallen into disorder, and the people suffered much hardship. Then 'there suddenly appeared, coming from the South, a white man of large stature and authoritative demeanour. This man had such great power that he changed the hills into valleys and from the valleys made great hills, causing streams to flow from the living stone'.

The early Spanish chronicler who recorded this tradition explained that it had been told to him by the Indians he had travelled among on his journeys in the Andes. And they heard it from their fathers, who in turn had it from the old songs which were handed down from very ancient times. They say that in many places he gave men instructions as to how they should live, asking them to love one another and to show charity to all. He was a scientist and an engineer, a sculptor and an architect. He caused terraces and fields to be formed on the steep sides of the ravines, and sustaining walls to rise up and support them. He made irrigating channels to flow and he went in various directions arranging many things. He was also a teacher and a healer and made himself helpful to people in need.

Before his coming it was said men lived in a condition of disorder, many went naked like savages, they had no houses or dwellings other than caves, and from these they went forth to gather whatever they could find to eat in the countryside. Viracocha was credited with changing all this and with initiating the long-lost golden age which later generations looked back on with nostalgia.

5.4 San Lorenzo, Mexico - The Olmec Enigma

San Lorenzo is an Olmec site lying south-west of Coatzecoalcos in the heart of the 'Serpent Sanctuary'. It was here that the earliest carbon-dates for an Olmec site (around 1500 BC) had been recorded by archaeologists. However, Olmec culture appeared to have been fully evolved by that epoch and there was no evidence that the evolution had taken place in the vicinity of San Lorenzo. In this there lay a mystery. The Olmecs, after all, had built a significant civilization which had carried out prodigious engineering works and had developed the capacity to carve and manipulate vast blocks of stone (several of the huge monolithic heads, weighing twenty tons or more, had been moved as far as 60 miles overland after being quarried in the Tuxtla mountains).

So where, if not at ancient San Lorenzo, had their technological expertise and sophisticated organization been experimented with, evolved and refined? Strangely, despite the best efforts of archaeologists, not a single, solitary sign of anything that could be described as the 'developmental phase' of Olmec society had been unearthed anywhere in Mexico (or, for that matter, anywhere in the New World). These people, whose characteristic form of artistic expression was the carving of huge Negroid heads, appeared to have come from nowhere. Here, at the dawn of history in Central America, the Olmecs had heaped up an artificial mound more than 100 feet high as part of an immense structure some 4000 feet in length and 2000 feet in width.

From the summit you can see for miles across the surrounding countryside. A great many lesser mounds are also visible and around about are several of the deep trenches the archaeologist Michael Coe had dug when he had excavated the site in 1966.

Coe's team made a number of finds here, which included more than twenty artificial reservoirs, linked by a highly sophisticated network of basalt-lined troughs. Part of this system was built into a ridge; when it was rediscovered water still gushed forth from it during heavy rains, as it had done for more than 3,000 years. The main line of the drainage ran from east to west. Into it, linked by joints made to an advanced design, three subsidiary lines were channelled.

After surveying the site thoroughly, the archaeologists admitted that they could not understand the purpose of this elaborate system of sluices and water-works. Nor were they able to come up with an explanation for another enigma. This was the deliberate burial, along specific alignments, of five of the massive pieces of sculpture, showing Negroid features, now widely identified as 'Olmec heads'. These peculiar and apparently ritualistic graves also yielded more than sixty precious objects and artefacts, including beautiful instruments made of jade and exquisitely carved statuettes. Some of the statuettes had been systematically mutilated before burial.

The way the San Lorenzo sculptures had been interred made it extremely difficult to fix their true age, even though fragments of charcoal were found in the same strata as some of the buried objects. Unlike the sculptures, these charcoal pieces could be carbon-dated. They were, and produced readings in the range of 1200 BC. This did not mean, however, that the sculptures had been carved in 1200 BC.

They could have been. But they could have originated in a period hundreds or even thousands of years earlier than that. It was by no means impossible that these great works of art, with their intrinsic beauty and an indefinable numinous power, could have been preserved and venerated by many different cultures before being buried at San Lorenzo. The charcoal associated with them proved only that the sculptures were at least as old as 1200 BC; it did not set any upper limit on their antiquity.

5.5 Children of the First Men, Palenque, Chiapas Province, Mexico

The Mayan Temple at Chiapas Province consisted of three chambers and rests on top of a nine stage pyramid almost 100 feet tall. There is a Palace, a spacious rectangular complex on a pyramidal base, dominated by a narrow, four-storied tower, thought to have been used as an observatory by Mayan priests. A number of other spectacular buildings lay half swallowed by the encroaching forest. These were the Temple of the Foliated Cross, the Temple of the Sun, the Temple of the Count, and the Temple of the Lion - all names made up by archaeologists.

In the central chamber of the Temple, set into the rear wall are two great grey slabs, and inscribed on them are 620 separate Mayan glyphs. These take the form of faces, monstrous and human, together with writhing, mythical creatures. No one knows what was being said because the inscriptions, a mixture of word pictures and phonetic symbols, have not been decoded.

To the left of the hieroglyphs is a steep descending internal stairway. This leads to a room buried deep in the bowels of the pyramid, where the tomb of Lord Pacal lay. This damp stairway had been a secret place from the date when it was originally sealed, in AD 683, until June 1952 when the Mexican archaeologist Alberto Ruz lifted the flagstones in the temple floor. The stairway had been intentionally filled with rubble by its builders, and it took four more years before the archaeologists cleared it out completely and reached the bottom. Entering a narrow chamber they found the skeletons of five young victims of sacrifice. A huge triangular slab of stone was at the far end of the chamber. When it was removed, Ruz was confronted by a remarkable tomb. He described it as 'an enormous room, a kind of grotto draped with curtains of stalactites, and from whose floor arose thick stalagmites like the dripping of a candle.

The room was 30 feet long and 23 feet high. Around the walls could be seen the striding figures of the Lords of the Night—the 'Ennead' of nine deities who ruled over the hours of darkness. Centre-stage, and overlooked by these figures, was a huge monolithic sarcophagus lidded with a five-ton slab of richly carved stone. Inside the sarcophagus was a tall skeleton draped with a treasure trove of jade ornaments. A mosaic death mask of 200 fragments of jade was affixed to the front of the skull. These, supposedly, were the remains of Pacal, a ruler of Palenque in the seventh century AD. The inscriptions stated that this monarch had been eighty years old at the time of his death, but the jade-draped skeleton the archaeologists found appeared to belong to a man half that age.

Pacal's coffin was made of solid stone and was uncompromisingly horizontal. It had all the features of the ancient Egyptians. Like the beliefs concerning the perils of the afterlife, might Pacal's sarcophagus not be an expression of a common legacy linking Ancient Egypt with the ancient cultures of Central America?

The heavy stone lid of the sarcophagus too seemed to have been modelled on the same original as the magnificent engraved blocks the Ancient Egyptians had used for this exact purpose. Indeed, it would not have looked out of place in the Valley of the Kings. But there was one major difference. The scene carved on top of the sarcophagus lid was unlike anything that ever came out of Egypt. It showed a clean-shaven man dressed in what looked like a tight-fitting body-suit, the sleeves and leggings of which were gathered into elaborate cuffs at the wrists and ankles. The man lay semi reclined in a bucket seat which supported his lower back and thighs, the nape of his neck resting comfortably against some kind of headrest, and he was peering forward intently. His hands seemed to be in motion, as though they were operating levers and controls, and his feet were bare, tucked up loosely in front of him.

Was this supposed to be Pacal, the Mayan king? If so, why was he shown operating some kind of machine? The Mayan's weren't supposed to have had machines. They weren't even supposed to have discovered the wheel. Yet with its side panels, rivets, tubes and other gadgets, the structure Pacal reclined in resembled a technological device. A tiny jade statuette was found lying close to the skeleton inside the sarcophagus, and it appeared to be much older than the other grave-goods also placed there. It depicted an elderly Caucasian, dressed in long robes, with a goatee beard.

5.6 A Computer for Calculating the End of the World

The Mayan's had legends handed down to them by their forefathers: They were endowed with intelligence; they saw and instantly they could see far; they succeeded in knowing all that there is in the world. The things hidden in the distance they saw without first having to move. Great was their wisdom; their sight reached to the forests, the rocks, the lakes, the seas, the mountains, and the valleys. In truth, they were admirable men. They were able to know all, and they examined the four corners, the four points of the arch of the sky, and the round face of the Earth.

The achievements of this race aroused the envy of several of the most powerful deities. 'It is not well that our creatures should know all,' opined these gods, 'Must they perchance be the equals of ourselves, their Makers, who can see afar, who know all and see all? Must they also be gods?' Obviously such a state of affairs could not be allowed to continue. After some deliberation an order was given and appropriate action taken: Let their sight reach only to that which is near; let them see only a little of the face of the Earth. Then the Heart of Heaven blew mist into their eyes which clouded their sight as when a mirror is breathed upon. Their eyes were covered and they could only see what was close only that was clear to them. In this way the wisdom and all the knowledge of the First Men were destroyed.

Anyone familiar with the Old Testament will remember the reason for the expulsion of Adam and Eve from the Garden of Eden had to do with similar divine concerns. After Adam had eaten of the fruit of the tree of the knowledge of good and evil, The Lord God said, 'Behold, the man has become as one of us, to know good and evil. Now, lest he put forth his hand and take also of the tree of life and eat and live for ever, [let us] send him forth from the Garden of Eden.'

The Popol Vuh is accepted by scholars as a great reservoir of uncontaminated, pre-Colombian tradition. It is therefore puzzling to find such similarities between these traditions and those recorded in the Genesis story. Moreover, like so many of the other Old World/New World links we have identified, the character of the similarities is not suggestive of any kind of direct influence of one region on the other but of two different interpretations of the same set of events.

Both the Popol Vuh and Genesis therefore tell the story of mankind's fall from grace. In both cases, this state of grace was closely associated with knowledge, and the reader is left in no doubt that the knowledge in question was so remarkable that it conferred godlike powers on those who possessed it. The Bible, calls it 'the knowledge of good and evil' and has nothing further to add.

The Popol Vuh is much more informative. It tells us that the knowledge of the First Men consisted of the ability to see 'things hidden in the distance', that they were astronomers who 'examined the four corners, the four points of the arch of the sky', and that they were geographers who succeeded in measuring 'the round face of the Earth'.

Geography is about maps. In The Mystery of the Maps we saw evidence suggesting that the cartographers of an as yet unidentified civilization might have mapped the planet with great thoroughness at an early date. Could the Popol Vuh be transmitting some memory of that same civilization when it speaks nostalgically of the First Men and of the miraculous geographical knowledge they possessed? Geography is about maps, and astronomy is about stars. Very often the two disciplines go hand in hand because stars are essential for navigation on long sea-going voyages of discovery (and long sea-going voyages of discovery are essential for the production of accurate maps).

Is it accidental that the First Men of the Popol Vuh were remembered not only for studying 'the round face of the Earth' but for their contemplation of 'the arch of heaven'? And is it a coincidence that the outstanding achievement of Mayan society was its observational astronomy, upon which, through the medium of advanced mathematical calculations, was based a clever, complex, sophisticated and very accurate calendar?

5.7 Knowledge out of place

In 1954 J. Eric Thompson, a leading authority on the archaeology of Central America, confessed to a deep sense of puzzlement at a number of glaring disparities he had identified between the generally unremarkable achievements of the Mayans as a whole and the advanced state of their astro-calendrical knowledge, 'What mental quirks,' he asked, 'led the Mayan intelligentsia to chart the heavens, yet fail to grasp the principle of the wheel; to visualize eternity, as no other semi-civilized people has ever done, yet ignore the short step from corbelled (stonework) to true arch; to count in millions, yet never to learn to weigh a sack of corn?'

Perhaps the answer to these questions is much simpler than Thompson realized. Perhaps the astronomy, the deep understanding of time, and the long-term mathematical calculations, were not 'quirks' at all. Perhaps they were the constituent parts of a coherent but very specific body of knowledge that the Maya had inherited, more or less intact, from an older and wiser civilization. Such an inheritance would explain the contradictions observed by Thompson.

We already know that the Maya received their calendar as a legacy from the Olmecs (a thousand years earlier, the Olmecs were using exactly the same system). The real question should be where did the Olmecs get it? What kind of level of technological and scientific development was required for a civilization to devise a calendar as good as this? Take the case of the solar year. In modern Western society we still make use of a solar calendar which was introduced in Europe in 1582 and is based on the best scientific knowledge then available: the famous Gregorian calendar.

The Julian calendar, which it replaced, computed the period of the Earth's orbit around the sun at 365.25 days. Pope Gregory XIII's reform substituted a finer and more accurate calculation: 365.2425 days. Thanks to scientific advances since 1582 we now know that the exact length of the solar year is 365.2422 days. The Gregorian calendar therefore incorporates a very small plus error, just 0.0003 of a day—pretty impressive accuracy for the sixteenth century. Strangely enough, though its origins are wrapped in the mists of antiquity far deeper than the sixteenth century, the Mayan calendar achieved even greater accuracy. It calculated the solar year at 365.2420 days, a minus error of only 0.0002 of a day. Similarly, the Maya knew the time taken by the moon to orbit the Earth. Their estimate of this period was 29.528395 days - extremely close to the true figure of 29.530588 days computed by the finest modern methods.

The Mayan priests also had in their possession very accurate tables for the prediction of solar and lunar eclipses and were aware that these could occur only within plus or minus eighteen days of the node (when the moon's path crosses the apparent path of the sun).

Finally, the Maya were remarkably accomplished mathematicians. They possessed an advanced technique of metrical calculation by means of a chequerboard device we ourselves have only discovered (or rediscovered?) in the last century. They also understood perfectly and used the abstract concept of zero and were acquainted with place numerations. These are esoteric fields. As Thompson observed, the cipher (nought) and place numerations are so much parts of our cultural heritage and seem such obvious conveniences that it is difficult to comprehend how their invention could have been long delayed. Yet neither ancient Greece with its great mathematicians, nor ancient Rome, had any inkling of either nought or place numeration. To write 1848 in Roman numerals requires eleven letters: MDCCCXLVIII. Yet the Maya had a system of place-value notation very much like our own at a time when the Romans were still using their clumsy method.

Isn't it a bit odd that this otherwise unremarkable Central American tribe should, at such an early date, have stumbled upon an innovation which Otto Neugebauer, the historian of science, has described as 'one of the most fertile inventions of humanity'.

5.8 Someone else's science?

Let us now consider the question of Venus, a planet that was of immense symbolic importance to all the ancient peoples of Central America. The Maya understood that Venus was both 'the morning star' and 'the evening star'. The cycle of a planet is the period of time it takes to return to any given point in the sky - as viewed from Earth. Venus revolves around the sun every 224.7 days, while the Earth follows its own slightly wider orbit. The composite result of these two motions is that Venus rises in exactly the same place in the Earth's sky approximately every 584 days.

Whoever invented the sophisticated calendrical system inherited by the Maya had been aware of this and had found ingenious ways to integrate it with other interlocking cycles. Moreover, it is clear from the mathematics which brought these cycles together that the ancient calendar masters had understood that 584 days was only an approximation and that the movements of Venus are by no means regular. They had therefore worked out the exact figure established by today's science for the average cycle of Venus over very long periods of time. That figure is 583.92 days and it was knitted into the fabric of the Mayan calendar in numerous intricate and complex ways.

For example, to reconcile it with the so-called 'sacred year' (260 days, which was divided into 13 months of 20 days each) the calendar called for a correction of four days to be made every 61 Venus years. In addition, during every fifth cycle, a correction of eight days was made at the end of the 57th revolution. Once these steps were taken, the tzolkin (count) and the cycle of Venus were intermeshed so tightly that the degree of error to which the equation was subject was staggeringly small - one day in 6000 years.

And what made this all the more remarkable was that a further series of precisely calculated adjustments kept the Venus cycle and the tzolkin not only in harmony with each other but in exact relationship with the solar year. Again this was achieved in a manner which ensured that the calendar was capable of doing its job, virtually error-free, over vast expanses of time.

Why did the 'semi-civilized' Maya need this kind of high-tech precision? Or did they inherit, in good working order, a calendar engineered to fit the needs of a much earlier and far more advanced civilization? Consider the crowning jewel of Maya calendrics, the so-called 'Long Count'. This system of calculating dates also expressed beliefs about the past -notably, the widely held belief that time operated in Great Cycles which witnessed recurrent creations and destructions of the world.

According to the Maya, the current Great Cycle began in darkness on a date corresponding to 13 August 3114 BC in our own calendar. As we have seen, it was also believed that the cycle will come to an end, amid global destruction, on 23 December 2012 in our calendar. The function of the Long Count was to record the elapse of time since the beginning of the current Great Cycle, literally to count off, one by one, the 5125 years allotted to our present creation.

The Long Count is perhaps best envisaged as a sort of celestial adding machine, constantly calculating and recalculating the scale of our growing debt to the universe. Every last penny of that debt is going to be called in when the figure on the meter reads 5125. So, at any rate, thought the Maya. Calculations on the Long Count computer were not, of course, done in our numbers. The Maya used their own notation, which they had derived from the Olmecs, who had derived it from ... nobody knows.

124

This notation was a combination of dots (signifying ones or units or multiples of twenty), bars (signifying fives or multiples of five times twenty), and a shell glyph signifying zero. Spans of time were counted by days (kin), periods of twenty days (uinat), 'computing years' of 360 days (tun), periods of 20 tuns (known as katun), and periods of 20 katuns (known as bactun). There were also 8000-tun periods (pictun) and 160,000-tun periods (calabtun) to mop up even larger calculations. All this should make clear that although the Maya believed themselves to be living in one Great Cycle that would surely come to a violent end they also knew that time was infinite and that it proceeded with its mysterious revolutions regardless of individual lives or civilizations.

6

Crop Circles

Signs on the Earth below - (Acts 2:19; Joel 2:30)

It seems that math's codes and geometric patterns have long been an important factor in crop circle formations and the images appearing now, in the present time, I see as a continuation of the esoteric fingerprints recorded throughout history, some of which have been included in this book. There are so many examples I could use of crop circles, ice and sand circles but the following I think is extremely interesting:

Mathematicians are perplexed after a highly complex crop circle appeared in a Wiltshire field in the UK - depicting a fundamental mathematical symbol. The circle is, apparently, a coded image representing a complex mathematical number — the first ten digits of pi — and even astrophysicists admit they find it "mind-boggling". The circular pattern was created in a barley field near Barbury Castle, an Iron Age hill fort, in June 2008.

The above is taken from www.timesonline.co.uk

Having read about these circles my research then took me to the following article that was written by Leslie Kean for the *Providence Journal* in San Francisco, and the contents takes the phenomena of these circles away from the realms of fiction to non-fiction.

Origin of Crop Circles Baffles Scientists

Since the recent release of the movie Signs, crop circles have been thrust into the limelight.

Such major publications as Scientific American and U.S. News and World Report have echoed the common belief that all crop circles are made by stealthy humans flattening plants with boards. This assumption would be fair enough if we had no information suggesting otherwise.

However, intriguing data published in peer-reviewed scientific journals clearly establishes that some of these geometric designs, found in dozens of countries, are not made by "pranks with planks." In fact, a study about to be published by a team of scientists and funded by Laurance Rockefeller concludes "it is possible that we are observing the effects of a new or as yet undiscovered energy source."

In the early 1990s, biophysicist William C. Levengood, of the Pinelandia Biophysical Laboratory, in Michigan, examined plants and soils from 250 crop formations, randomly selected from seven countries. Samples and controls were provided by the Massachusetts-based BLT Research Team, directed by Nancy Talbott.

Levengood, who has published over 50 papers in scientific journals, documented numerous changes in the plants from the formations. Most dramatic were grossly elongated plant nodes (the "knuckles" along the stem) and "expulsion cavities" - holes literally blown open at the nodes - caused by the heating of internal moisture from exposure to intense bursts of radiation. The steam inside the stems escaped by either stretching the nodes or, in less elastic tissue, exploding out like a potato bursting open in a microwave oven.

Seeds taken from the plants and germinated in the lab showed significant alterations in growth, as compared with controls. Effects varied from an inability to develop seeds to a massive increase in growth rate - depending on the species, the age of the plants when the circle was created and the intensity of the energy system involved.

These anomalies were also found in tufts of standing plants inside crop circles - clearly not a result of mechanical flattening - and in patches of randomly downed crops found near the geometric designs. These facts suggested some kind of natural, but unknown, force at work.

Published in *Physiologia Plantarum* (1994), the international journal of the European Societies of Plant Physiology, Levengood's data showed that "plants from crop circles display anatomical alterations which cannot be explained by assuming the formations are hoaxes." He defined a "genuine" formation as one "produced by external energy forces independent of human influence." A strange brown "glaze" covering plants within a British formation was the subject of Levengood and John A. Burke's 1995 paper in the *Journal of Scientific Exploration*. The material was a pure iron that had been embedded in the plants while the iron was still molten. Tiny iron spheres were also found in the soil.

In 1999, British investigator Ronald Ashby examined the glaze through optical and scanning electron microscopes. He determined that intense heat had been involved - iron melts at about 2,700 degrees Fahrenheit - administered in millisecond bursts. "After exhaustive inquiry, there is no mundane explanation for the glaze" he concluded.

In another paper for *Physiologia Plantarum* (1999), Levengood and Talbott suggested that the energy causing crop circles could be an atmospheric plasma vortex - multiple interacting electrified air masses that emit microwaves as they spiral around the Earth's magnetic-field lines. Some formations, however, contain cubes and straight lines.

Astrophysicist Bernard Haisch, of the California Institute for Physics and Astrophysics, says that such "highly organized, intelligent patterns are not something that could be created by a force of nature."

But Haisch points out that since not all formations are tested, it is unknown how many are genuine. Nor is it likely that such complex designs could evolve so quickly in nature. "Natural phenomena make mountain ranges and form continents - they don't learn geometry in ten years," says Haisch, who is the science editor for the *Astrophysical Journal*.

In 1999, philanthropist Laurance Rockefeller made possible the most definitive - and most revealing - study to date. The BLT Research Team collected hundreds of plant and soil samples from a seven-circle barley formation in Edmonton, Canada. The plants had both elongated nodes and expulsion cavities, and the soils contained the peculiar iron spheres, indicating a genuine formation. The controls showed none of these changes.

Mineralogist Sampath Iyengar, of the Technology of Materials Laboratory, in California, examined specific heat-sensitive clay minerals in these soils, using X-ray diffraction and a scanning electron microscope. He discovered an increase in the degree of crystallinity (the ordering of atoms) in the circle minerals, which statistician Ravi Raghavan determined was statistically significant at the 95 percent level of confidence.

"I was shocked," says Iyengar, a 30-year specialist in clay mineralogy. "These changes are normally found in sediments buried for thousands and thousands of years under rocks, affected by heat and pressure, and not in surface soils." Also astounding was the direct correlation between the node-length increases in the plants and the increased crystallization in the soil minerals - indicating a common energy source for both effects.

Yet the scientists could not explain how this would be possible. The temperature required to alter soil crystallinity would be between 1,500 and 1,800 degrees F. This would destroy the plants.

Understanding the possible ramifications of these findings, Talbott sought the expertise of an emeritus professor of geology and mineralogy at Dartmouth College, Robert C. Reynolds Jr., who is former president of the Clay Minerals Society. He is regarded by his colleagues as the "best-known expert in the world" on X-ray diffraction analysis of clay minerals. Reynolds determined that the BLT Team's data had been "obtained by competent personnel, using current equipment."

The intense heat required for the observed changes in crystallinity "would have incinerated any plant material present," he confirms in a statement for the Rockefeller report. "In short, I believe that our present knowledge provides no explanation."

Meteorologist James W. Deardorff, professor emeritus at the College of Oceanic and Atmospheric Sciences at Oregon State University, and previously a senior scientist at the National Center for Atmospheric Research, states in a 2001 Physiologia Plantarum commentary that the variety, complexity and artistry of crop circles "represent the work of intelligence," and not a plasma vortex. "That is why the hoax hypothesis has been popularly advocated," he says.

However, he points out, the anomalous properties in plant stems thoroughly documented by Levengood and Talbott could not possibly have been implemented by hoaxers. Deardorff describes one 1986 British formation in which upper and lower layers of crop were intricately swirled and bent perpendicular to each other, in a fashion that "defies any explanation."

"People don't want to face up to this, and scientists have to deal with the ridicule factor," he said in a recent interview. Adding to the puzzle, professional filmmakers have documented bizarre daytime "balls of light" at crop-circle sites. Light phenomena were observed by multiple witnesses at the site of the Canadian circle so meticulously examined under the Rockefeller grant.

Eltjo Hasselhoff, a Dutch experimental physicist, has taken on the study of what he describes as "bright, fluorescent flying light objects, sized somewhere between an egg and a football."

Scientists face real and serious questions in confronting this mystery. Could this be secret laser technology beamed down from satellites? Is it a natural phenomenon? Is there a consciousness or intelligence directing an energy form yet unknown to us?

"To look at the evidence and go away unconvinced is one thing," says astrophysicist Haisch. "To not look at the evidence and be convinced against it is another. That is not science." It's not good journalism either.

The above was taken from:
www.projo.com/opinion/contributors/content/projo_20020916_kean.21cb0 .html

7

What is religion?

A religion is a set of beliefs and practices, often centred upon specific supernatural and moral claims about reality, the cosmos, and human nature, and often codified as prayer, ritual, and religious law. Religion also encompasses ancestral or cultural traditions, writings, history, and mythology, as well as personal faith and mystic experience. The term "religion" refers to both the personal practices related to communal faith and to group rituals and communication stemming from shared conviction.

The above was taken from Wikipedia, the free online encyclopedia.

7.1 The word of the Creator

I think the word of the Creator can be found in many places, including ancient text. As an example, it would seem the Christian Bible was written by about forty different people over a period of approximately 1,600 years. The writers of the Bible were men who lived in different places at different periods of time. They had varying occupations and in many cases, the writers did not know each other. Dotted throughout the Bible and hidden amongst the text are scientific facts about this world modern man only just understands. The words of the Creator are obviously spoken through the pages via man but a lot of what is written in the Bible is at the mercy of the writers and those who perhaps employed the writers and so is open to interpretation. During my research I was fascinated to find the following:

Scientific Facts

Columbus and Magellan proved the Earth is round. That was just 500 years ago. The Bible told us the Earth was round thousands of years before anybody ever heard of Columbus or Magellan. "It is He who sits above the circle of the Earth" (Isaiah 40:22). "When He prepared the heavens, I was there: When He drew a circle on the face of the deep" (Proverbs 8:27).

The Bible also tells us we are not able to number the stars. In 1940, astronomers finally came to the conclusion they were not able to count all of the stars in the universe. Almost 2,500 years ago, Jeremiah recorded: "As the host of heaven cannot be numbered, nor the sand of the sea measured: so will I multiply the descendants of David My servant and the Levites who minister to Me" (Jeremiah 33:22). Almighty God cannot only count the stars, he can call them by name (Psalm 147:4).

"In the beginning God created the heavens and the Earth" (Gen. 1:1) This was written by Moses through the inspiration of the Holy Spirit about 1500 B.C. In 1820 A.D. a man named Hubert Spencer gave the world five scientific principles by which man may study the unknown. They are time, force, energy, space, and matter. However, Moses, by inspiration, gave us those scientific principles in Genesis 1:1. "In the beginning" - God; "created" – energy; "the heavens" - space; "and the Earth"- matter. All of Spencer's scientific principles are right there in Genesis 1:1.

The Bible also says each star is unique. Corinthians 15:41 "There is one glory of the sun, another glory of the moon, and another glory of the stars; for one star differs from another star in glory." All stars look alike to the naked eye. Even when seen through a telescope, they seem to be just points of light. However, analysis of their light spectra reveals each is unique and different from all others. (We understand that people can perceive some slight difference in colour and apparent brightness when looking at stars with the naked eye, but we would not expect a person living in the first century A.D. to claim they differ from one another.)

The Bible describes the precision of movement in the universe. Jeremiah 31:35,36 "Thus says the Lord, Who gives the sun for a light by day, The ordinances of the moon and the stars for a light by night, Who disturbs the sea, And its waves roar."

The Bible describes the suspension of the Earth in space. Job 26:7 "He stretches out the north over empty space; He hangs the Earth on nothing".

The Bible describes the circulation of the atmosphere, which is consistent with Meteorology. Ecclesiastes 1:6 "The wind goes toward the south, and turns around to the north. The wind whirls about continually and comes again on its circuit."

The Bible includes some principles of fluid dynamics. Job 28:25 "To establish a weight for the wind, and apportion the waters by measure."

Statements Consistent With Biology

The book of Leviticus (written prior to 1400 BC) describes the value of blood. Leviticus 17:11 "For the life of the flesh is in the blood, and I have given it to you upon the altar to make atonement for your souls; for it is the blood that makes atonement for the soul."

The Bible describes biogenesis (the development of living organisms from other living organisms) and the stability of each kind of living organism. Genesis 1:11,12 "Then God said, Let the Earth bring forth grass, the herb that yields seed, and the fruit tree that yields fruit according to its kind, whose seed is in itself, on the Earth"; and it was so. And the Earth brought forth grass, the herb that yields seed according to its kind, and the tree that yields fruit, whose seed is in itself according to its kind. And God saw that it was good." Genesis 1:21 "So God created great sea creatures and every living thing that moves, with which the waters abounded, according to their kind, and every winged bird according to its kind. And God saw that it was good." Genesis 1:25 "And God made the beast of the Earth according to its kind, cattle according to its kind, and everything that creeps on the Earth according to its kind. And God saw that it was good." The phrase "according to its kind" occurs repeatedly, stressing the reproductive integrity of each kind of animal and plant. Today we know this occurs because all of these reproductive systems are programmed by their genetic codes.

The Bible describes the chemical nature of flesh. Genesis 2:7
"And the Lord God formed man of the dust of the ground, and breathed into his nostrils the breath of life; and man became a living being."

Genesis 3:19
"In the sweat of your face you shall eat bread till you return to the ground, for out of it you were taken, for dust you are, and to dust you shall return."

Statements Consistent With Hydrology

The bible includes descriptions of the hydrologic cycle. Psalm 135:7 "He causes the vapours to ascend from the ends of the Earth, he makes lightning for the rain, He brings the wind out of His treasuries." Jeremiah 10:13 "When He utters His voice there is a multitude of waters in the heavens, and He causes the vapours to ascend from the ends of the Earth. He makes lightning for the rain, He brings the wind out of His treasuries." Job 36:27-29 "For He draws up drops of water, which distil as rain from the mist, which the clouds drop down And pour abundantly on man. Indeed, can anyone understand the spreading of clouds, the thunder from His canopy?"

The Bible describes the recirculation of water. Ecclesiastes 1:7 'All the rivers run into the sea, Yet the sea is not full; To the place from which the rivers come, There they return again. Isaiah 55:10 For as the rain comes down, and the snow from heaven, and do not return there, but water the earth, and make it bring forth and bud, that it may give seed to the sower and bread to the eater,'

The Bible refers to the surprising amount of water that can be held as condensation in clouds. Job 26:8 'He binds up the water in His thick clouds, yet the clouds are not broken under it.' Job 37:11 'Also with moisture He saturates the thick clouds; He scatters His bright clouds.'

Hydrothermal vents are described in two books of the Bible written before 1400BC - more than 3,000 years before their discovery by science. Genesis 7:11

'In the six hundredth year of Noah's life, in the second month, the seventeenth day of the month, on that day all the fountains of the great deep were broken up, and the windows of heaven were opened.' Job 38:16 'Have you entered the springs of the sea? Or have you walked in search of the depths?'

Statements Consistent With Geology
The Bible describes the Earth's crust (along with a comment on astronomy). Jeremiah 31:37 Thus says the Lord: "If heaven above can be measured, And the foundations of the Earth searched out beneath, I will also cast off all the seed of Israel

For all that they have done, says the Lord." (Although some scientists claim that they have now measured the size of the universe, it is interesting to note that every human attempt to drill through the Earth's crust to the plastic mantle beneath has, thus far, ended in failure.)

The Bible described the shape of the Earth centuries before people thought that the Earth was spherical. Isaiah 40:22 'It is He who sits above the circle of the Earth, and its inhabitants are like grasshoppers, who stretches out the heavens like a curtain, And spreads them out like a tent to dwell in.' The word translated "circle" here is the Hebrew word *chuwg* which is also translated "circuit," or "compass" (depending on the context). That is, it indicates something spherical, rounded, or arched—not something that is flat or square. The book of Isaiah was written sometime between 740 and 680 BC. This is at least 300 years before Aristotle suggested that the Earth might be a sphere in his book *On the Heavens*.

Statements Consistent With Physics

The Bible suggests the presence of nuclear processes like those we associate with nuclear weaponry. This is certainly not something that could have been explained in 67 AD using known scientific principles (when Peter wrote the following verse). Peter 3:10 But the day of the Lord will come as a thief in the night, in which the heavens will pass away with a great noise, and the elements will melt with fervent heat; both the Earth and the works that are in it will be burned up.

The above was taken from:
http://www.clarifyingchristianity.com/science.shtml

7.2 The Great Masters/Teachers

I think there have been many great Masters who have been born in various places throughout the world and in different periods of time who have come as Messengers or Agents of the Creator to impart knowledge and teach the people by example, to help to move humanity on (and not all of them have been recognised). What the ancient Masters taught has had a huge impact on mankind and their legacy can still be seen today but the interpretation of the words of these Masters is at the mercy of man with their cultural differences and differing agendas, and historically this has sometimes caused problems for mankind. Following are some of the great Masters/Teachers.

Krishna was born in India about 3000BC. When he was a baby he spent all his time singing and dancing with the Gopis (milkmaids). He was always smiling and happy, and full of joy and laughter. When he grew up and saw others were not happy he spent many years experiencing the pain and suffering of others to find out why. Finally, in a forest hermitage he met a great Rishi (a spiritual teacher) who explained to him all life is one. Everything from the lowest insect to the greatest king is part of he same life, part of God, and the reason why people are unhappy is they did not realise this in their hearts. The Rishi also told Krishna that he had a very special mission, which was to bring this knowledge to other people by the example of his own life. Krishna did this and many people in India followed him on the joyful path. The teachings of Krishna, which were given to his beloved disciple, Arjuna, are contained in a book called the *Bhagavad Gita* (an important book in the world's literature), which means 'The Lord's Song'.

Buddha. Siddhartha Gautama Buddha was born a prince in India 563 BC. He was brought up in a palace surrounded by luxury. Because of a prophecy about what would happen if he saw anyone sick, old or dead, or a holy man, his father the king tried to keep him from seeing what life is really like, allowing him to see only beauty and happiness. But when he was thirty the prophecy came true and he saw people suffering, and then he saw a holy man and this man was very calm and peaceful in spite of the suffering. He was no longer content and left his family, his palace and wealth to search out the meaning of life and death and suffering. At first he followed a very severe path, nearly starving himself to death, but then he realised the 'middle path' is better, not having too much or too little.

One day, during a long meditation lasting seven days in which he remembered many of his past lives he received his great awakening and became 'Buddha' the enlightened one. Then he spent the rest of his life helping others understand 'The Four Noble Truths' and follow 'The Noble Eightfold Path'.

Mohammed was born in Mecca (in present day Saudi Arabia) in 570 AD. Both his parents died when he was young and he was brought up by his uncle, a merchant in Mecca, where at that time people believed in many 'Gods' and that the way to please them was to kill animals in holy places. But as Mohammed grew up he met people who were Christians and Jews and became convinced that there was one God of all people. He started to meditate on his own in a quiet cave away from the noise of Mecca.

Then one day he heard a voice saying 'You are the Messenger of Allah', (God). During further meditations he saw the Angel Gabriel and was given many messages from God. These were written down by his friends, with whom he shared what was happening and were eventually put into a book called the Koran (the bible of Islam). Mohammed told people they must submit to the will of Allah. Islam means the inner peace which comes when one does this.

Moses. The story of Moses is told in the Old Testament of the Christian Bible. When all Hebrew babies were ordered to be killed by the wicked Pharaoh, Moses was hidden in the rushes of the Nile and found by the Pharaoh's daughter. When he grew up he became aware of God talking to him. This first happened when he saw a great fire in the bush, but the flames did not burn anything. He knew he had to lead his people, called the children of Israel, out of Egypt as they were cruelly treated as slaves and he had to take them to safety in the Promised Land. Before they could leave Egypt many plagues and terrible things happened (brought about by God so the story goes, to make the Pharaoh let them leave). These are symbols of the tests and difficulties we have to face in Earth life. When they did escape from Egypt they wandered for a long time in the wilderness (a symbol of caring only about worldly, selfish things), but when they were hungry God sent 'manna' to eat (spiritual food).

During this time Moses was called to the top of Mount Sinai to receive from God the tablets of the law, the Ten Commandments. When he came down he found his people worshipping a golden calf (symbol of material things), having forgotten about God. Moses was so upset he broke the tablets but later he went up the mountain again and after forty days and forty nights he returned with new tablets and his people eventually did all the things they were told.

Just before Moses died, aged over one hundred and twenty years, he was shown 'the Promised Land' to which he had so faithfully led his people.

Jesus. It is said he was born to Mary and Joseph in a stable in Bethlehem and that three wise men followed the star to find him and angels told shepherds where to look. He prepared for many lives for his incarnation as a world teacher, when he was able to bring a very special blessing to the world and the Christ Spirit, the Son of God, shone brightly through him.

Jesus told parables to teach his followers and he chose twelve disciples to be his helpers and their names were Simon, Peter, Andrew, Philip, Nathanael, two called James, John, Thomas, Simon, Judas Lebbeus and Judas Iscariot. After Jesus' death his followers started to insist that only he was the Son of God, and people could only be saved by believing in him. Jesus himself did not mean people to worship him, he knew he was being used by God to help the people of Earth. Jesus' teaching was that of love and we can make the 'Kingdom of God' come here and now in our lives, not in the distant future. His most famous words are the Lord's Prayer, in which he explained how we should pray to God, and his summary of the ten commandments of Moses.

The above was taken from the book *Great Teachers* by Jenny Dent

8

What is science?

"Great spirits have always encountered violent opposition from mediocre minds." Professor Albert Einstein.

In its broadest sense, science (from the Latin *scientia*, meaning "knowledge") refers to any systematic knowledge or practice. In its more usual restricted sense, science refers to a system of acquiring knowledge based on scientific method, as well as to the organized body of knowledge gained through such research.

The above was taken from Wikipedia, the free online encyclopedia.

I think if you investigate the history of science you will find it wasn't long ago that some scientists shunned the existence of a Creator and life after death, and any scientist who worked in the arena of consciousness might lose credibility. Now however we have brave, frontier scientists who are working in the field of quantum physics and its astonishing implications. The well-designed experiments conducted by some of these scientists tells us consciousness is a substances outside the confines of our physical bodies. It is thrilling for those who, like me, have experienced unexplained happenings and now as a result of the work of these frontier scientists are able to view these experiences in a more tangible way.

Science cannot give us all the answers because the overall picture is too huge. However, I have heard some modern day scientists tell us they have come to the conclusion this Earth came about by a random chance and not by the hand of a Creator and when the physical body dies then that is the end of that persons existence.

I have also heard other scientists say it appears that if there was a Creator it has since left the universe to evolve and does not now intervene in it

That disappoints me greatly and I would say to these scientists 'look again' because there are so many people who, like me, have had experiences that contradict these findings, and there are so many other strands to consider as well.

8.1 The unfolding science of the atom

• The unfolding science of the atom, with its many different compositions, tells us there is so much more to learn but shows us that everything is connected.

What are atoms? Atoms are the basic building blocks of matter that make up everyday objects. A desk, the air, even you are made up of atoms! There are about 90 naturally occurring kinds of atoms known to man, the difference in their numbers of protons, neutrons, and electrons give them different physical properties. Scientists in labs have been able to make about 25 more man-made atoms, probably the most well known of which would be the atomic bomb.

Atoms are made out of three basic particles:

Protons carry a positive charge.

Neutrons carry no charge.

Protons and neutrons join together to form the nucleus – the central part of the atom

Electrons carry a negative charge and circle the nucleus.

In 1968 scientists discovered new particles within the proton and the neutron. They called these particles quarks and there are three quarks inside the proton and the neutron, held to each other by other particles called gluons.

Electrons are very small and extremely light. It is easy to strip electrons off of atoms and use them for electrical power and in devices like television sets. Electrons can be used to probe inside of atoms. Higher energy electrons can detect smaller features inside of atoms.

Scientists learn about the inside of atoms by watching how electrons bounce off the atom, and by how the atom changes as a result of being hit by an electron.

The above was taken from http://education.jlab.org/atomtour/

I think there are plenty more natural compositions of the atom waiting to be discovered, one of which is consciousness, and it seems a lot of scientist are now accepting that consciousness exists outside of the physical body but what they don't yet know is, what is the composition of spirit/ consciousness?

8.2 Quantum physics

Quantum physics is a sub-branch of physics whose subjects are phenomena connected with the quantum. It deals with the behaviour of matter and energy on the minute scale of atoms and subatomic particles. Quantum mechanics is a fundamental physical theory which extends and corrects Newtonian mechanics, especially at the atomic and subatomic levels. The term *quantum* (Latin for quantity) refers to the discrete units that the theory assigns to certain physical quantities, such as the energy of an electromagnetic wave. The terms quantum physics and quantum theory are often used as synonyms of quantum mechanics. Some authors refer to "quantum mechanics" in the restricted sense of non-relativistic quantum.

The above was taken from Wikipedia, the free online encyclopedia

8.3 An explanation of the atom by Professor Gary Schwartz of the Human Energy Systems Laboratory, America

In my early academic life I studied electrical engineering and carried out numerous experiments with television sets. The brain is a mass of physical cells in which a lot of electrical activity takes place. My experiments on the TVs were similar in principle to those that neurosurgeons carry out on brains, and they have concluded the mind is inside the brain. But at the end of my experiment I did not come to the conclusion the TV signals (which carry all the information) were emanating from inside the television set.

Neuroscientists can tell you what is happening physically within the brain, but they cannot tell you the location of consciousness – which you could compare to the huge amounts of information contained in the TV signals, which are transmitted to the set via a host of frequencies. A TV set is both a receiver and a transmitter and so is a human brain. Consciousness or the 'incoming information' could be inside the head or outside. To test this theory, if you put a television set inside a shielded chamber you block the signal coming into that set and it won't work. If you put a medium inside a shielded chamber this does not prevent them from receiving specific, verifiable information which they transmit to us and the sitter. Experiments are ongoing but research indicates the human brain is a receiver and transmitter of energy and information from outside our physical bodies. The brain is merely a tool through which consciousness or the universal mind works.

The idea that you can generate matter is something most people think is impossible and the majority of people have never witnessed it. The question is - what is the relationship between matter and energy?

With quantum physics we now understand that what is primary is energy and what we call matter is a special kind of energy – its organized energy. All material things in the universe, including us, are ultimately made from atoms, which in turn are made from subatomic particles – and atoms are pieces of matter. For instance, one type of atom could be hydrogen and another atom, oxygen. They come together and make water. Molecules are made of atoms – cells are made of molecules that are made of atoms – organs are made of cells, which are made of molecules, which are composed of atoms. In simple terms, the atom is the fundamental unit of organized matter – and in the birth of the universe one of the first atoms to be born out of energy was hydrogen.

In physics, we explain that as the temperature of the early universe cooled down and the frequencies within it slowed down, then energy congealed into subatomic particles and ultimately atoms. But what you really need to get your head around is that when atoms congeal into matter, that matter is still almost entirely empty space.

Imagine there is an atom in front of you – and atoms are extremely tiny and can only be seen with the most sensitive microscopes. Let's say we have a hydrogen atom – and pretend that this atom is the size of the empire state building. Now, in the centre of every atom is a nucleus – which is where most of the mass (matter) is. How big do you think the nucleus is in comparison to the atom? The nucleus is only the size of a grain of sand but that grain of sand constitutes almost the entire weight of that building, but it still means that what you think of as solid matter is more than 99.9 percent empty space. So, matter equals organized energy and organised energy is mainly empty space. Therefore, the trick to creating matter is to organize the energy. And what organizes energy? The mind - mind and consciousness comes first. Max Planck, the father of quantum physics said "I regard consciousness as fundamental. I regard matter as a derivative of consciousness."

It is important to realise that materialization is not transforming nothing into something. It is taking energy and organizing it into a form that is sufficiently concentrated or dense, so that it can be experienced in our three-dimensional world via our physical senses. Think of glass, which is solid but we can see through it. Just because you cannot see something doesn't mean to say it's not there.

Our research and that of others indicates that millions of people have far more than the five accepted senses of sight, taste, hearing, touch and smell. Mediums and people like them are extra sensitive. Mediums, psychics and clairvoyants are sufficiently sensitive that they can 'see' more spectrums of light (which are frequencies), than the majority of us. They can also hear a greater range of frequencies. They see 'dead' people.

So you now know that cells are made of atoms. Think of the atomic bombs that were dropped in Japan in 1945. Small bombs, split atoms – which resulted in a devastatingly huge explosion of energy. It was a relatively small object which contained enormous power. The ALL is in the small, no matter how small it is everything, all information, is within it.

Let's talk about God. Most people think of God as a dead white, black, Chinese or any other size or shape male. If God, or what I prefer to call the Guiding Organizing Designer, is the fundamental guiding, organizing, designing process in the universe, with the potential to create all organised energy, then God exists in everything, including atoms, and even sub atomic particles.

The table does not have consciousness as we do, as there are many levels of consciousness. Also the table does not have eyes to convert protons of light into a visual experience, but it does have 'awareness' of the organised energy with which it can resonate.

Imagine the global implications if we could all comprehend what quantum physics is now telling us – religion as we know it could be transformed. The way we view our world would be shattered forever. To know that we all contain God and that everything has this infinite potential and knowledge inside itself that just keeps being recycled is amazing.

If somehow you were able to make your atoms vibrate faster than the speed of light then you would no longer be visible. But most atoms never travel at the speed of light because their mass would become infinitely heavy. However, our thoughts may travel at the speed of light or even faster. Only things that are mass-less can travel at the speed of light and this includes 'dead' people. A 'ghost' which is a ball of energy, has no mass and can therefore walk through what we experience as everyday three-dimensional matter – they are totally unobstructed.

Healers talk of a light passing through them, out from their hands and into a patient. We have just finished analyzing data from experiments we conducted in 2002. We invited an experienced healer to come to our lab for five days to teach a group of 26 doctors and nurses how to give healing. Firstly, you need to understand that cosmic rays are super high-frequency gamma rays – which are the highest frequency that we can measure. We measured levels of frequencies being absorbed and emitted by these people before and after the five days. We found that after the training the subjects were absorbing gamma cosmic rays, but emitting more x-rays, which vibrate at a lower frequency than the cosmic rays. In other words the human body seemed to be acting as a transformer, stepping down the cosmic ray frequencies into x-ray frequencies before pulsing them into another person. So we now have good evidence that we have the capacity – through intention – to absorb super high-frequency cosmic rays which could be what the Chinese call chi, the Indians call prana, and so on. We can absorb them through the breath, through our pores and through intention. In these ways the participants become more absorbent of the higher frequencies.

In our research we know that all things both reflect and absorb light. Plants emit light, but they also absorb various frequencies from full-spectrum light which they then convert into matter; that's how plants grow. The eye also receives light and emits light.

So what about sound therapy, when researchers have sung certain tonal notes when people were, say, bleeding after accidents, and the bleeding stopped whilst the tone was being sung? Sound is organised energy – or frequency – which is ultimately information. Sound is vibration – vibration is information.

What about the past? We can perceive the past but we cannot take our bodies back in time. The atoms formed shortly after the big bang are all around us. Atoms have been here since that moment and are just being re-cycled, re-circulated. So the past is all around us and I believe time travel is accessing the recycled information (energy) within the atoms that are in the here-and-now. The past is like a video that is playing in the present but you would need to access the specific 'tape' that you want to see.

For example, when remote viewers, who are highly sensitive people, are given co-ordinates for any location on the planet, they 'travel' there in their minds. The mind can be anywhere and some of them will see a specific location as it looked in the past. Their information has been verified as being highly accurate. What I believe is happening is that they are 'reading' the information of the past via atoms that are here in the present.

If the weather were bad we can create a 'storm' around us if our thoughts (energy and information) are in chaos. Imagine you have a microphone; you plug it into an amplifier and now point the micro-phone towards the speaker – and what happens?

You get feedback as the sound is amplified and if you go on and on doing this and don't turn the microphone away, it can amplify to the point of literally blowing the speakers. In the same way if you became connected to a storm by energy, you can feed the storm and the storm can feed you. It is even possible to create a weather storm if our thoughts (energy and information) were in chaos.

Right now we are in a transitional stage in our evolution. If I were to make a guess I would say that around six million or so people out of a potential six billion people on the planet, are opening up to what is possible. Spiritually we have a long way to go, but how do you scale a mountain? Inch by inch .....

An explanation of the atom by Professor Gary Schwartz of the Human Energy Systems Laboratory, America was taken from Hazel Courtney's book, *The Evidence for the Sixth Sense*.

When Garry Schwartz tells us about the mind creating a storm, it made me think about the Native American Indians when they did the rain dance. They probably knew how to get their mind to a state where they could connect with the elements and create a storm to make rain come in a controlled way.

I also thought about poltergeist activity and I think it is the same thing only whereas the Indians were able to create a storm to make rain in a controlled way, the person creating the energy for poltergeist activity to take place has no control over it and are unaware of their involvement. This activity usually takes place around pubescent teens when their hormones are raging, thus the energy they are creating is wild and raging as well.

8.4 The Big Bang

100 years ago this year, Albert Einstein published three papers that rocked the world. These papers proved the existence of the atom, introduced the theory of relativity, and described quantum mechanics. His equations for relativity indicated that the universe was expanding. This bothered him, because if it was expanding, it must have had a beginning and a beginner. Since neither of these appealed to him, Einstein introduced a 'fudge factor' that ensured a 'steady state' universe, one that had no beginning or end. But in 1929, Edwin Hubble showed that the furthest galaxies were fleeing away from each other, just as the Big Bang model predicted. So in 1931, Einstein embraced what would later be known as the Big Bang theory, saying, "This is the most beautiful and satisfactory explanation of creation to which I have ever listened." He referred to the 'fudge factor' to achieve a steady-state universe as the biggest blunder of his career. Einstein's theories have been thoroughly proved and verified by experiments and measurements.

But there's an even more important implication of Einstein's discovery. Not only does the universe have a beginning, but time itself, our own dimension of cause and effect, began with the Big Bang. That's right -- time itself does not exist before then. The very line of time begins with that creation event. Matter, energy, time and space were created in an instant by intelligence outside of space and time. About this intelligence, Albert Einstein wrote in his book *"The World As I See It"* that the harmony of natural law "Reveals an intelligence of such superiority that, compared with it, all the systematic thinking and acting of human beings is an utterly insignificant reflection."

The Big Bang theory was totally rejected at first. But those who supported it had predicted that the ignition of the Big Bang would have left behind a sort of 'hot flash' of radiation. If a big black wood stove produces heat that you can feel, then in a similar manner, the Big Bang should produce its own kind of heat that would echo throughout the universe. In 1965, without looking for it, two physicists at Bell Labs in New Jersey found it. At first, Arno Penzias and Robert Wilson were bothered because, while trying to refine the world's most sensitive radio antenna, they couldn't eliminate a bothersome source of noise. They picked up this noise everywhere they pointed the antenna. At first they thought it was bird droppings. The antenna was so sensitive it could pick up the heat of bird droppings but even after cleaning it off, they still picked up this noise.

This noise had actually been predicted in detail by other astronomers, and after a year of checking and re-checking the data, they arrived at a conclusion: This crazy Big Bang theory really was correct. In an interview, Penzias was asked why there was so much resistance to the Big Bang theory. He said, "Most physicists would rather attempt to describe the universe in ways which require no explanation. If you have a universe which has always been there, you don't explain it, right?

"Somebody asks you, 'How come all the secretaries in your company are women?' You can say, 'Well, it's always been that way.' That's a way of not having to explain it. So in the same way, theories which don't require explanation tend to be the ones accepted by science, which is perfectly acceptable and the best way to make science work."

But on the older theory that the universe was eternal, he explains: "It turned out to be so ugly that people dismissed it. What we find - the simplest theory – is a creation out of nothing, the appearance out of nothing of the universe." Penzias and his partner, Robert Wilson, won the Nobel Prize for their discovery of this radiation.

The Big Bang theory is now one of the most thoroughly validated theories in all of science. Robert Wilson was asked by journalist Fred Heeren if the Big Bang indicated a creator. Wilson said, "Certainly there was something that set it all off. Certainly, if you are religious, I can't think of a better theory of the origin of the universe to match with Genesis."

If the universe had expanded a little faster, the matter would have sprayed out into space like fine mist from a water bottle - so fast that a gazillion particles of dust would speed into infinity and never even form a single star. If the universe had expanded just a little slower, the material would have dribbled out like big drops of water, and then collapsed back where it came from by the force of gravity. A little too fast, and you get a meaningless spray of fine dust. A little too slow, and the whole universe collapses back into one big black hole. The surprising thing is just how narrow the difference is. To strike the perfect balance between too fast and too slow, the force, something that physicists call "the Dark Energy Term" had to be accurate to one part in ten with 120 zeros. If you wrote this as a decimal, the number would look like this:

0.0000000000000000000000000000000000 0000000000000000000000000000000000 0000000000000000000000000000000000 00000000000000000000000000000001

In their paper "*Disturbing Implications of a Cosmological Constant*" two atheist scientists from Stanford University stated that the existence of this dark energy term "Would have required a miracle. An external agent, external to space and time, intervened in cosmic history for reasons of its own." Just for comparison, the best human engineering example is the Gravity Wave Telescope, which was built with a precision of 23 zeros. The Designer, the 'external agent' that caused our universe must possess an intellect, knowledge, creativity and power trillions and trillions of times greater than we humans have.

Now a person who doesn't believe in a creative intelligence has to find some way to explain this. One of the more common explanations seems to be "There were an infinite number of universes, so it was inevitable that things would have turned out right in at least one of them."

This print contains a message. It contains information in the form of language. The message is independent of the medium it is sent in. Messages are not matter, even though they can be carried by matter (like printing this text on a piece of paper). Messages are not energy even though they can be carried by energy (like the sound of my voice.) Messages are immaterial.

Information is itself a unique kind of entity. It can be stored and transmitted and copied in many forms, but the meaning still stays the same. Every cell in your body contains a message encoded in DNA, representing a complete plan for you. OK, so what does this have to do with a creative intelligence? It's very simple. Messages, languages, and coded information ONLY come from a mind, a mind that agrees on an alphabet and a meaning of words and sentences, a mind that expresses both desire and intent. Whether we use the simplest possible explanation, such as the one given here, or if we analyze language with advanced mathematics and engineering communication theory, we can say this with total confidence:

"Messages, languages and coded information never, ever come from anything else besides a mind. No one has ever produced a single example of a message that did not come from a mind."

Nature can create fascinating patterns - snowflakes, sand dunes, crystals, stalagmites and stalactites, tornados and turbulence and cloud formations. But non-living things cannot create language. They cannot create codes. Rocks cannot think and they cannot talk. And they cannot create information.

It is believed by some that life on planet Earth arose accidentally from the "primordial soup," the early ocean which produced enzymes and eventually RNA, DNA, and primitive cells. But there is still a problem with this theory: It fails to answer the question, 'Where did the information come from?'

DNA is not merely a molecule. Nor is it simply a "pattern." Yes, it contains chemicals and proteins, but those chemicals are arranged to form an intricate language, in the exact same way that English and Chinese and HTML are languages. DNA has a four-letter alphabet, and structures very similar to words, sentences and paragraphs, with very precise instructions and systems that check for errors and correct them. To the person who says that life arose naturally, you need only ask:

"Where did the information come from? Show me just ONE example of a language that didn't come from a mind."

Matter and energy have to come from somewhere. Every-one can agree on that. But information has to come from somewhere, too! Information is a separate entity, fully on par with matter and energy. And information can only come from a mind. If books and poems and TV shows come from human intelligence, then all living things inevitably came from a super intelligence.

Every word you hear, every sentence you speak, every dog that barks, every song you sing, every email you read, every packet of information that zings across the Internet, is proof of the existence of a creative intelligence, because information and language always originate in a mind. In the beginning were words and language. In the beginning was Information. When we consider the mystery of life - where it came from and how this miracle is possible - do we not at the same time ask the question where it is going, and what its purpose is?

The above was taken from Peter Marshall:
http://www.ublimewill.blogspot.com/2005/07/part-1-where-did-universe-come-from.html

I think when you consider consciousness exists outside of the physical body and we are all connected by a single organism of interconnected energy fields, and then when you throw into the equation that some people are able to harness the energy in the way the native American Indians did, then it is not impossible to imagine an immense power such as the Creator could have focused its mind, splitting atoms to cause the big bang that created our universe and world.

8.5 The Quest for a Theory of Everything

Over the past century, physicists have unlocked the secrets behind radio and television, nuclear energy and the power of the sun. Now they're seeking the ultimate prize: a 'theory of everything' that could reveal a bizarre realm of interdimensional wormholes and time warps.

Such a theory would give us the ability to 'read the mind of God' says Cambridge cosmologist Stephen Hawking. And in Hawking's opinion, there is a 50-50 chance that someone will discover the Holy Grail within the next twenty years. It won't be easy though, the discoverer would have to find the harmony underlying two themes as discordant as light Bach and heavy rock.

On one side is Albert Einstein's theory of general relativity. Einstein saw the large-scale universe as a smooth, curved surface in four dimensions (the three dimensions of space plus time). The gravitational force that binds us to the Earth arises from the very structure of that space-time continuum.

On the other side is quantum theory. Beginning in the 1920's, a generation of scientists defined the small-scale universe as a collection of fuzzy phantoms. These subatomic particles couldn't be precisely located in space and time, but their interaction could be described in statistical terms.

Both theories are proven successes but taken together, they're out of joint. The equations that describe the gravitational field are completely different from those for electromagnetism and subatomic interactions.

Moreover, each theory is incomplete by itself. Relativity cannot tell us how the big bang gave rise to the universe as we know it, or what lies within the black holes created by the collapse of massive stars. Quantum theory, meanwhile, only describes an assortment of particles, mathematical constants and equations, without divining the sense and symmetry underlying them all.

For decades, theorists have tried various strategies to roll up the gravitational field and the quantum field into one set of equations. Most of the attempts failed. 'Whenever we tried to calculate numbers from these theories, we would arrive at meaningless infinities,' said theoretical physicist Michio Kaku.

But one bizarre approach is gaining popularity. It turns out that the equations of quantum theory can mesh perfectly with the theory of relativity if we look at them from the perspective of a ten-dimensional universe.

The concept is called 'superstring theory' because theoreticians imagine the core components of the universe as tiny loops of string or membranes vibrating in ten dimensions. Different resonances of the vibrations correspond to different types of particles. Thus, electrons, neutrinos and other elementary particles fit on a grand scale, just as the notes A, B and C fit on a musical scale.

Kaku says it should come as no surprise that the universe makes more sense in higher dimensions. After all, Einstein made the universe seem more sensible by including time as the fourth dimension.

But if the universe we only dimly understand as having four dimensions really has ten, where are the other six dimensions? Kaku and his fellow string theorists contend that when the big bang inflated our four dimensions into the universe as we know it, the extra six dimensions collapsed into loops smaller than the smallest observed subatomic particle.

If humans could somehow identify and harness those dimensions, it might become possible to manipulate those interdimensional fields. You could create stable 'wormholes' for rapid transit across the universe. You might even be able to drop into parallel 'quantum universes' that operate under physical laws completely different from our own.

Exploring such science-fiction possibilities would require resources of science-fiction proportions.

There are millions of possible solutions for the superstring equations, and figuring out the right solution for our universe would be like picking a needle out of a galaxy sized haystack. Even if the theory turns out to be right, probing the shrunken dimensions would require energies approaching the scale of the big bang, trillions of trillions of times more powerful than a hydrogen bomb.

However, outer space could open a window to the hidden dimensions and at least provide some confirmation of superstring theory. By observing the patterns of particles and antiparticles flying through space, researchers just might find indirect evidence to back up a 'theory of everything'.

The above was written by Alan Boyle on October 8th 1998, Science Editor, MSNBC, based on material from 'Hyperspace' and 'Visions' by Michio Kaku..

8.6 CERN, Geneva - the God particle

CERN, the European Organization for Nuclear Research, is one of the world's largest and most respected centres for scientific research. Its business is fundamental physics, finding out what the Universe is made of and how it works. At CERN, the world's largest and most complex scientific instruments are used to study the basic constituents of matter — the fundamental particles. By studying what happens when these particles collide, physicists learn about the laws of Nature.

The instruments used at CERN are particle accelerators and detectors. Accelerators boost beams of particles to high energies before they are made to collide with each other or with stationary targets. Detectors observe and record the results of these collisions.

Founded in 1954, the CERN Laboratory sits astride the Franco–Swiss border near Geneva.

The above is taken from http://public.web.cern.com

I was so excited when on 10 September 2008 CERN successfully steered the first particle beam around the full twenty seven kilometres of the Hadron Collider, the world's most powerful particle accelerator. This was an historic event watched by the sixty participating countries around the world that are funding the project which could determine the existence of the Higgs boson, named after Professor Peter Higgs, a theoretical particle physicist who formulated the theory behind the sub-atomic particle named after him in the 1960s. His theory could help to unify the many disparate forces of the universe. Dubbed the "God particle" by Nobel Prize-winning physicist Leon Lederman, the Higgs boson is a controversial particle believed to bestow mass on all other particles.

Finding this particle would give an insight into why particles have certain mass and this unexplored territory should be accessible using the Large Hadron Collider.

One of the things CERN might find as a result of this colossal experiment is the existence of parallel universes. How absolutely thrilling this would be, because if they do find these other universes then it would only take a small leap to recognise this is where our spirit/consciousness goes when we 'die'. If this theory proves to be correct then the death of the physical body and the continued existence of the spirit is a scientific process, not reliant on any belief system, religion etc.

It was equally thrilling to me to learn the Director of CERN, who got to switch on the Hadron Collider, is Dr Lynn Evans who has been dubbed 'Evans the Atom' and he is originally from Aberdare in Wales, some twenty miles from where I live.

Go Wales!

9

Thoughts and feelings are real and exist outside of the physical body

It used to be thought we could keep our thoughts and feelings to ourselves, that they were internal. Science is now discovering not only are our thoughts and feelings internal but they are also external, and they impact on everything around us. Internally, thoughts and feelings can manifest physical illness [as can environment, lifestyle etc] and the cells in our bodies respond to not just our thoughts and feelings but also our words. Thoughts, feelings and words are energy in motion and as our bodies are energy moving at a different rate (atoms), then the molecular substance of our bodies is susceptible to thought and emotion. If we continually think in a restrictive way and suppress negative emotions such as resentment, anger, bitterness, and hatred then this can eventually manifest as illness in our bodies.

Externally, thoughts and feelings have an impact on many things, including plants and water which are both vital to our survival, and when you consider we humans are approximately two thirds water as are all living things, and the Earth is made up of more than 70% water, then we can begin to realise what a devastating impact bad and negative thoughts and feelings can have on us, our environment and the world.

The next few chapters give a solid foundation to what is mentioned above and from them you will see as everything is connected by a single organism of interconnected energy fields, we can create our own future singularly but we also contribute to the future of the whole.

9.1 Matthew Manning - Healer

Matthew Manning is a world famous healer who has participated in a wide range of experiments designed to test what effect, if any, his thoughts would have on a wide range of biological systems. The following experiment is taken from his book 'The Healing Journey'.

'If red blood cells are put in ordinary tap water the red corpuscles will expand and eventually burst, releasing haemoglobin. This process is known as haemolysis. However, if the water is made slightly saline, the red corpuscles are buffered and will remain intact for longer. As haemolysis proceeds, the blood-saline solution changes from cloudy to clear, providing researchers with a measure of the rate of decay. This particular experiment consisted of ten trials, each one measuring the rate of haemolysis of ten blood samples. Five of these were control samples and five were samples that I attempted to influence. During the control trials I tried not to think of the test tube of blood cells. When I was trying to heal, I placed my hands above the tube without touching it while imagining the cells surrounded by a brilliant white light. I assured the cells that the light and energy would protect them and that they would remain intact and resistant to the surrounding solution.

The test results showed that the cells remained intact four times longer in the experiments in which I tried to heal than they did in the trials where I removed my influence. R. Williams Braud, one of the scientists involved in the experiment later told a newspaper: "By concentrating his mind on the test tube of blood, Matthew was able to slow down the death of the cells. Normally the blood cells would break down and die within a maximum of five minutes, but he was able to slow down the destruction so that the blood cells were still intact as long as twenty minutes later."'

Also in his book under a chapter entitled 'Immunity and the nervous system' it says: 'An Australian scientific researcher, R.W.Bartrop and his colleagues in New South Wales had been carefully studying the effects of bereavement and in particular its effect on physical health and immune function. They followed twenty-six surviving spouses of patients who had been either killed in accidents or died from natural causes.

As well as offering counselling to the bereaved, they recorded the changes in their immune functions in the weeks following the losses. By taking blood samples from the bereaved spouses and comparing them with samples from a non-bereaved group, they discovered that the immune system of the grieving spouses showed a much-lowered activity of the T cells.

It was the very first time that anybody had been able to show a measurable depression of immune function following severe psychological real life stress'.

9.2 Water experiments

The groundbreaking work of Japanese Dr Masaru Emoto has led to a new consciousness of Earth's most precious resource - water.

What has put Dr. Emoto at the forefront of the study of water is his proof that thoughts and feelings affect physical reality. By producing different focused intentions through written and spoken words and music and literally presenting it to the same water samples, the water appears to "change its expression".

Essentially, Dr. Emoto captured water's 'expressions.' He developed a technique using a very powerful microscope in a very cold room along with high-speed photography, to photograph newly formed crystals of frozen water samples. Not all water samples crystallize however. Water samples from extremely polluted rivers directly seem to express the 'state' the water is in.

Dr. Masaru Emoto discovered that crystals formed in frozen water reveal changes when specific, concentrated thoughts are directed toward them. He found that water from clear springs and water that has been exposed to loving words shows brilliant, complex, and colourful snowflake patterns. In contrast, polluted water, or water exposed to negative thoughts, forms incomplete, asymmetrical patterns with dull colours.

Dr. Emoto's work provides us with factual evidence that human vibrational energy, thoughts, words, ideas and music, affect the molecular structure of water, the very same water that comprises over seventy percent of a mature human body and covers the same amount of our planet.

Dr. Emoto has been visually documenting these molecular changes in water by means of his photographic techniques. He freezes droplets of water and then examines them under a dark field microscope that has photographic capabilities. His work clearly demonstrates the diversity of the molecular structure of water and the effect of the environment upon the structure of the water. Dr Emoto's work provides evidence that we can positively heal and transform ourselves and our planet by the thoughts we choose to think.

The above is taken from www.hado.net

9.3 Plant experiments

Cleve Backster is a leading lie-detector expert. In 1966 when watering plants at his office he wondered if it might be possible to measure the length of time it would take water to travel up the stem of a plant from the roots and reach the leaves, particularly in a cane plant with an especially long trunk. It occurred to him that he could test this by connecting the cane plant to one of his polygraph machines; once the water reached the spot between the electrodes, the moisture would contaminate the circuit and be recorded as a drop in resistance.

A lie detector is sensitive to the slightest change in the electrical conductivity of skin, which is caused by increased activity of the sweat glands, which in turn are governed by the sympathetic nervous system. The polygraph galvanic skin response (GSR) portion of the test displays the amount of the skin's electrical resistance, much as an electrician's ohmmeter records the electrical resistance of a circuit. A lie detector also monitors changes in blood pressure, respiration, and the strength and rate of the pulse. Low levels of electrical conductivity indicate little stress and a state of calm. Higher electrodermal activity (EDA) readings indicate that the sympathetic nervous system, which is sensitive to stress or certain emotional states, is in overdrive – as would be the case when someone is lying. A polygraph reading can offer evidence of stress to the sympathetic nervous system even before the person being tested is consciously aware of it.

In 1966 the state-of-the-art technology consisted of a set of electrode plates, which were attached to two of a subject's fingers, and through which a tiny current of electricity was passed. The smallest increases or decreases in electrical resistance were picked up by the plates and recorded on a paper chart, on which a pen traced a continuous, serrated line.

When someone lied or in any way experienced a surge of emotion (such as excitement or fear), the size of the zigzag would dramatically increase and the tracing would move to the top of the chart.

Backster sandwiched one of the long, curved leaves of the cane plant between the two sensor electrodes of a lie detector and encircled it with a rubber band. Once he watered the plant, what he expected to see was an upward trend in the ink tracing on the polygraph recording paper, corresponding to a drop in the leaf's electrical resistance as the moisture content increased. But as he poured in the water the very opposite occurred. The first part of the tracing began heading down-ward and then displayed a short-term blip, similar to what happens when a person briefly experiences a fear of detection.

At the time Backster thought he was witnessing a human style reaction, although he would later learn that the waxy insulation between the cells in plants causes an electrical discharge that mimics a human stress reaction on polygraph instruments. He decided that if the plant were indeed displaying an emotional reaction, he would have to come up with some major emotional stimulus to heighten this response.

When a person takes a polygraph test, the best way to determine if he is lying is to ask a direct and pointed question, so that any answer but the truth will cause an immediate, dramatic stress reaction in his sympathetic nervous system. In order to elicit the equivalent of alarm in a plant, Backster knew he needed to somehow threaten its well-being. He tried immersing one of the plant's leaves in a cup of coffee, but that did not cause any interesting reaction on the tracing – only a continuation of the downward trend. If this were the tracing of a human-being, Backster would have concluded that the person being monitored was tired or bored. It was obvious to him that he needed to pose an immediate and genuine threat – he would get a match a burn the electroded leaf.

At the very moment he had that thought, the recoding pen swung to the top of the polygraph chart and nearly jumped off. He had not burned the plant, he had only thought about doing so. According to his polygraph the plant had perceived the thought as a direct threat and registered extreme alarm. He ran to his secretary's desk in a neighbouring office for some matches. When he returned the plant was still registering alarm on the polygraph. He lit a match and flickered it under one of the leaves. The pen continued on its wild, zigzag course. Backster then returned the matches to his secretary's desk. The tracing calmed down and began to flat-line.

He hadn't known what to make of it. He had long been drawn to hypnosis and ideas about the power of thought and the nature of consciousness. He had even performed a number of experiments with hypnosis during his work with the Army Intelligence Corps and the CIA, as part of a campaign designed to detect the use of hypnosis techniques in Russian espionage.

But this was something altogether more extraordinary. This plant, it seemed, had read his thoughts. It wasn't even as though he particularly liked plants. This only could have occurred if the plant possessed some sort of sophisticated extrasensory perception. The plant somehow must be attuned to its environment, able to receive far more than pure sensory information from water or light.

Backster modified his polygraph equipment to amplify electrical signals so that they would be highly sensitive to the slightest electrical change in the plant. He and his partner, Bob Henson, set about replicating the initial experiment. Backster spent the next year and a half frequently monitoring the reactions of the other plants in the office to their environment.

They discovered a number of characteristics. The plants grew attuned to the comings and goings of their caretaker. They also maintained some sort of 'territoriality' and so did not react to events in the other offices near Backster's lab. They even seemed to tune in to Pete, his Doberman Pinscher, who spent his days at the office.

Most intriguing of all, there seemed to be a continuous two-way flow of information between the plants and other living things in their environment. One day when Backster boiled his kettle to make coffee, he found he had put in too much water. But when he poured the residue down the sink, he noticed that the plants registered an intense reaction.

The sink was not the most hygienic; indeed his staff had not cleaned the drain for several months. He decided to take some samples from the drain and examine them under a microscope, which showed a jungle of bacteria that ordinarily lives in the waste pipes of a sink. When threatened by the boiling water, had the bacteria emitted a type of mayday signal before they died, which had been picked up by the plants?

Backster, who knew he would be ridiculed if he presented findings like these to the scientific community, enlisted an impressive array of chemists, biologists, psychiatrists, psychologists and physicists to help him design an airtight experiment. In his early experiments, Backster had relied upon human thought and emotion as the trigger for reactions in the plants. The scientists discouraged him from using intention as the stimulus of the experiment because it did not lend itself to rigorous scientific design. How could you set up a control for a human thought, an intention to harm say? The orthodox scientific community could easily pick holes in his study. He had to create a laboratory barren of any other living things besides the plants to ensure the plants would not be, as it were, distracted.

The only way to achieve this was to automate the experiment entirely. But he also needed a potent stimulus. He tried to think of the one act that would stir up the most profound reaction, something that would evoke the equivalent in the plants of dumbfounded horror. It became clear that the only way to get unequivocal results was to commit the equivalent of mass genocide. But what could he kill *en masse* that would not arouse the ire of anti-vivisectionists or get him arrested? It obviously could not be a person or a large animal of any variety. He did not even want to kill members of the usual experimental population, like rats or guinea pigs. The one obvious candidate was brine shrimp. Their only purpose as far as he could tell was to become fodder for tropical fish. Brine shrimp were already destined for the slaughterhouse. Only the most ardent anti-vivisectionist could object.

Backster and Henson rigged up a gadget that would randomly select one of six possible moments when a small cup containing the brine shrimp would invert and tip its contents into a pot of continuously boiling water. The randomizer was placed in the far room in his suite of six offices, with three plants attached to polygraph equipment in three separate rooms at the other end of the laboratory. His fourth polygraph machine, attached to a fixed valve resistor to ensure that there was no sudden surge of voltage from the equipment, acted as the control.

Microcomputers had yet to be invented, as Backster set up his lab in the late sixties. To perform the task, Backster created an innovative mechanical programmer, which operated on a time-delay switch, to set off each event in the automation process. After flipping the switch, Backster and Henson would leave the lab, so that they and their thoughts would not influence the results. He had to eliminate the possibility that the plants might be more attuned to him and his colleague than a minor murder of brine shrimp down the hallway.

Backster and Henson tried their test numerous times. The results were unambiguous, the polygraphs of the electroded plants spiked a significant number of times just as the point when the brine shrimp hit the boiling water. Years after he made this discovery – and after he became a great fan of *Star Wars* – he would think of this moment as one in which his plants picked up a major disturbance in the Force, and he had discovered a means of measuring it. If plants could register the death of an organism three doors away, it must mean that all life forms were exquisitely in tune with each other. Living things must be registering and passing telepathic information back and forth at every moment, particularly at moments of threat or death.

The above is taken from The Intention Experiment, Lynne McTaggart.

9.4 Dr. Kenneth Ring's NDE Research of the Blind

Vicki Umipeg, a forty-five year old blind woman, was just one of the more than thirty persons that Dr. Ken Ring and Sharon Cooper interviewed at length during a two-year study concerning near-death experiences of the blind. The results of their study appear in their newest book Mindsight. Vicki was born blind, her optic nerve having been completely destroyed at birth because of an excess of oxygen she received in the incubator. Yet, she appears to have been able to see during her NDE. Her story is a particularly clear instance of how NDE's of the congenitally blind can unfold in precisely the same way as do those of sighted persons. As you will see, apart from the fact that Vicki was not able to discern colour during her experience, the account of her NDE is absolutely indistinguishable from those with intact visual systems.

Vicki told Dr. Ring she found herself floating above her body in the emergency room of a hospital following an automobile accident. She was aware of being up near the ceiling watching a male doctor and a female nurse working on her body, which she viewed from her elevated position. Vicki has a clear recollection of how she came to the realization that this was her own body below her. The following is her experience:

"I knew it was me, I was pretty thin then, I was quite tall and thin at that point and I recognized at first that it was a body but I didn't even know it was mine initially. Then I perceived that I was up on the ceiling and I thought "well, that's kind of weird, what am I doing up here?" I thought, "Well this must be me, am I dead?" I just briefly saw this body and I knew that it was mine because I wasn't in mine"

In addition, she was able to note certain further identifying features indicating that the body she was observing was certainly her own.

"I think I was wearing the plain gold band on my right ring finger and my father's wedding ring next to it, but my wedding ring I definitely saw. That was the one I noticed the most because it's most unusual. It has orange blossoms on the corners of it."

There is something extremely remarkable and provocative about Vicki's recollection of these visual impressions, as a subsequent comment of hers implied.

"This was," she said, "the only time I could ever relate to seeing and to what light was, because I experienced it."

She then told them that following her out-of-body episode, which was very fast and fleeting, she found herself going up through the ceilings of the hospital until she was above the roof of the building itself, during which time she had a brief panoramic view of her surroundings. She felt very exhilarated during this ascension and enjoyed tremendously the freedom of movement she was experiencing. She also began to hear sublimely beautiful and exquisitely harmonious music akin to the sound of wind chimes. With scarcely a noticeable transition, she then discovered she had been sucked head first into a tube and felt that she was being pulled up into it. The enclosure itself was dark, Vicki said, yet she was aware that she was moving toward light. As she reached the opening of the tube, the music that she had heard earlier seemed to be transformed into hymns and she then "rolled out" to find herself lying on grass. She was surrounded by trees and flowers and a vast number of people. She was in a place of tremendous light, and the light, Vicki said, was something you could feel as well as see. Even the people she saw were bright.

"Everybody there was made of light. And I was made of light. What the light conveyed was love. There was love everywhere. It was like love came from the grass, love came from the birds, love came from the trees."

Vicki then becomes aware of specific persons she knew in life who are welcoming her to this place. There are five of them. Debby and Diane were Vicki's blind schoolmates, who had died years before, at ages 11 and 6, respectively. In life, they had both been profoundly retarded as well as blind, but here they appeared bright and beautiful, healthy and vitally alive and no longer children, but, as Vicki phrased it, "in their prime." In addition, Vicki reports seeing two of her childhood caretak-

ers, a couple named Mr. and Mrs. Zilk, both of whom had also previously died. Finally, there was Vicki's grandmother, who had essentially
raised Vicki and who had died just two years before this incident. In
these encounters, no actual words were exchanged, Vicki says, but only
feelings, feelings of love and welcome. In the midst of this rapture, Vicki
is suddenly overcome with a sense of total knowledge.

"I had a feeling like I knew everything and like everything made sense.
I just knew that this place was where I would find the answers to all the
questions about life, and about the planets, and about God, and about
everything. It's like the place was the knowing".

As these revelations are unfolding, Vicki notices that now next to her is
a figure whose radiance is far greater than the illumination of any of the
persons she has so far encountered. Immediately, she recognizes this
being to be Jesus. He greets her tenderly, while she conveys her excitement to him about her newfound omniscience and her joy at being there
with him. Telepathically, he communicates to her.

"Isn't it wonderful? Everything is beautiful here, and it fits together. And
you'll find that. But you can't stay here now. It's not your time to be here
yet and you have to go back." Vicki reacts, understandably enough, with
extreme disappointment and protests vehemently, "No, I want to stay
with you."

But the being reassures her that she will come back, but for now, she "has
to go back and learn and teach more about loving and forgiving." Still
resistant, however, Vicki then learns that she also needs to go back to
have her children. With that, Vicki, who was then childless but who "desperately wanted" to have children (and who has since given birth to
three) becomes almost eager to return and finally consents. However,
before Vicki can leave the being says to her, "but first watch this." And
what Vicki then sees is "everything from my birth" in a complete
panoramic review of her life, and as she watches, the being gently com-
ments to help her understand the significance of her actions and their
repercussions. The last thing Vicki remembers, once the life review has
been completed, are the words, "You have to leave now." Then she experiences "a sickening thud" like a roller-coaster going backwards, and
finds herself back in her body.

Such reports, replete with visual imagery, were the rule, not the exception, among Ring and Cooper's blind respondents. Altogether, 80% of
their entire sample claimed some visual perception during their near-

death or out-of-body encounters. Although Vicki's was unusual with respect to the degree of detail, it was hardly unique in their sample.

Sometimes the initial onset of visual perception of the physical world is disorienting and even disturbing to the blind. This was true for Vicki, for example, who said:

"I had a hard time relating to it (i.e., seeing). I had a real difficult time relating to it because I've never experienced it. And it was something very foreign to me. Let's see, how can I put it into words? It was like hearing words and not being able to understand them, but knowing that they were words, and before you'd never heard anything. But it was something new, something you'd not been able to previously attach any meaning to."

Taken from:
http://www.near-death.com/experiences/evidence03.html

9.5 A Day in the Life of Oscar the Cat

Oscar the Cat awakens from his nap, opening a single eye to survey his kingdom. From atop the desk in the doctor's charting area, the cat peers down the two wings of the nursing home's advanced dementia unit. All quiet on the western and eastern fronts. Slowly, he rises and extravagantly stretches his two-year-old frame, first backward and then forward. He sits up and considers his next move.

In the distance, a resident approaches. It is Mrs. P., who has been living on the dementia unit's third floor for three years now. She has long forgotten her family, even though they visit her almost daily. Moderately dishevelled after eating her lunch, half of which she now wears on her shirt, Mrs. P. is taking one of her many aimless strolls to nowhere. She glides toward Oscar, pushing her walker and muttering to herself with complete disregard for her surroundings. Perturbed, Oscar watches her carefully and, as she walks by, lets out a gentle hiss, a rattlesnake-like warning that says "leave me alone." She passes him without a glance and continues down the hallway. Oscar is relieved. It is not yet Mrs. P.'s time, and he wants nothing to do with her.

Oscar jumps down off the desk, relieved to be once more alone and in control of his domain. He takes a few moments to drink from his water bowl and grab a quick bite. Satisfied, he enjoys another stretch and sets out on his rounds. Oscar decides to head down the west wing first, along the way sidestepping Mr. S., who is slumped over on a couch in the hallway. With lips slightly pursed, he snores peacefully - perhaps blissfully unaware of where he is now living. Oscar continues down the hallway until he reaches its end and Room 310. The door is closed, so Oscar sits and waits. He has important business here.

Twenty-five minutes later, the door finally opens, and out walks a nurse's aide carrying dirty linens. "Hello, Oscar," she says. "Are you going inside?" Oscar lets her pass, then makes his way into the room, where there are two people. Lying in a corner bed and facing the wall, Mrs. T. is asleep in a foetal position. Her body is thin and wasted from the breast cancer that has been eating away at her organs. She is mildly jaundiced and has not spoken in several days. Sitting next to her is her daughter, who glances up from her novel to warmly greet the visitor. "Hello, Oscar. How are you today?"

Oscar takes no notice of the woman and leaps up onto the bed. He surveys Mrs. T. She is clearly in the terminal phase of illness, and her breathing is laboured. Oscar's examination is interrupted by a nurse, who walks in to ask the daughter whether Mrs. T. is uncomfortable and needs more morphine. The daughter shakes her head, and the nurse retreats. Oscar returns to his work. He sniffs the air, gives Mrs. T. one final look, then jumps off the bed and quickly leaves the room. Not today.

Making his way back up the hallway, Oscar arrives at Room 313. The door is open, and he proceeds inside. Mrs. K. is resting peacefully in her bed, her breathing steady but shallow. She is surrounded by photographs of her grandchildren and one from her wedding day. Despite these keepsakes, she is alone. Oscar jumps onto her bed and again sniffs the air. He pauses to consider the situation, and then turns around twice before curling up beside Mrs. K.

One hour passes. Oscar waits. A nurse walks into the room to check on her patient. She pauses to note Oscar's presence. Concerned, she hurriedly leaves the room and returns to her desk. She grabs Mrs. K.'s chart off the medical-records rack and begins to make phone calls.

Within a half hour the family starts to arrive. Chairs are brought into the room, where the relatives begin their vigil. The priest is called to deliver last rites. And still, Oscar has not budged, instead purring and gently nuzzling Mrs. K. A young grandson asks his mother, "What is the cat doing here?" The mother, fighting back tears, tells him, "He is here to help Grandma get to heaven." Thirty minutes later, Mrs. K. takes her last Earthly breath. With this, Oscar sits up, looks around, then departs the room so quietly that the grieving family barely notices.

On his way back to the charting area, Oscar passes a plaque mounted on the wall. On it is engraved a commendation from a local hospice agency: "For his compassionate hospice care, this plaque is awarded to Oscar the Cat." Oscar takes a quick drink of water and returns to his desk to curl up for a long rest. His day's work is done. There will be no more deaths today, not in Room 310 or in any other room for that matter. After all, no one dies on the third floor unless Oscar pays a visit and stays awhile.

Note: Since he was adopted by staff members as a kitten, Oscar the Cat has had an uncanny ability to predict when residents are about to die. Thus far, he has presided over the deaths of more than 25 residents on the third floor of Steere House Nursing and Rehabilitation Center in Providence, Rhode Island. His mere presence at the bedside is viewed by physicians and nursing home staff as an almost absolute indicator of impending death, allowing staff members to adequately notify families. Oscar has also provided companionship to those who would otherwise have died alone. For his work, he is highly regarded by the physicians and staff at Steere House and by the families of the residents whom he serves.

Article from *The New England Journal of Medicine*, written by David M. Dosa, MD, MPH

Taken from :
http://content.nejm.org/cgi/content/full/357/4/328

10

Universal language of symbols

There is a universal language of symbols beyond the power of words. This symbolic form of communication transcends the spoken language and we can receive these symbols either internally or externally and in our sleep state and waking time. Symbols give a knowledge which concerns the deeper mysteries of man and the universe and helps the universe orchestrate events more easily. It is a language that connects one world to another and allows communication between those worlds.

I think there is a universal language made up of symbols. It has been handed down through the ages and can be found in places such as ancient cultures, religious text, historical structures etc. It is another piece of the puzzle and a way for the Creator, the universe, spirit workers and our higher selves to communicate with us and give us guidance to lead us forward in life. Symbols are sometimes picture images that everyone can understand. If we were illiterate and could not read or write, to communicate with someone other than being face to face we would have to draw a picture, and the picture would be symbolic. For instance, if you could not make an appointment you might draw a clock with the hands set at a certain time. You might then put a big cross over the clock, and this would convey you could not make the appointment.

We use symbols in our everyday, modern lives, and they can be found in places such as on the roads, in offices, hotels and shops, conveying to us a symbolic instruction. When we dream our dreams are full of symbols and if we can understand this universal language then we can interpret the guidance received in our sleep state via our subconscious database, the universal database and from those living in a parallel universe of thought/spirit.

We can also receive symbols in our waking hours and it is a subtle and cryptic form of communication. Symbols can also be an event, happening, smell, feeling etc. that has a symbolic meaning. For instance, if the radio changed channel on its own it might mean you need to change your way of thinking. If a bad smell appeared from nowhere it could be telling you something doesn't smell right.

Just by speaking in our mind we can ask for help and guidance with specific issues, such as 'please help me to achieve what ever it is I have come to Earth to achieve' and by doing this you can be led down a long, long road which requires you to be strong, brave and truthful about yourself and your motives and requires you to develop and balance your intellect, intuition and emotions. It is a proper journey but one where you have an unseen navigator at your side, showing you the way.

11

Us - the computer

I think of the physical body (outer casing) and the spirit that animates the physical body as being like a computer which has a wireless connection.

Our physical body can be likened to the hardware of a computer, (the plastic casing, screen, keyboard etc.).

Our spirit, which is the animating force within us and all living things, has a mind. The mind of the spirit is like the hard drive of the computer (where all documents and data is stored) and all our data, (everything we think, feel, experience and learn) is stored in the database of the mind which is located in the storage facility/aura, and we are constantly populating that database with more data.

The third eye is like the mouse of the computer and is animated by our six senses and it is part of the mind of the spirit. The third eye interacts with the brain of the physical body, firing and activating the brain so our thoughts can be put into action, and our five physical senses as well as the sixth sense, utilised.

The brain is a mass of electric circuits through which the mind expresses itself.

When we die the hardware (physical body) is redundant, it is no longer needed and can be scrapped by what ever means is acceptable to us.

The spirit with all the data contained therein, all we have thought, felt, experienced and learnt etc. lives on, just like everything stored in the hard drive of the computer lives on once removed from the hardware.

When the spirit breaks free upon the death of the physical body all the chakras of the spirit collapse back into one another. All the chakras fit perfectly one inside the other so you are left with one wheel/orb that contains all.

We – that conscious part of us – never die.

The spirit exists in a parallel universe where upon entering the mind is unlocked and everything that has gone before is downloaded and merges with what we have learnt whilst here on Earth this time around.

11.1 The database of the mind

I think we are like a computer and I think our mind is like the database of the computer. Everything we think, feel, experience and learn is entered, filed and saved in the storage medium/aura of the mind. In our sleep state there seems to be some kind of mechanism that sees the mind retrieving from the storage medium data/memories that it uses to speak to us in a symbolic language of symbols. We have the capacity to translate this language if we take the trouble to learn. This is the same symbolic language that has been used throughout history via such things as ancient text, monuments etc. for our higher self, the universe and spirit workers to give us cryptic and subtle messages for guidance and to help us achieve what ever it is we have come here on Earth to experience, achieve etc. It is a language that allows communication from one world to another.

The mechanism that allows us to retrieve data/memory from the database in the storage medium/aura of the mind is a mystery to me. However I would use our similarity with the computer to try to find some understanding of this mechanism.

Everything that we have learnt during our lifetime is not in our conscious memory at any one time. These things when needed have to be moved from the storage medium/aura of the mind to our consciousness, and that's exactly how a computer works. The mechanism is very similar. A computer can have practically any amount of storage attached but when operating all of this information is not being processed, it is waiting to be called upon and moved (loaded) into RAM (memory).

11.2 The universal database

Garry Schwartz has explained to us thoughts and feelings are real, they are atoms, and I have used such examples as water and plant experiments to show how science is understanding and accepting this fact. I have also used blind Vicki's story to show we can see, think and feel when we are outside of the body, and Oscar the Cat's story demonstrates animals can 'read' the data in the empty space that is all around us. I think all our thoughts and feelings are stored internally (in our own database/aura), as well as existing and stored externally 'out there' in a universal database. Is the universal database the aura of Mother Earth? I think it probably is.

If we need guidance or help and the symbolic reference is not in the database of our mind it seems to me we can access the universal database to tell us what it is we need to know. For example:

Friedrich August Kekule was a scientist and was having problems with discovering the properties of Benzine. One night he had a dream and part of the dream was of snakes and one of the snakes had seized hold of is own tail. The snake seizing its own tail gave Kekule the circular structure idea he needed to solve the Benzine problem.

I wonder if there was someone else in the world thinking about the structure of Benzine and had put the pieces of the puzzle together? If so this would have been entered into the universal database and Kekule could somehow have accessed it.

Or perhaps those in the parallel universe (spirit workers) provided Kekule with the symbolic missing piece of the Benzine puzzle to help in the process of discovery and take humankind forward a little.

Another interesting point is when people have prophetic dreams. There is a very touching example from Wales where I live of a ten years old Welsh girl who was killed in the Aberfan disaster, when a coal tip (where waste from the mining process was dumped) slid into the school. On the morning of the disaster this little girl told her mum she dreamt she went to school and there was no school there, something black had come down all over it.

This little girl went off to school and at 9.15am that morning the coal tip gave way, sending tons of coal sludge, water and boulders to the village below. The avalanche mowed down everything in its path, including stone houses, trees and the school. In all one hundred and forty four people were killed, most of them children at the school.

We know everything emits a frequency and we also know the frequency will contain data or information. The coal tip would have been emitting a frequency telling of its distress as it was shifting position. It is probable in her sleep state this child accessed the frequency of the coal tip from the universal database and her mind somehow converted the data into the universal language.

Science is telling us a quantum energy field connects everything in the universe, including human beings and their thoughts, and everything emits a type of frequency which contains data. It is apparent to me we are somehow able to access this data from a universal database even if it is sometimes not specific enough for us to understand what the data is telling us.

12

We are body and spirit and are here on Earth to learn lessons

We have seen the Age of Pisces was to teach us we were body and spirit, and I think the spirit contains a mind and a soul. The mind is for thought and thinking and lies over the heart area of the physical body. The soul is for feelings and emotions and lies over the stomach (gut) area of the physical body. The spirit is present at conception, when the sperm and the egg meet, and if it were not present then there could be no life, no animation. I think the mind of the spirit is locked so everything that has gone before and the reason we have come to Earth is not known to us.

We are at the mercy of those workers in the spirit world or parallel universe who know our plan and have agreed to work with us and help us to learn, experience and achieve what ever it is we have come to Earth for. I see planet Earth like a school or university with the people living on Earth being at all different levels of learning, depending on the individual's spiritual growth achieved over different lifetimes.

When we wake in the morning imagine a periscope rising from the heart area and travelling up to the forehead. The periscope has an eye and this is called our third eye.

In our sleep state I think our spirit can leave the body and go to a parallel universe for guidance from spirit workers who know our plan and what we are supposed to achieve. When the spirit returns to the body, if we wake up too soon then we are paralysed, (just like your computer would be paralysed if you disengaged the mouse). This can be a frightening experience but until the spirit is back in place and the third eye is activating the brain there can be no animation, we cannot move or speak.

However there is no need to be frightened because it is quite natural and eventually, once the spirit is settled, you will be able to move and see again.

We do not normally remember we have received guidance from a parallel universe but the guidance sits there in our database and upon waking we might just have an answer to our problems, or the data/guidance might present itself to our consciousness at the right time.

12.1 Mind - Heart / Soul - gut

In Lynne McTaggart's book *The Intention Experiment* in the Chapter entitled 'Hearts that beat as one', she tells about research subjects who were registering psychological responses before they saw certain photos. She goes on to tell us:

'Dr Rollin McCraty, Executive Vice-President and Director of Research for the Institute of HeartMath, in Boulder Creek, California was fascinated by the idea of shared physical foreboding of an event, but wondered where exactly in the body this intuitive information might first be felt. He used the original design of Radin's study with a computerized system of randomly generated arousing photos, but hooked up his participants to a greater complement of medical equipment.

McCraty discovered that these forebodings of good and bad news were felt in both the heart and brain, whose electromagnetic waves would speed up or slow down just before a disturbing or tranquil picture was shown. Further-more, all four lobes of the cerebral cortex appeared to take part in this intuitive awareness. Most astonishing of all, the heart appeared to receive this information moments before the brain did. This suggested that the body has certain perceptual apparatus that enables it continually to scan and intuit the future, but that the heart may hold the largest antenna. After the heart receives the information, it communicates this information to the brain'.

'McCraty's conclusion – that the heart is the largest 'brain' of the body – has now gained credibility after research findings by Dr John Andrew Armour at the University of Montreal and the Hopital du Sacre-Coeur in Montreal. Armour discovered neurotransmitters in the heart that signal and influence aspects of higher thought in the brain.

McCraty discovered that touch and even mentally focusing on the heart cause brain-wave entrainment between people. When two people touched while focusing loving thoughts on their hearts, the more 'coherent' heart rhythms of the two began to entrain the brain of the other.

Armed with this new evidence about the heart, Dean Radin and Marilyn Schlitz decided to explore whether remote mental influence extended to anywhere else in the body. An obvious place to explore was the gut. People speak about intuition as a 'gut instinct' or 'gut feeling'. Certain researchers have even referred to the gut as a 'second brain'. Radin wondered if a gut instinct was accompanied by an actual physical effect.

Radin and Schlitz gathered 26 student volunteers, paired them, and this time wired them up to an electrogastrogram (EGG), which measures the electrical behaviour of the gut; monitors on the skin usually closely match the frequencies and contractions of the stomach. Although the Freiburg study has shown otherwise, Radin and Sclitz believed that familiarity could only help to magnify the effects of remote influence. In case some sort of physical connection was indeed important, Radin asked all the participants to exchange some meaningful object first.

Radin put one participant from a pair in one room. The other sat in another, darkened room, attached to an electro-gastrogram, viewing live video images of the first person. Images periodically flashed on another monitor, accompanied by music to arouse particular emotions: positive, negative, angry, calming or just neutral. The results revealed another example of entrainment – this time in the gut. The EGG readings of the receiver were significantly higher and correlated with those of the sender when the sender experienced strong emotions, positive or negative. Here was yet more evidence that the emotional state of others is registered in the body of the receiver – in this case, deep in the intestines – and that the home of the gut instinct is indeed the gut itself.'

12.2 The psychic centres - chakras

I think that chakras are wheels of consciousness and I have observed how subtle energies affect us mentally, emotionally and physically. If I am feeling imbalanced in any way I focus my thoughts on my chakras and imagine them opening and closing and I can physically feel them responding to my thought. I experience a mild sensation over my face and head that feels as though I have walked into a cobweb. My temples seem to pulsate and my forehead gets tight. I also sometimes experience an increased heartbeat and a fluttering sensation in my stomach. I visualise all the chakras resonating in harmony with one another. In this way I become balanced and am able to act in a reasoned way, responding in the right way to any situation that might be problematic, and keeping the emotions out of it.

My understanding is a chakra is the wheel of consciousness at each of the seven main energy centres of the spirit and they are activated by thought and feeling. These chakras function as pumps and valves, regulating the flow of energy (which contains information) through our energy system. Our thoughts and feelings open and close these valves and they filter the world around us, absorbing that which matches how we are feeling, is on our level of understanding, belief systems etc. We are consciously made aware of this information when it is expressed via the brain.

The chakras interact with the physical body through two major vehicles, the endocrine system and the nervous system. Each of the seven chakras is related to one of the seven endocrine glands, and intersecting nerves Thus, each chakra can be associated with particular parts of the body and particular functions within the body controlled by those nerves or the endocrine gland associated with that chakra.

Everything we sense and how we perceive it, in accordance with our default setting at birth, life experiences, belief systems etc., can be divided into seven categories. Each category can be associated with a particular chakra. Thus, the chakras correspond to not only particular parts of your physical body, but also particular parts of your consciousness.

When you feel anxious, you feel it in the chakra associated with that part of your consciousness experiencing the anxiety, and in the parts of the physical body associated with that chakra. The anxiety in the chakra is detected by nerves, and transmitted to the parts of the body controlled by those nerves. When the anxiety continues over a period of time, or to a particular level of intensity, the person creates a symptom on the physical level.

So what this means is chakras accept and transmit information, and everything that is accepted and transmitted has its own path through the body. The information is then stored in the database of the mind of the spirit, and the database of the mind of the spirit is the aura, where everything you have ever thought, felt, experienced, learned etc is stored.

12.3 The Aura

I think the aura is an energy field (which contains data) that surrounds the physical body, and that includes the body of humans, animals, birds, fish, insects, plants, trees and any living thing. If I concentrate by looking at any of these living things, particularly when there is a solid background behind them, I am able to see the aura.

In works of art, ancient text and such like, we are told the auras of the ancient Teachers/Masters extended outward from the body for several miles, drawing crowds of followers to them where ever they travelled. Many Teachers/Masters are portrayed as having a halo, and this is probably a representation of the aura. I think the Native American Indian's headdress is also a representation of the aura.

I think the aura is of the mind of the spirit and is like a storage facility which contains all our thoughts and feelings, everything we are thinking and feeling now at this moment, as well as every thought and feeling we have ever had in this life, and it contains everything we have experienced or learnt this time around. The aura is the database of the mind of the spirit.

I think we leave part of our energy/data everywhere we go and this is how people are able to practice psychometry, reading information from an object that has been handled by someone else. Thoughts and feelings that are particularly intense such as, fear, sorrow etc are read easier than the more mundane type.

However, we do not have to handle an object for our energy/data to be read. If something very dramatic happened in a building or an area, such as people fighting and experiencing lots of violence, pain, fear and such like it is thought these intense feelings and emotions can be stored in the natural iron of stone etc.

We are told iron is everywhere in nature and it holds information if it is magnetised in the right way. It is probable ghosts are repeats of information stored in natural iron and not, as some people think, distressed spirits.

Every single thing we think or feel is a frequency that has a pitch (sound) associated with it. Scientists tell us everything vibrates and thus everything emits sound and just because you can't hear a sound it doesn't mean a sound is not being made, it just means it is off our range of hearing. Also, every single thing we think or feel has a colour associated with it.

In Roger Coghill's book *The Healing Energies of Light*, in chapter 5 Healing with Light, it says 'In 1911 Dr Walter Kilner (who invented the famous Kilner Jar for preserving fruit), risked his position as director of the X-ray department at St Thomas's Hospital in London, by publishing an heretical book called *The Human Atmosphere Or The Aura Made Visible with the Aid of Chemical Screens*. In it he reported that an emanation from human bodies can be seen through specially made spectacles which allowed vision in the ultraviolet part of the spectrum. These had a double screen containing a liquid dye called dicyanin dissolved in alcohol.

This emanation according to Kilner consisted of three zones:

• A thin dark layer close to the skin
• A vapourous layer with rays pointing away from the skin
• A tenuous outer layer about 15 centimetres (6 inches) across, with varying density and colours.

Kilner found that these layers varied according to age, sex, mental energy, and health state. He went so far as to use them tentatively to diagnose diseases such as hepatitis, appendicitis, cancer, epilepsy and psychological states'.

I think Kilner was very brave to risk his position at the hospital and also his credibility, as so many people who were rigid in their way of thinking would have ridiculed him. I think in the not too distant future Kilner's findings will be expanded upon and could see us using the aura as a means of diagnosing mental and physical conditions in mainstream medicine.

Science tells us light comprises the seven colours of the rainbow and more. The writer and Physicist Andrade said 'every kind of light has it's beginnings in atoms'.

Although science still has not unlocked the secrets of the aura it is now readily accepted it does exist. As you develop and strengthen your chakras and third eye you can see the aura. It is recognised our thoughts and feelings are atoms which create different colours that can be seen in the aura. For instance, when someone is imbalanced in any way such as being angry, they are on the red frequency or channel, and you will see the imbalance and anger in the aura as red. It is probably where the saying 'I saw red' comes from.

If you are negative that is the frequency or channel you will transmit and receive on and you will see the colour of negativity as a dark or murky green, and you will transmit your negativity to others and you will draw negativity to you. You could liken this as tuning into a particular radio channel.

We are constantly exchanging energy (information) with everything and everyone. This is why when we meet someone we can be attracted, repelled or indifferent to them, according to the way in which an energy connection is established. We are constantly processing the energy we are exchanging, with the chakras absorbing, pumping and filtering in line with the frequency we are tuned into.

We receive and transmit energy through our aura, via the chakra system. If we meet someone our chakras seek to connect with the appropriate chakras of that person.

We can come away from that person feeling strong or weak, according to the exchange of energy. Supposing one person felt inadequate they could unintentionally project their inadequacy on to another person if that other person was not confident and was therefore on the same wavelength, and in this way the first person would temporarily strengthen and empower themselves and the victim could walk away feeling weakened. We are in a constant dance with everyone and everything around us. However, once we become aware of this just by changing our way of thinking we can alter our frequency and can filter out any unwanted energy connections and absorb that which is more on our new wave length.

When all chakras resonate at the same frequency, we are in tune with that person. If we are around someone constantly our chakras can start to tune in to the other person and start to resonate on their frequency, and we can become like them. If you have a group of women of menstruation age working together, over time they will all start to menstruate at the same time as they become attuned to each other. We are like musical instruments with an unseen tuning fork acting as a conductor and tuning us in to resonate with other instruments.

When we first meet a person we might say we feel 'totally comfortable' with them. However whether this is a good or bad thing depends on the frequency we occupy. For instance, if you were brought up with an alcoholic parent then without you knowing you could attract an alcoholic to you, as this is a frequency you have been tuned into all your life.

In order to get off a destructive frequency and break possible repeated patterns that appear throughout our life and relationships, we have to learn to use the mind and not emotions. Our mind needs to be stronger than the emotion.

We have to get rid of restricted belief systems and change the way we think, perhaps by recognising the truth of our childhood and being able to make a conclusion about it and allow closure in a healthy way, and that type of thing.

12.4 Psychics and Mediums

I think every single living thing in this world has a spirit and so that means every living thing in this world is psychic, capable of processing information from everything that's out there in the empty space/universal database, via frequencies/ data absorbed through the chakras.

This age is to do with things of the air and telepathy, part of the psychic ability, will come to the fore in this age and is achieved by working with waves of the air. In this age telepathy will become an accepted form of communication.

In chapter 8.3 'An explanation of the atom by Professor Garry Schwartz' you will have read: 'The table does not have consciousness as we do, as there are many levels of consciousness. Also the table does not have eyes to convert protons of light into a visual experience, but it does have 'awareness' of the organised energy with which it can resonate'.

An example of this would be, supposing a very heavy weight was put on the table and the table was going to collapse, then the table would emit a frequency to all in its surroundings which would tell of its distress and imminent collapse. If there were an animal lying near the table it is possible the animal would absorb the frequency emitted by the collapsing table via its chakra system and then the animal would move out of the way. This is probably the explanation for natural disasters when animals appear to leave affected areas before the disaster happened. It is possible we humans would also pick up on the frequency but whilst we might tend to ignore or not understand what we absorbed the animal probably would not ignore it.

If the process of weighting the table was over a period of time, adding to the weight bit by bit, it is possible in our sleep state we could pick up on the frequency of warning being emitted by the table that it was on the verge of collapse via a dream. However, mostly we would not understand what the symbols in the dream meant and it is only after the event we might realise we had had a premonition of what was to happen.

You have read in chapter 9.3 of the plant experiments, and this is an example of how plants absorb and process the frequencies, thoughts and feelings of everything around them and demonstrates how everything is connected.

We all have psychic ability, it is the sixth sense and intuition, that gut feeling that when ignored usually sees things going badly for us and we find ourselves saying 'why didn't I listen?'. The problem is we process what we absorb via the brain, and our personalities, belief systems etc. occupy the same space and so we could seek to rationalise away what we have sensed.

We might think 'it's just me being silly', or we might think our sensing is something to be feared etc. according to our beliefs. We now know thoughts are real and feelings are real, they exist inside and outside of the physical body and they are atoms. When we think or feel we are creating atoms that have an effect on, and connect to, everything. You will have read atoms contain protons, neutrons and electrons, and protons carry a positive charge, neutrons carry no charge and electrons carry a negative charge.

Does this mean that when we are happy, confident and all those good things, that we are creating and releasing protons that can have a positive effect on us, and everything and everyone around us? Perhaps when nothing in particular is going on and our thoughts and feelings are neutral then we are creating and releasing neutrons that have no effect.

Things that have a negative effect on us would be depression, fear, unhealthy love, hate, obsession, violence etc. Does this mean the thoughts and feelings associated with these negative things produce electrons?

I wonder if when we walk into a building or any place where we sense a negative atmosphere, this means whoever has been there before has been negative, and have they left behind free floating clouds of electrons we pick up on? If we ourselves were negative this would probably make us feel much worse and if we believed in evil spirits etc. we could even think an evil spirit had attached itself to us as a result of visiting the building or place.

People who work as psychics usually have a more developed psychic ability and are more able to read the atoms/data contained in the aura, as well as the atoms/data left on objects and in the environment. However, we must be aware the psychic has to interpret what it is they are reading and then we are at the mercy of the psychic's personality, belief systems and their level of knowledge. The symbolic universal language will also form part of what is being read, and this is where it gets complicated. I have found a lot of psychics know nothing about the mechanism behind their psychic ability, and they know little about the universal language and often they read the symbolism as literal.

For instance, if a psychic felt a sitter had toothache and the sitter denied this, the psychic might say, 'Get your teeth checked as you are going to have a problem', they might not explore with the sitter whether there was something the sitter was aching to say. If the psychic then felt the sitter had a demon around them, if they themselves believed in demons they might say, 'You are possessed by a demon', whereas actually the sitter had a symbolic demon such as a person, alcohol, drugs, gambling etc. and they needed to overcome their demon; and perhaps this demon was the reason for the toothache and, if explored further, the psychic could have got to the root of the problem.

At this point perhaps I should mention I personally do not think there are demons or evil spirits that possess/attach themselves to people and their auras as some people believe. I do not think demons and evil spirits are separate entities, rather I think this is something we all have the potential to be and is an aspect of the personality. We have free will and it is up to us whether we do good or bad.

You don't have to be a bad person to feel you have a demon or an evil entity with you, rather you could have low self esteem and that sort of thing. This means your chakras/ aura might connect with people who will feed your low self esteem but you can also connect with the unseen frequencies of every person and thing whether living or dead via the universal database which occupies the empty space around you and are on your frequency, and you can feel even more insecure by absorbing this. Your thoughts can be dark and you could feel as though these thoughts are not of you but they are, as it is you that is interpreting the data in the frequency to which you are connected or tuned into.

However this is only a frequency that you can connect with, it is not anything you are attached to or anything that is attached to you. Your low self esteem and insecurity can be a devil and is your demon and in order to get rid of your demon you need to work on yourself and eventually you will resonate at a different frequency and attract different people and situations to you. You need to put as much care into your mental and emotional health as you do your physical health.

I have come to this conclusion about so-called demons and evil entities not just because what science is now telling us but also from working over the years in the arena of the mind. I have had people come to me believing they were possessed, and sometimes they have had that possession confirmed by someone who seemed to be knowledgeable in these things, reinforcing their fear. However, when you investigate what is really going on in their life you can always find some negative aspect to their personality. This might be because of their life experiences, suffering childhood abuse or that type of thing.

In order to change this negative aspect they need to empower themselves through knowledge. They have to learn to quiet the emotions, start to learn about life and people and challenge any restrictive belief systems so they can make a considered judgement of their past. In this way they change the way they think and feel and they can also change frequency, no longer attracting or resonating with harmful frequencies, people and situations, and generally de-cluttering their life.

Whilst everyone is a psychic, not all psychics are mediums but most people have the ability to be a medium or at the very least be their own medium. A medium is able to tune into a higher frequency and communicate with those who have died (discarded the physical body) and are living in a parallel universe in spirit form. The gift can be used to prove evidence of survival to someone who is grieving, or it can be used for help and guidance to who ever needs it. There are many people who are natural mediums and develop their gifts on their own, and there are others who might not be natural but have a desire to develop.

One of the keys to developing mediumship is to expand the mind with knowledge, reading about the mysteries of the world and about spiritual matters and investigating the science of consciousness. This should help you get rid of any restrictive belief systems and concentrate on self-improvement, taking time to quiet the mind and using meditation techniques to help with this. You will then be able to tune into different frequencies or channels.

Mediumship comes in different forms but unfortunately the wonderful physical and direct voice gifts which brought in this age have all but disappeared and we are left with mostly mental mediumship.

Mental Mediumship can be separated into three forms; Clairvoyance, Clairaudience and Clairsentience. Each has a different way of receiving information:

Clairvoyance
The meaning of the word clairvoyance is 'clear seeing'. A clairvoyant medium will 'see' the spirit person who is communicating and will give evidence of this by giving the sitter a detailed description of the spirit person who the medium 'sees' via their 'third eye'. It is like looking at a photograph or a moving picture, as though watching television.

Clairaudience
The meaning of the word clairaudience is 'clear hearing'. A clairaudient medium will 'hear' the spirit person either by 'hearing' a voice inside their head, or as though someone was standing beside them and talking into their ear.

Clairsentience
The meaning of the word clairsentience is 'clear sensing and feeling'. A clairsentient medium will 'sense or feel' the spirit person. The clairsentient medium will experience things associated with the spirit

person when living on Earth such as symptoms of illness, depression and so on. All the senses can be involved including smell and taste.

13

Examples of dreams and their meanings

I had a dream where a cheque came through the post made out to me and it was for £750. I seemed to be questioning where could this cheque have come from and didn't seem pleased to receive it. I woke up and got on with my day and later went to take a shower but my shower packed up. I called an electrician and he told me I was very lucky because the wrong fuse was used and it should have been a 750 fuse. It might sound silly but because my dream and the fuse both mentioned the figure 750 I wondered if there was any connection?

There certainly is a connection as money is currency which symbolises power and I think you were being told to check the power and in particular the 750 fuse. How amazing you received the guidance before having confirmation from the electrician there was a problem with the fuse in your shower. If only you had realised the significance you could have saved yourself some money. There is definitely someone looking after you and I am confident it will make you take notice of your dreams in future.

–

I had a dream where I was told I had cancer of the brain. I was then outside walking and in front of me was a man and woman, and the man was holding a gun to the woman's head. I called the police to come and help the woman by taking the gun off the man. They came and disarmed the man and when the man spoke he seemed to be a politician. However, the police were not impressed by him and took him away. The woman was so relieved and was able to walk away skipping.

Is there a man who is inside your head, eating away at you and is like a cancer? Perhaps you feel defenceless to protect yourself, and it might be his character is very persuasive and he has an unpleasant influence on you. There is a universal force or power (police) that is there for all of us. You can call on this power and ask for help to go forward with your life, free of this oppressive influence.

–

The other night I had the strangest of dreams. I was eating a sandwich, but as I bit into it my mouth filled with ants. I remember desperately trying to spit them out, but as I did there just seemed to be more of them. I've never dreamed of ants before, what does it mean?

I think you are being forced down a road and you don't have much choice in the matter. You are being 'sandwiched' in. Ants are workers and are very industrious in their endeavours and work for the good of the whole. There is obviously also a connection related to communication (mouth) and so perhaps you are being told you help others by communicating in some way. For instance, it could be you are a teacher and have been chewing over whether to leave your profession and the dream is encouraging you to stop thinking this because the way you work is of immense help to those you teach. I hope this makes sense to you and you can find the area of your life it relates to.

—

In my dream I was with two ex boyfriends and we were in a showroom buying a car for me. There were some really smart looking cars and some bangers. I saw a beautiful old Mercedes and it felt so right. However my two ex's had decided old bangers were suitable for me. One had chosen a red and dented car and the other had chosen a black and tatty car. They were arguing with each other and with me about this. I was disappointed at their interference and when I looked outside a traffic warden was writing a ticket on the car we had arrived in.

I think you might need to move on with your life as you have parked in this situation for too long and if you don't move on there will be a price to pay. Also there are those around you who do not know your worth. You are changing and it will not always be pleasing to others as they would like to keep you down. However, you cannot let others interfere with your progression and sometimes this means we have to leave them behind. You can be that Mercedes, that wise person who has learnt from life and is now comfortable with their self.

—

In my dream I saw myself on television, it was the back view and I was dressed all in white. I was stood at a skip taking something out and there were a couple of other people taking out of this skip as well. The commentator on television was saying people were caught stealing artefacts. I was so upset to see myself on television as I thought what was in the skip was discarded. I felt quite paranoid but when I went out and about I was relieved to see people did not recognise me as the person that was on television.

Television is communication and I think you are being told something from the past is being communicated to others in the wrong way. An artefact is of historical interest and I think you have retrieved something from the past that has been discarded, but could be of interest to others. However your motives are for the good as you are balanced in your actions (white). It could be something like someone having a business idea they shared with you but they didn't follow it through and you have taken it up. Don't worry as others will not recognise you as a person who has done something wrong.

—

In my dream I was with a lady and we had a baby. It belonged to both of us and we were taking it in turns to push the baby in its pram. When it was her turn she would put a cover or some kind of wrap on its head. When it was my turn I would take the cover off, but I would do this in a placating way, like as though she was in charge. This was the theme of the dream, with her in a position of dominance and me trying to assert myself, but not quite succeeding.

You might be in a partnership or some kind of joint venture with someone. If so, you are both trying to push ahead with your baby, or your project, but whereas you want things to be out in the open for ahead, your partner wants to cover something up. Perhaps your partner feels things would be too exposed if the wraps were off. As it is both your baby you should insist on an equal say.

—

I had a dream where I am back in my parents' house. I see myself lying in their bed and I am childlike, sucking my thumb. I hear my mother calling me to get up but I don't want to move. She keeps calling I have been in the bed for too long and I feel irritated by this and stubbornly refuse to get up. She comes to the top of the stairs with her arms open and just stands there. As I have not spoken to my parents for some years, to dream of them is rather unsettling.

I think the dream is telling you that you are being childlike regarding the situation with your parents. You have been in this situation for too long and you should wake up to the fact time is passing. I am sure you have reasons to feel irritated at the thought of contacting them but you will regret your stubbornness should anything happen to them. I think your mother is thinking of you and would welcome you back with open arms.

—

In my dream I was walking barefoot on shale. It was awful and my feet were cut and bleeding. There were other people walking but they had stout shoes on and there was a track beneath their feet. I was crying and thinking 'how on Earth did this happen to me?' I was desperately trying to get off the shale and I realised I had a bike with me, but I wasn't riding it. It took some effort to get on the bike, and peddling with my cut feet over this uneven ground was very difficult. However, I started to make some headway. I was concentrating on peddling when the dream ended.

Feet, shoes and what is underfoot are all to do with your direction. I think you have no protection for your direction because you haven't been using the power at your disposal. I am glad to hear you have realised you have resources on hand that, although hard work, can get you to be where you are supposed to be, back on track.

—

I am retired due to ill health and I loved my job and got on well with the lads. I frequently dream I am back in my old job but stairs I once knew lead to nowhere and I end up in a maze of corridors. The lifts take me to high levels with just a sheer drop in front of me and the walls seem to be crumbling. I try to communicate to my mates but they cannot understand me.

Your dream is all about your mind and I think you are starting to think on a much higher level with belief systems and thought structures changing. You now have the time to think and learn about things you didn't bother with before. It is a time of change for you, with all that was familiar now shifting as you expand your mind, and this can be quite confusing. There is so much to learn and that sheer drop is symbolic of the barriers in your mind coming down and leaving it wide open for exploration.

—

In my dream I was on a boat on the sea in some sort of bay. I was stood at the front as the boat glided around this bay. I could even feel the spray from the ocean. It was a beautiful sunny day and the sea was clear and beautiful, I could see rocks beneath and fish. I saw a great big basking whale, she was enormous. We glided round her gently. We circled the bay twice and then took off into the open sea away from the bay. I don't know who the 'we' were, but I knew I was not alone. The dream was so clear and felt so real. It really was beautiful.

The sea is the sea of life and your view is so clear. I think the whale is the spiritual power that is with you but is just basking at the moment. You wait until it takes off and takes you with it. Your life will open up and you are ready for it. I am so pleased for you. Well done.

—

My husband had a terminal illness and passed away six weeks ago and I am grief stricken. Last night I dreamt I was walking in the country and I came across a lovely bridge. I put my hands on the bridge to look at the flowing water and I was bitten by a long green snake and then as I walked away my hand was bruised. One of my large back teeth just fell out of my mouth.

A bridge can be a symbol of passing over to the other side and your husband has passed to spirit, and of course a river takes you back to the sea of life. Perhaps it is time for you to get back into life because I am sure your husband's illness and death has been like a snake coiling and twisting your insides and this has left you crushed and bruised you but you cannot stay in this state. Teeth are symbolic of words and the back teeth are for chewing. Perhaps you have chewed over this for too long and need to spit it out of your system? Your husband would not want you to suffer.

—

I am a woman over sixty and have had a strange dream. I went soundly off to sleep to awaken screaming loudly, heart racing because this very tall dark figure was standing over me with a club, about to hit me over the head. I was terrified. This thing was all black with no facial signs - just black and was about seven foot tall. Can you explain this - it was truly frightening.

I can assure you this apparition was not real but was a symbolic message for you. Is there something or someone in your life that is over-shadowing you? As there was no facial signs, does this mean it is hard for you to read the situation that is overshadowing you? For instance, you could have a hunch about something but not understand where your feelings are coming from because there are no obvious signs. What ever this is, I feel the club represents you being forced to acknowledge it. I hope this explanation makes sense to you and allays your fears.

—

I have had three dreams in quick succession. In my first dream I was stood with a person and we were really close. We were so close our skin was rubbing against each other and I realised my skin was blistered. I then had a terrifying dream where I was being raped. I made no attempt to defend myself and allowed it to happen. In the third dream I was being chased and who ever is running after me didn't catch me but I am left feeling thoroughly tired.

I think someone you are close to is rubbing you up the wrong way, really irritating you and getting under your skin. You feel violated and it is as though you are being forced into a situation and you feel vulnerable. You are allowing this to happen and you should take control and defend yourself. It is no good running away from this person. Perhaps it is about time you stood your ground and confronted this issue as to continue in this way will take all your energy. What fantastic guidance.

—

My partner and I both dreamt the same dream. She dreamt she was in church taking several steps down the aisle to marry me, but she could only see the sides of the seating. Me and my best man were in front of her with happy expressions on our faces. Then I dreamt I saw my partner walking down the aisle but I was only able to see the side of the seating. She was wearing a white wedding dress, with an expression of happiness on her face. When she got to me, she stopped and turned to face me smiling.

You both seem to have been given guidance about the same thing. A marriage is symbolic of a new way of life and you are not seeing the whole picture of something you have been sitting on, for an example it could be you are sitting on an idea to emigrate or that kind of thing. I would say whatever the situation is it would be a very positive and happy new way of life for you both.

—

I dreamt I was in my boyfriend's sailing boat but he wasn't with me. It was awful as out of nowhere the wind came and the seas turned rough. I didn't know how to control the boat and was hanging on to the sides, frightened to let go. I was looking around, trying to stop the panic rising, concentrating on how to take control. I knew I had to unfurl the sails but there were three sails on different masts which had to open up together and if I did this one at a time the boat would violently turn around and around. However I was one person and realised it was impossible to achieve this synchronized manoeuvre.

Are you in a situation where a person's actions have whipped up a storm around you and you didn't see it coming? You obviously feel things are out of control and it is natural for you to want to stabilise the situation but it seems it is just not possible. Perhaps it is time to bail out of the relationship?

I dreamt I had cancer of the face. I was told this by a doctor and I was so angry with her for telling me this. I would not accept it, even though she tried all ways to convince me of the reality of my situation. I can still remember the intense feeling of anger I felt towards her, it was so real. It seemed I could see no sign of this cancer and so I left the doctor. I then saw myself horrified, as my face was covered by a weeping sore. I went back to the doctor and she told me she was glad I had returned and acceptance would help my situation.

Is there something that is eating away at you? It could be a person or a situation and is something you have to face and admit to yourself, otherwise it will do you no good. The doctor is that part of you that wants you to heal and acceptance will help as you cannot continue to ignore this. You need to heal yourself.

I dreamt I was a cleaner for a house and the floor in the entrance hall was covered in sand, even though I had cleaned it the night before. The owner of the house (a domineering and negative woman) was not amused and when we looked in the other rooms we found they were all a shambles with the furniture tipped over. I wanted to call the police but the woman would not let me..

I think the house is you and you are attempting to clean up your act and make personal changes as things are chaotic in your life. Sand represents time, and you are being told this cannot happen overnight. The domineering owner is the side of you which is over critical and negative. You are starting to recognize the spiritual side of you, that force that is with you so don't let your negative side stop your progression. Cleaning away your negative thoughts and taking responsibility for your actions will enable you to tidy up your present situation, bringing law and order to your life.

My son committed suicide and I keep dreaming similar dreams where he kills himself but not always in the same way. Sometimes I see his coffin but he's not really dead as he moves around. Also when I go to bed

I close my eyes but something tells me to open them and I see faces. I seem to sense things happening before they do and this makes me uneasy. My late mum seems to be with my son and like my son she too moves in her coffin as if they are not really dead.

I think your son is telling you there are many different ways to die but it does not stop us surviving. He and your mother have both survived and are in the same place so you should try to lay them to rest (coffin), in other words stop the intense grieving. Your grief has tuned you into a different frequency and you are entering the world of clairvoyance. It is a wonderful tool and you can use it to help yourself and others.

—

14

Symbolic happenings

There is some kind of evil spirit in my house and I think it is jealous of my new partner. He moved in with me and my kids three months ago and I am sure that my mum orchestrated this. She died five months ago and within two weeks of her dying I had met this new man. The alarm keeps going off even though it has not been set, the doorbell rings and there is no-one there and the toilet is flushing on its own and when these things happen there is a terrible stench. Please help us as we are frightened.

I think your mum is telling you there is something you need to be alarmed about and you need to open up to what is really going on and flush this out as something doesn't smell right in your house. Please do not be frightened as there is nothing evil about this symbolic form of communication, it is just your mum looking out for you and your kids as she always did.

—

I have miscarried my much wanted baby and I feel absolutely distraught but have noticed a really unusual thing. When I leave my house and go out the front door a little tiny butterfly appears and flies in front of me. It is absolutely tiny, about the size of my fingernail, and is pure white. I didn't think you could get baby butterflies and have certainly never seen one before. It is as though this butterfly waits for me. Is it trying to tell me something?

I am so sorry to hear of your loss but you are right as you are being given a message. A butterfly is a symbol of transformation and transition. The front is the future and I think you are being told your baby has made that transition to the next life, has been transformed and has a future. I hope this helps with the grieving process and please be assured not one of us ever dies and when it is your turn you will meet up with the spirit that was your baby.

—

I woke up from sleep and even though it was dark I could see a bug on the lamp which is next to my bed. The bug was really fat and looked as though it was full of eggs. I thought "I have to catch that bug otherwise it will lay its eggs." I slid out of bed and put the main light on but the bug disappeared. I searched my bedroom and it wasn't there. Eventually I turned the light off and got back in to bed. I then heard a loud buzzing. I turned the light on and the buzzing stopped, I turned the light off, and it started again. This went on for ages. Is there a rational explanation?

I think there is someone around you who is bugging you. This person has lots of opportunities coming their way and so you need to see them in a more spiritual light, otherwise they will continue to bug you. You are thinking negative and it will do you no good in the long run.

—

My beloved sister died In November of last year. She was only forty-nine. At her funeral a butterfly was hovering around my shoulder. It was with me as I walked into the church and re-appeared when I left the church. It was a dismal, dark day but as we left the church the sun came out and lit up everything. I cannot get these events out of my mind and recognise a butterfly should not be around in November. I wondered if there was a spiritual connection.

I am so sorry to hear of your loss but you are right, there is a spiritual connection to these events. A butterfly is a fantastic symbol. It starts life as a caterpillar and then forms into a chrysalis and emerges as a butterfly. It is a symbol of transition and transformation and the struggle from one life to another. Your sister has made that transformation and she is free. She is enjoying the warmth and brightness of her new surroundings and wanted you to know that.

—

I came home last night and my house was securely locked with the security alarm on and it had not been activated. On the stairs was a bottle of Bach Flower Remedy called Wild Oat. Nobody had been in the house and it did not belong in the house. Does this have a meaning? Also, later that night my kitchen lights were turning on / off, on / off but the light switch was not moving. I feel quite freaked by these things. Is there any explanation you can think of?

You are so lucky; the bottle is called an apport – a physical gift from the spirit world/universe that brings a symbolic message. I have looked up Wild Oat and it is the remedy for people who feel they want to do something worthwhile with their lives but do not know in which direction they should move. It helps people to find their true role, putting them back in touch with their own basic purpose in life so the way ahead seems obvious. The kitchen symbolically is where you prepare to serve others and the lights were making the message clearer to you. There is obviously something you are meant to be doing that will help others and I truly wish you all the best with this.

—

I am having night terrors. I go to sleep but start to wake up and I am paralysed. I can't move my body or open my eyes. A horrible, demon like man is with me and he stands before me and I am frightened of him. I have tried to ignore him but that makes him mad and he jumps up and down, shaking his fists at me. His appearance is absolutely grotesque. I am frightened of going to sleep at night.

I am so sorry to hear of this dreadful experience and can understand why you are frightened. I think you are being told you need to confront your demons. Your demons could be something like alcoholism, drug addiction, gambling or some such thing. What ever this is, it is paralysing and disabling you. The next time this happens speak to the demon with your mind and tell him you want to confront him and ask for his help. You will be amazed at how you can be supported to help you with your demon, supposing that is you are ready for this.

—

My grandfather has died and I sat with him for hours before he passed. As soon as I left the room he went, and I was distraught because he was on his own. Two days after he died I had a vivid dream. My mobile phone was ringing in the dream and when I looked at the display it said 'granddad'. When I woke up I immediately looked in the directory of my mobile and I was stunned to see 'granddad' listed as calling me.

You would be surprised how many times loved ones have sat at the bedside of the dying and when they leave the room for a moment the person they were keeping vigil over has died. The dying person holds on, not wanting to leave their loved ones. I think it is sometimes easier for the spirit to leave the body when they are on their own. The mobile phone represents communication, your granddad is letting you know he is alright, and he has confirmed this by ensuring his call was listed in your directory.

—

My husband has died and I am distraught. I have been begging him to let me know he is still with me and a few things have happened that are weird. I have a door stop that holds the back door open and it has vanished. My porch light keeps coming on, although I haven't pushed the switch and all my clocks have gone forward. Does this mean anything?

I think your husband is communicating with you symbolically. He is telling you to close the door on the past, as the back represents the past. By putting the porch light on he is saying there is light in the future, as the front represents the future. A clock is symbolic of time and he is encouraging you to go forward. Speak to him in your mind and ask for strength and guidance and take comfort in the fact we all survive bodily death and are living a life on Earth for a purpose. You still have work to do in this life and I am confident you can now go forward.

–

My son aged 41 died suddenly over two years ago. From a few months after his death our doorbell has been ringing on and off with no-one there. Is he trying to show me he is still with me?

I truly believe your son is telling you to 'open up' to him. He has left the physical world and is now back in the world of thought or spirit. Let him in by acknowledging he still exists and speak to him in your mind asking for strength and guidance. He can answer you via dreams, thought transference, sensing, coincidence etc.

–

When I met my partner about four years ago, a five pence piece showed up frequently and in unusual places. I felt someone in spirit was trying to get my attention and I linked it to my new relationship. However, the relationship has now finished because I felt he was abusing me. I am finding these five pence pieces more and more often and so is my son. I can't help feeling somebody from my family who has passed is trying to contact me.

Money or currency is symbolic of power. When we have life experience and learn lessons, we gain power. We become wiser and more confident and our decisions are based on thought and the sixth sense rather than emotions. I feel you and your son have suffered in some way. You are both open to the spiritual side of life because you made the symbolic connection to the five pence pieces. Speak in your mind and ask for guidance and you will be amazed at how you can follow the symbolic communication with just a little balanced thought.

–

Can we have messages via symbols in our everyday lives? I ask this because my mother has died recently and her favourite song was the war song We'll Meet Again. You very rarely hear this but I have heard it three times in the last few days when passing a café, turning on the radio, that type of thing. Also, although I live in a third floor flat, three times recently I have had a butterfly fly in, which has never happened before. In the last few days, on three separate occasions, the clock has stopped at 3pm, which was the time my mother died. Am I reading too much into this?

I think your mother is telling you that you will meet again, she has made the transition from one life to the next, symbolised by the butterfly and she is reinforcing the three in the symbolic happenings as her heart stopped ticking at 3pm. She has survived and when it is your turn, so will you. What a wonderful message from mum.

—

Please can you put my mind at rest, this actually happened a few days before my husband passed away of kidney failure. When he was in hospital I got up to find a large glass and a small glass of dirty water on the draining board, and the glasses did not belong to me. I can't understand how they got there as I live on my own in a one-bedroom bungalow which is doubled glazed and all doors locked. I think about it every day, hope you can help? Thank you.

Symbols are received in our sleep state via dreams but also in our waking hours via coincidence, physical phenomena, apports etc. They tell us something in a universal language. I think you were being prepared for your husband's death by those who have already passed on, perhaps family members, and the symbolic message was the kidneys were not draining properly and your husband was filling up with dirty water. One kidney was probably larger than the other and they were not doing their job properly. Also to consider is, if those who have passed on are not dead it must mean even though your husband has passed, like them, he is not dead. He has just discarded the physical body and in time you will meet again. I hope my response does put your mind at rest.

15

Case studies

Over the years of working in the spiritual arena I have met many different people, and all of them have a story to tell. People normally find themselves contacting me when they have unexplained happenings, coincidence or dreams that are troubling them. They also contact me when they are bereaved and are hurting, or perhaps have had some tragedy or negative experience that has affected them. Some people contact me because they are fascinated with my work, or others contact me because they too are on the same wave-length as me. Nearly all of them that make contact are looking for answers, and I see my task as helping them to look at life, the world and the universe in a different way, thereby connecting them to the higher frequencies and teaching them about the universal language so their true journey can begin.

That this world is in trouble cannot be disputed, as it is clear for all to see. The behaviour of man has deteriorated globally and Mother Earth, as well as the wider universe and all living things, are suffering as a result. The symptom of this suffering is expressed in nature via climate change etc. and is telling us we are having a negative impact on our surroundings, and man's inhumanity to man and other living things demonstrates our need to change.

We really do have to listen, as the years leading up to 2012 are vital. Graham Hancock tells us in his book *The Fingerprints of the Gods* about the Mayan calendar and says:

'Consider the crowning jewel of Maya calendrics, the so-called 'Long Count'. This system of calculating dates also expressed beliefs about the past - notably, the widely held belief that time operated in Great Cycles which witnessed recurrent creations and destructions of the world.

According to the Maya, the current Great Cycle began in darkness on a date corresponding to 13 August 3114 BC in our own calendar. As we have seen, it was also believed the cycle will come to an end, amid global destruction, on 23 December 2012 in our calendar. The function of the Long Count was to record the elapse of time since the beginning of the current Great Cycle, literally to count off, one by one, the 5125 years allotted to our present creation.'

I think the Mayan's ancient words were again another example of symbolism and pieces of the jigsaw provided by the Creator. I do not think our world will stop on 23 December 2012 but I do think our world will have undergone a dramatic change and we can already see this change happening. Whether this change will be achieved with our input or will see us unwillingly being dragged along is for us to collectively decide.

As I am sat typing these words I have the television on in the background and a newsreader is reporting on the spiralling rise in fuel prices and the resulting impact on business and the individual. This made me think of Mother Earth and how her joints must be aching, as we bleed her of the fluid of protection (oil) that sits underneath her crust, and how eventually she will react.

This is just one example of how we can all be unwillingly dragged along down the road of global destruction. It could be Mother Earth will shift her body as she tries to adapt to her loss of fluid and the results can be what we term 'natural disasters' and people will stubbornly ask 'why did God do this'. As oil is running out, fuel prices might continue to spiral and the machinery that drives our world might stop and life as we know it would be in chaos and it too would come to a stop. Symbolically this will result in global destruction – or karma – cause and effect – what goes around comes around, and we will be forced to change.

However, with our technological capability we are more than able to come up with an alternative fuel. Yes it will cost us to change the way we fuel our lives, and many things such as machinery, processes and vehicles would have to be adapted or would be redundant but it has to happen even though this would cause chaos, and the fuel situation is just one example.

There are many, many more examples such as the financial decline, moral decline and ethical decline of individuals, businesses and even countries and there is always a price to pay, especially when you cannot use ignorance as an excuse. We do know better and whatever the Creator's plan is for this age, it will happen whether we are willing participants or not. We will learn.

The following few pages are examples of how individuals are waking up spiritually, and they are happy to share their inspiring stories with you for the benefit of the whole, and as the spiritual student and wonderfully talented singer-songwriter Rees advises,

Enjoy the journey

Let the old journeys end.....and new ones in.....
.......Life is beautiful.......
Relax....Watch....Enjoy.....
Let the story begin.....
Magnificent play unfolding -
Given to you from the sky.
Put down your worries and open your heart,
It has always been you "The Star"...
that the glorious creator chose for this path xxx

15.1 Julia

From a young age I have searched for answers to life. I felt there had to be more to life than I was being taught at home, in church and in school. There were so many different ideas that were conflicting. and didn't seem to add up to a complete belief system that fitted how I viewed the world. The feeling was an inner knowing but incredibly hard to describe. I just always felt there was more to life than what seemed to be on offer, something more profound and therefore important.

As I grew older I read everything I could on spiritual matters. I had a longing to know more and make sense of my life journey because my father had sexually abused me in my childhood. There were times when life had lost all appeal to me and it was the feeling there was something more that kept me in this world, kept me fighting to search for answers that would give me some faith and encouragement that I was worth more than the upbringing I had suffered.

I met Yvonne ('Yve') in 2004. I contacted her by telephone after seeing her details in the telephone directory, because I was in a bad way both mentally and physically. I viewed life in a very negative way and was struggling to come to terms with the impact my childhood had had on me. I was married by this point to my husband Jon and had two small daughters, yet we were all living in chaos because of my fragile state.

A few months prior to contacting Yve, I had taken a step towards obtaining some form of resolution over my past, and had gone with my husband to the police to report the historical sexual abuse that had clouded my life for over fifteen years. I handed over a tape recording I had made of a conversation between my father and I that secretly captured my father at long last admitting he had abused me. As a young child I had attempted to voice what was happening in my home but my father had denied it and I was labelled a fantasist and he was able to carry on the abuse. My mother acted as though she had never heard me.

Having then started the process of seeking justice I had to wait for what was eventually a year for the CPS to investigate my allegations and decide whether they could prosecute my father for his abuse of me. It was a few months into this wait that I first contacted Yve. I told her of my background and that I was waiting for a decision from the CPS. I explained I was not able to function and had terrible conflicting thoughts, feelings and emotions of guilt, shame, sorrow, anxiety etc. that were not only disabling me, but were also disabling my husband and my daughters.

I made an appointment to see Yve and she told me to view her work with me as life coaching. She put her arms around me and hugged me and said that she was connected to me and would lend me her strength to help me to help myself. She told me it was not just she that was connected to me but it was the whole of the universe, and the universe would also give me the strength to help myself. We sat for ages and she told me about life, not the life that was my reality but the life that defied reality because it was not tangible. As Yve was able to back up everything she said it made perfect sense to me, and things started to slot into place. She told me that mentally and emotionally I had not been 'knitted together' properly and we needed to unravel the faulty thoughts and feelings and replace them with new thoughts and feelings/'stitches', and my thoughts had to be stronger than my feelings and emotions.

I was told it was my thoughts, feelings and emotions that were disabling me as they were knotted together, and I had to learn to work with my mind and see clearly in order to heal. In order to do that my mind needed to be expanded. She said this mind expansion would enable me to connect with a parallel universe where workers were waiting to work with me, to help and guide me.

She said she did not think that anybody came on Earth to be abused, those actions were the freewill of the abuser, but I could turn that negative into a positive to help myself and subsequently help others. From that very first meeting Yve told me I was capable of writing a book that could reach many, many people and in this way I could share my experience to help others and empower myself.

She suggested I join her course and this I readily did. I cannot express how fragile I was at this stage and I really do think I had suffered an undiagnosed nervous breakdown and so for me to be able to do this was a huge step forward but it just felt so right.

I joined the course with about eight other people and in the first lessons we were told we needed to challenge our belief systems, as the more restricted our belief systems the more confined our mind is. To enable us to expand our mind we explored the esoteric fingerprints that are here on Earth, which included historical writing and structures, religion, astrology, symbolism and the ages of Pisces and Aquarius. We learnt there is not just a plan for our lives on Earth, there is also a plan for the Earth and the universe but we are at the mercy of random events and the freewill of not just ourselves but the freewill of others as well. We did a workshop in the second part of the lesson and I was hooked from that time on.

We had folders to take home with us that contained details of all the things we had learnt, as well as lots of information and case studies to back up everything else we would be taught as the course progressed. I sat with my husband Jon each night after the course and as we went through the folder he was thrilled to see Yve brought science into the structure of the course and had researched the science of consciousness. Jon is a proper science buff and he was so pleased this element was present in the course as it enabled him to expand his own knowledge.

Yve and I would talk regularly and she would tell me I needed to be brave. She helped me to unravel the chaos inside me and advised, every time a wave of emotion came over me, to speak in my mind and ask for help. She also told me to push the negative thoughts away and think about the wonders of the world so as to concentrate on things outside of me. She gave me a visualization exercise to do, where I would visualize white light coming from above and pouring through the top of my head and lighting up the whole of me. I also learnt about the spirit and its chakra system and I would visualise the chakras opening and resonating in harmony with each other. These meditative exercises really helped and soon started to have a positive effect on my ability to cope and my life in general.

As my mind started to expand and I took on board the lessons I was learning, my previous conflicting emotions of guilt and sorrow were replaced with ones of anger and outrage. I felt so angry that I had allowed my father to manipulate me in such a way that I had carried the burden of guilt for him, and began to have my own judgment of my past instead of bathing in a turmoil of conflicting emotions.

Even more stunning was the fact Yve told the class when we spoke in our mind we could be answered. These answers would be shown to us in the form of thoughts, dreams, symbols, coincidence etc and in the folder we were given a list of all forms of spirit communication. She started to teach us this universal language, to be able to communicate and interpret received communication ourselves.

As the weeks went on all of us attending the course could feel the shift in energies and we were all amazed when we started to receive communication. It was unbelievable, but when you asked a question you would eventually get some sort of an answer back.

During this period I felt as though the CPS's decision would never come, and I had almost lost all hope of obtaining some resolution to my past. My entire life seemed to be in a state of limbo, as I felt unable to fully progress with my personal development until I had some sort of response to enable me to move forwards. I took on board the lessons I had learnt during the course, and asked in my mind for some reassurance that an answer would come.

I had been given so many dates by the police when the CPS would reach their decision and each time that date came, no answer followed. I had been given a further date in the middle of August, and felt all my hopes and dreams were pinned and focused on that date. I asked before I fell asleep if I would receive a response on that date, and prayed for some form of communication to give me some hope to carry on.

That night I had a dream. I dreamt I was a student at university, waiting for my examination results. I asked my university professor when my results would be published, and I was told I would receive my results in November. When I awoke I studied the symbolism of this dream and realized this was the answer to my question. The professor symbolized a higher and wiser power that was teaching me about life, and I would receive an answer from the CPS not in August but in November. I took on board this response, and no longer pinned my hopes on the original date in August, and held my belief that if I waited until November; I would not be let down.

Sure enough August came and went, and in November 2004 the CPS informed me my father was to be charged with thirteen counts of various sexual offences and would indeed stand trial.

I began to get back some balance in my life and by the time the course had finished there was a huge difference in me. I joined up for a second course and my husband Jon came with me as he was fascinated by the transformation in me, and the communication I was receiving. During this time I spent a week away with a friend for a much needed break, and during my absence Jon could hear crying coming from downstairs. Half asleep, Jon walked downstairs to see if one of our daughters had got up, but found the house completely silent, and the girls fast asleep in their beds. On inspection of the parameters of the house, Jon found the light in the back garden shed had been switched on, and was shining light into the house.

There was no open access to our garden as the side gate was kept locked. Jon felt extremely reassured and was able to interpret the symbolism of this act as reassurance that there was light coming in to do with the past, we had all the tools we needed and all would be well.

By the time my father's trial came to Court I was a different person. I was able to stand on my own two feet and was completely strong and resilient to anything life could throw at me. I felt empowered in the knowledge that I was not alone, and there were greater forces at work to guide and support me through the entire process. I was able to stand tall in the witness stand secure in the knowledge I had done nothing wrong, and this was my opportunity to hand back the burden of the weight I had been carrying to its rightful owner, my father.

As a result of my determination to see this through, and with Yve and Jon at my side to maintain my focus, the jury found my father guilty of all counts of acts committed against me, and he was sentenced to eight years imprisonment. Just as Yve had initially told me, I was then in a position where the negativity of my early years had resulted in the complete opposite. I felt positive about life and in my own ability to communicate that positivity to others.

I approached the NSPCC and worked over the coming months as an ambassador for the charity, speaking out on national television and radio about my experiences in an attempt to comfort others going through the process of dealing with childhood abuse.

A few months after the trial I had another dream. I had been concerned about my family, as my mother and brothers had all stood by my father throughout the court process and maintained his innocence despite his subsequent conviction. I dreamt that I was in a car taking a lady to a hospital to commence a rehabilitation program for her alcoholism. She was very upset and nervous, yet I could do nothing to help.

When I woke, I further examined this dream, and realized that the woman symbolized my own mother. She had lived her life under my fathers influence and now she had to detox. In taking my father to court I had taken my mother on a journey, but I could not carry her through the process following his conviction. It was now in her hands to make the decision to heal and walk away from his influence if that be the path she chose.

When things had settled down Yve reminded me that I had a book to write and so that is what I did. I wrote a book about my childhood and the devastating impact the abuse had on my life. When the book was finished incredibly I did not have to peddle my way to a round of agents/publishers because the spirit workers had it all planned. I sent the manuscript to an agent who was a contact of Yve's, who felt the book was extremely powerful and wanted to sign me to their agency.

Within a couple of weeks I received a call from this agent (1), explaining another agent (2) had contacted them and amongst other things had discussed my story after hearing an interview I had aired for the NSPCC on the radio, having no idea the agent (1) she was talking to was about to sign me. This agent (2) specialized in non fiction and when she realised agent (1) was in the process of signing me, she begged to be given my contact details. As I had still not signed to a specific agency, I met with this second agent as a result of a further dream.

I had dreamt that my work would be published by the second source approached, which had initially seemed improbable due to the interest of the first agency. As a result of this I felt drawn to the second agent, who indeed signed me and had the book published with the first publishing house approached. I was desperate to help others by sharing what had happened to me and by writing a best selling book I would have the ideal tool. I know without any doubt we are here on Earth to learn lessons, and that we all have human frailties with the potential to be good or bad, kind or evil. That is what is meant by free will.

I did not come here on Earth to be abused but rather I was a victim of such abuse. I am no longer a victim. Life is now settled and productive. Jon and I have had a third child, our son Zackary, and have a fantastic life with the family we have created. I am currently working as a full time PA, and continue to receive contact from other survivors as a result of the continued success of my book 'Daddy's Little Girl'. Spiritually, Jon and I continue to receive messages, often to nudge us in the right direction when daily life commitments take over. Recently our son Zackary put our house phone in a glass of water, which resulted in us buying another phone. Within a couple of days a vase of water fell on the new phone, disabling it yet again. During this period, Jon's mobile phone fell into water also, making it three instances of our ability to communicate being withdrawn. By this point Jon and I saw the humour in the messages we were receiving!

Water represents life, and we were being told in no uncertain terms that our hectic lives were affecting our ability to communicate with spirit and listen to their guidance. Jon and I now ensure that we take the time to ask for help, direction and guidance in any aspect of our lives that feels uncertain, and more importantly to listen to the communication received, if only to reduce our bills at the phone shop!

I now continue to work with any instances that come my way of others that need my help and support. The book was written and published for a reason, to allow spirit to communicate my message and for me to continue to help and support others. As a result of this I have attended court with other victims of historical child abuse and supported them through the same process, to endeavour to help them to help themselves, and gain their own strength and direction.

If I meet someone who is hurting I put my arms around them and hug them and I tell them I am connected to them and will lend them my strength and help them to help themselves. I tell them it is not just me that is connected to them but it is the whole of the universe, and the universe will also give them the strength to help themselves as life is about the journey and overcoming obstacles we meet on the road.

15.2 Luke

I was the only child of a single mother who had me when she was sixteen. My mother had grown up in care and had no family support network to rely upon, and therefore it was just me and mum. I had always known that mum was fragile and the least little thing would make her unbalanced. We lived on a large council estate with loads of others around us, but only had a handful of friends. My mum rarely went out and was always very fearful, and in turn I was fearful too.

I was a very sensitive child and I loved music and drama and my school encouraged this. I always had the lead role in plays, and always sang solo in concerts. I got a lot of attention because of my talent and I had dreams of going to drama school but my dreams came to a sudden end when my mother died. She was thirty three and had ovarian cancer. By the time she went to the doctor and was diagnosed it was too late. l was seventeen years of age when she died.

After my mum's death the fear of being homeless and alone kicked in. I would pray to my mum 'please mum help me, I don't know which way to go, if you can hear me please guide me'. I felt suicidal and could see no way out and sat with my mum's strong medication in my hand, trying to find the courage to join her. Just as I put the first tablet to my mouth a friend of my mother's called. She was working in a large department store and had called to encourage me to apply for employment there. She saw the state I was in and took charge of me and my future. And so it was I left my South Wales Valleys home and came to the big city, Cardiff. I started work in the department store and I lived in shared accommodation. I did my best to fit in and took advantage of any opportunity that came my way.

If my work colleagues invited me out I went; if my housemates invited me out I went, and in this way I started to make a new life for myself. I was the entertainer everywhere I went and people liked having me around because I made them laugh. I always had a nagging fear in the background of being on my own and so I was a real people pleaser, saying yes to everything and everyone. I was determined everyone would like me and I wouldn't be left on my own.

I had always known I was gay and once in Cardiff I lived the life of a gay male. I was very promiscuous and said 'yes' to everything and everyone. I never wanted to be on my own and so was very compliant, although I never achieved a long term relationship as in those circumstances I was high maintenance, as I needed lots of reassurance. I was popular, everyone loved me, I had many friends and was busy. When eventually I moved into my own little flat I could never be on my own and so I always had people there, and would do anything to keep them with me. And then HIV hit the scene!!

HIV was on the television, it was in the newspapers, everyone was talking about it and the gay community were treated like lepers. I was frightened and my friends were frightened and everyone looked at everyone else with suspicion. For me it changed everything as accountability now started to creep in. I was no longer seventeen years old and a naive adolescent; I was in my late twenties and had many years of life experience under my belt and I knew that I had to change as I now loved life and didn't want to die. I went to my doctor and told her everything. I told her about my mother, my lifestyle and my fear and she suggested I went into counselling.

Luckily for me my counsellor was a spiritual gay male, who was able to give me a type of diagnosis about how my life experiences had shaped my life and how I had responded. He helped me to understand me and my fear, and he showed me how to live my life better and he put things in a spiritual context.

This all happened over twenty years ago and I am now in my fifties and no longer live with fear. I am a completely changed person and I work in a hostel for homeless people. I look at the people that we help and I know every one of them has a story to tell, and how easy it would be to be in their shoes. None of them have chosen to be homeless but circumstances have led them there.

I heard about Yvonne and her work when the time was right and I have sat Yvonne's courses and I now fully embrace the spiritual way of life. I constantly ask for help and guidance and follow the symbolic language that comes my way, and I know when I sent a plea to my mother when she died all those years ago, she sent an Earth angel to help me in the form of her friend. This experience helped me to totally buy into the concept that we are all spiritual beings living a life in a physical body to learn lessons and I know we are like computers and everything gets entered, filed and saved and that faulty data will eventually cause problems, just as I absorbed my mother's fear and this caused problems for me. I see evidence of this faulty data all around me, as there are so many walking wounded, people who are afraid of life and don't know how to live properly. It leads you to ask the question 'What are we as a civilised society doing wrong?' There is such a high percentage of dysfunctional people around that have not been parented properly, or whose life experiences or environment has polluted them, just like a virus, and we should now be asking 'What do we have to do to make it right?'.

I believe I am where I am supposed to be at the present time, and for me life is now my stage, as I play my part in helping others and I know I am doing good as whenever I have the opportunity I explain about life to the homeless people, and I encourage them to speak in their mind and ask for help and guidance. I tell them they are body and spirit and are here for a purpose and I explain about the universal language and hopefully, on some level and in time they might just hear.

15.3 Dawn

I was born in the USA to a hardworking family who had many deep-rooted secrets and as a result were dysfunctional in many ways. My life was full of contradictions because of this dysfunction and the secrets that had to be continually covered up. This resulted in lies and covert behaviour but despite this, and maybe because of this, I have always known there was more to life.

At the age of five I remember sitting on my living room floor with my baby sitter, Janey, sitting on the settee smoking a cigarette. The smoke from her cigarette formed a picture of my great-grandmother (who I lovingly called 'boo') sitting in a high backed chair and waving good-bye. I looked at Janey and said, "boo has died." Janey did not quite know what to say and proceeded to tell me this was not the case. Within five minutes of this happening Janey then received a phone call from my stepdad telling her my great-grandmother had just died.

As a child, other incidents included always knowing when my mum would be coming around the corner from work before she ever got there. I would instinctively know the phone was going to ring and who the caller would be just before it would ring. I was also a very religious child, brought up within a very strict Polish, catholic family. I attended church six days a week and confession on at least one of those days. I recall having numerous discussions with the priest in respect of whether GOD existed, and how did we know? What happened when we died? Was there life after death?

When I was twelve years old I had a phone call from my grandmother (my mum's mum). I had just come in from school when the phone had rung. My mum and my stepdad were both home at the time. My grandmother told me she had to leave. She said that I was to be brave and good, and to take care of myself, and she said she would always be with me. I told her I loved her and I would not forget her and we both hung up. My mum asked me who was on the phone and I told her it was grandma saying good-bye to me as she had to leave. My mum said this was impossible as my grandma had died the previous day and they did not know how to tell me. I told my mum not to bother as grandma had already told me herself.

My family did not understand any of the regular incidents I experienced as a child. Whilst they could not explain them, they also did not believe them. As time went on I learned to keep the things that happened quiet, but my belief in what happened never faltered and only assisted in convincing me there was more to life and death than we knew and could explain.

These incidents and questions have never left me and have in fact guided and shaped me into who and where I am now - living in the UK. Looking back I can see there has been an unseen hand guiding me through all the many trials and hardships, from living with the many secrets in a dysfunctional family, joining the American Military as a way out of my situation, and eventually coming to live in Wales in the UK. This guiding hand has led me to Yvonne and the journey I am currently on. I met Yvonne in the summer of 2005. There was a psychic fair in Llandaff, Cardiff I wanted to attend. It was during the lunchtime and I was looking after my daughter who was poorly. I said in my head I would like to go and if it was meant to be, let my husband come home at lunchtime and say he was working from home. At lunchtime my husband walked in and said he was working from home for the rest of the day. I knew I was meant to go.

When I turned up at the psychic fair, Yvonne was sat right next to the door selling her books and publicising her course. She was the first person I was drawn to and the first person I saw. The cynic in me says this was due to where she was sat, but in fairness the light blocked her out upon first entering the door. We introduced ourselves and I knew Yvonne was the reason for me going to the fair.

I bought a copy of her book, *The Making of a Spiritual Medium* to read whilst on holiday and I asked her to send me details of her classes commencing in the autumn. In October 2005, I began her spiritual education and psychic development class for the first time. I say for the first time as I ended up doing the class numerous times. It is a lot to comprehend and understand especially from a standing start. And for me, it was impossible to remember it all in just one course. For me, the classes provided an explanation to all those unanswered questions as well as offered a way forward.

Yvonne did not expect me to just accept what was said and nor would I. I had spent my life questioning everything, there was no way I could just 'accept' what was being said or taught without challenging this and continually testing it. So I did. I carried out test after test. I would ask a question in my head and see if an answer was provided. And it would be. The answers would come in different ways, sometimes through a thought in my head, other times a song on the radio, a licence plate of a car, a road sign etc. I just needed to get better at recognising the answers when they were provided.

At the same time as starting Yvonne's course, I had also given up my full-time job to get my MSC in Human Resource Management and my University course had also commenced. This was a full-time Masters Degree course I had undertaken to complete in one year. Not for the faint hearted, but I was determined to complete it.

As part of the course we were also required to undertake a placement. Having worked in HR for over twenty years I was not looking forward to this, particularly as it was a voluntary placement and we did not get paid. I really did not want to give away my expertise for free, so I asked for an alternative option to present itself. The next day in class we were advised of two additional placements available as research assistants at the university and these were paid positions.

We were told that if we were interested, we needed to turn up at a specific room at 2:00 p.m. Well, I turned up at the room expecting the whole class to be there, and there was no one. Whilst I waited, another girl turned up. As things transpired, we were the only two who had turned up for the positions and subsequently they were ours by default. I was so grateful. And this meant I had a little bit of money as well.

By the time I had come to the exam stage of the MSc course, I had completed Yvonne's course. I asked in my head for help with the exams and to provide a sign as to what areas I needed to study, and performance management kept coming up. I told the study group that I was with we should look at this and yet they did not want to. Not wanting to be separate from the group, I studied those areas they wanted to look at. When we took the exam, five questions were on performance management. A lesson well learnt.

During this time, we also had to choose our dissertation topics. We had to write a 20,000-word dissertation. I had already started work on sickness, absence and retention levels as my topic, but by the time I came to the end of Yvonne's course I felt I wanted to do a different topic.

I subsequently chose 'Intuition' as my dissertation choice, clearly a different subject from those on my MSc course who were looking at sickness levels, retention, performance management, strategy etc. Whilst the dissertation was difficult, I did feel guided along the way. A professor located in a room across from me discovered that Intuition was my topic and he offered to loan me a friend's dissertation on 'Intuition'. And the journey continued. I became involved with those working on Intuition in the university. I became increasingly aware of the models that assess both analytic and intuitive ability. My knowledge on 'Intuition' from the academic perspective increased. I also got to know several of the PhD students and thought, 'well maybe I could carry on and do my PhD'.

On the day that I submitted my MSc HRM dissertation, I also submitted my PhD application for a studentship. Again the topic for my proposed PhD was 'Intuition'. In December I was asked to sit an interview for the PhD studentship application, which I did. This was the most difficult interview I had ever taken part in. I then found out I had been accepted for a full PhD studentship and that the topic I had chosen (i.e. 'Intuition') had also been accepted. I also found out I had achieved a 2:1 for my MSc Dissertation.

On the day of my MSc HRM graduation, we had just sat in the car to drive to the ceremony and Leona Lewis' 'A Moment Like This' came on the radio. I did feel it was for me for two reasons, the first being that my deceased grandmother's name was Leona and secondly, I had waited my whole life to get a degree and now I had achieved this. And who would have thought I would also be accepted on a full PhD studentship with a topic of 'Intuition'. The sceptics may call it coincidence, I would say I just followed the symbols/signs and guidance provided.

At this point in time I am just finishing my PhD. Whilst studying for this, I have presented my work in Cardiff, Canada and Belgium, and am very aware of the need for additional research to be undertaken on this subject. I can honestly say I am walking the walk in respect of both Yvonne's course and in respect of my own PhD topic of 'Intuition', and as I walk this walk the opportunities continue to present themselves, and I continue to work with them.

Whilst Yvonne's course and the book you are reading are aimed at the individual, my PhD and research work are aimed at the organisation and the individual within this. In both cases it is about increasing awareness, in the first instance - awareness of self, but in the second instance - awareness of what's around us.

We need to challenge the archaic belief systems that we may have been brought up with. We need to continually seek answers to questions that have not yet been answered, we need to challenge, long held habitual behaviours in a desire to move forward in an increasingly complex and evolving world, where we ourselves are also evolving.

The signs and symbols are there as guidance and firstly we need to learn to recognise these symbols to know which direction to take. When we learn this and follow this guidance, the journey becomes a limitless opportunity and adventure, open to all possibilities.

Over the years I have become much better at identifying the symbols and signs provided. I now use them consistently in my daily life and I genuinely feel I am on the road I am meant to be on. I can see why I had to be born into my particular family, and why I had to experience life prior to achieving academic qualifications, as this has allowed me to gain valuable experience of how our intuition works. As a child I did not understand that the uncomfortable feeling in certain situations meant I was picking up when something was not right, but my life experience has led me to recognise this feeling as my 'intuition', and it alerts me when I need to take notice of something or someone for whatever reason. Of course, I also recognise this intuition can guide me in my choices etc., and this, coupled with all other forms of the universal language, is an important tool to help me on my journey.

I want to continue my spiritual journey and achieve what ever I have come on Earth to achieve. The first part of my life has been about experience and this middle part is about achieving academic qualifications. I hope the next part is about putting it all together, and will give me the credibility to enable me to work in the arena of consciousness, and allow me the opportunity to help move science and humanity   forward.

15.4 Paula

I am a thirty-six-year-old ordinary girl, living an extraordinary life, and all because of the toolkit I am now armed with since taking Yvonne's spiritual education and psychic development course. I know, absolutely, the life I am living now could have been so different had I not taken the lessons and understood and used the tools that are available from the universe to help me on my journey through life.

I first met Yvonne ('Yve') through a coincidence, I accompanied a friend who had booked a reading with her, and ended up spending a good few hours discussing 'spiritual stuff' after my friends reading. I was intrigued to learn that the coincidences and experiences I was having in my life all meant something.

For the first four years of my life I had been brought up in my grandparent's house as my mum was a single mum. I had an incredibly close relationship with both my grandfather and grandmother. My mum eventually met and married my step-dad ('dad') and they took me to live with them in their new home. My mum and dad went on to have three children together and so I was the oldest of four.

My dad treated me as his own and it was a happy, secure and loving household but with one glaring difference - I was the only mixed race person. Now, even though my childhood was loving and happy, the race issue was something that played on my mind and visually I was so obviously different from the rest of my family and outside of the home people would ask me questions. The circumstances surrounding my birth was not something that was ever spoken about inside the home and in all honesty, because my childhood was so good, it seemed the wrong thing to do to ask the question.

I wanted to, but when I thought about doing so my body would react and I would break out in a sweat, have palpitations and would have a horrible, intense feeling inside. It was this that stopped me asking about my heritage.

216

Not long after my sixteenth birthday my granddad died. I had idolised him and I was devastated when he died and found it very difficult to control my emotions. I was a high achiever academically and a natural sportswoman but the emotional part of me was not strong and as I got older my emotions were starting to control my life but at the time I didn't realise this.

I went through school and college and gained a higher degree. I went on to forge a great career and was a high earner but I always had problems interacting with my colleagues as I would take things personally and had an inability to speak up, with the usual symptoms of breaking out in a sweat, having palpitations and the horrible, intense feeling being present on these occasions.

It was like I was two people, one was a high achiever and then the other was emotionally dysfunctional. Also my personal life left a lot to be desired. Don't get me wrong, I had friends and was always out and about socialising, but I surrounded myself with people who were constantly in a crisis and together we all whipped up a storm of tears, tantrums and gossip, feeding off one another's energy. As a result my relationships never seemed to work out as I would have expected.

Up until the time I started the spiritual course I had moved from broken relationship to broken relationship and I always seemed to make wrong decisions and end up unhappy, thinking 'why me?'. I also found myself moving jobs as when difficulties presented themselves with my work colleagues, instead of tackling the issue I would walk away.

The physical symptoms and intense feeling I experienced would not allow me to confront any issues and even though I was technically skilled and efficient at what I did, I would let the other side of me dominate my life.

When I started the course and learnt all about the unexplained mysteries on Earth, former civilisations and all those things I was absolutely fascinated. Each week we went through all these different stages of learning about things that are 'out there' but I had never known about. The science was incredible and made me realise how I was attracting to me all this dysfunction because I was dysfunctional. Slowly I began to see things in a different way.

In each lesson we would all speak about our week and report any dreams, coincidence and such like, and to see what was happening in other peoples lives as a result of using these new tools was powerful. Yve would then speak to us for about an hour, expanding our mind step-by-step and backing up everything she said with science etc. We would then have a tea break and after that would do workshops that included   meditation and visualisation, and then progressed to practising psychometry (reading from an object) and eventually we read for people who we didn't know and that Yve had brought in for the occasion.

The purpose of reading from objects and people was to show us how on a subtle level we read things from people, the environment and everything that is around us all the time. When we are unaware of this subtle communication we can react to what we are feeling on an emotional level and personalise what it is we are receiving. In other words if we absorbed a feeling of paranoia, instead of thinking 'what am I picking up, is that person feeling paranoid?' We might take on the paranoia as our own, thinking that person doesn't like me and consequently feeling paranoid about it.

The classes showed us how reacting with emotions, being impulsive, judgmental, critical, unreasonable etc were symptoms of insecurity, low self-esteem, learnt behaviour, and all those types of things.

During the visualisation exercises we received symbols from our sub-conscious, the universe, and also spirit workers for us to decipher. These symbols, once deciphered, told us about ourselves, what our issues were and how to overcome them.   We were taught the universal language used by those living in a parallel universe and each week we would be given techniques or tools to use to help us go forward. This programme of mind expansion and self-development was incredible and it is absolutely fascinating how coincidences and signs present themselves all the time.

One of the most incredible events that has happened in my life was brought about by a series of unbelievable coincidences. It concerned my biological father and how I had never asked any questions about him. It was always going to be a really difficult subject to raise with my mum because for so many years the subject had never been spoken about. At the time, whilst I was growing up I thought that it was all down to me not being worthy, but now I totally understand that my mum didn't know how to approach the subject as she was so mindful of not wanting me to feel different from the others. She genuinely felt if I had any questions to ask then I would ask them and if I didn't want to know then she would not push the knowledge on me. My mum also felt as uncomfortable about the subject as I did and this was down to her own insecurities and so it was easier just to let things be.

After completing the course I knew I had to confront head on things I had not confronted before. I had to overcome the physical symptoms and intense feelings I experienced that had stopped me from tackling these issues.

I had become more confident and realised knowing who my biological father was is a right of mine, and I shouldn't feel guilty or bad about myself for wanting to know. A good friend of mine had recently discovered who her biological father was but I was still working out how to ask the question. As we had been taught in the class, each day I spoke in my mind and asked the person who was working with me for help with this. Yve had taught us the answers might not come immediately and we had to be patient and consistent and that meant asking the same questions each day until the answer came.

A few weeks later I got a new job and part of this job meant I had to fill out some detailed forms regarding my background, and one of the questions on the form was that of my 'natural' parents. How incredible the question had been taken out of my hands and I had to ask from a career perspective rather than a personal one.

But the discovery was to get even more incredible. Armed now with a name, I went down to Yve's to tell her the news. I told her the name and unbelievably she knew my biological father. Even though she had not seen him for over thirty years she was able to tell me all about him and even had a picture to show me.

It felt strange seeing my father's picture and just thinking about contacting him gave me the old symptoms and I knew I was not ready to take matters any further at that time. Even though I was making such a huge effort to change, my old ways were very ingrained in me and I still surrounding myself with weak and damaged people but now I was aware of it. All the time I was speaking in my mind and asking for help and guidance and saying to this unseen person who was working with me I wanted to change.

The new job I had taken was on a short contract basis and when the contract was coming to an end a serious of dreams, coincidence and symbolic happenings presented me with a fantastic opportunity to work on contract in a different country. This unseen person told me I needed to cut myself off completely from the old way of life. Just like anyone with an addiction I needed to go to a symbolic 'rehab' so that I could detox.

Even though the prospect was scary to me and the old symptoms came every time I thought about moving away, I went to work overseas and put myself in a self imposed exile. It was the loneliest, toughest but best time of my life. Looking back on it now I grew and learned so much as a person. It was obvious that to reach my true potential I had to change as a person, but in order to do that I had to be away from my home surroundings and everything that was familiar to me. I had to stop feeding off the old energy I was connected to and just as though I was a radio I had to change channels. It was the familiar and old channel that kept luring me back to the 'old me' and my 'old life', so being away was the only way to do it.

As each month went by whilst I was away I could feel myself changing, I was becoming stronger, more confident and happier. When I had to tackle a person or an issue and the old, intense symptoms appeared I would tell myself this was just such a situation that I had to confront and I would take a step back and use my mind and my instinct.

When my overseas contract finally came to an end I stayed living where I was but started to look for jobs back in the UK, and now had the guts to reach high and go for a more senior role, confident I was up to the challenge. Previously, although being more than capable of this higher position, I had shied away knowing it would inevitably bring conflict with colleagues, as this came with the territory.

When my time abroad was done and I had secured my senior position, I accompanied Yve on a Thursday morning to the radio station where she was co-hosting a show. This was an exciting trip out. Little did I know what was going to happen when we got there. Yve, knowing that my father had been a musician when she knew him all those years ago, asked the DJ of the show if she knew him. The DJ said she did and she then mentioned to the guy that managed the radio station who my father was. The manager also knew my father and astonishingly had his number in his mobile phone. Without even consulting me he rang my father and handed me the phone, telling me to 'speak to your father'! I had never expected that to happen and neither had Yve!

Of course I was too shocked to speak to him there and then, so I took his number and said I would speak to him later. I went back to Yve's for a coffee and phoned him there and it was a really strange moment. We spoke for a while and I then understood all about the circumstances of my birth. We arranged to meet up the next day and it was an amazing time.

To be finally meeting my biological father was cathartic and I looked so much like him. However, I knew I would not have been able to do it before as I wasn't ready for it. I did not have the mental and emotional maturity and would probably have reacted badly to him. When my mum knew I had met my father she was so happy, but you could also see the relief in her eyes. It could not have been easy for her all those years ago to have been an unmarried mother and give birth to a mixed race child. I think this will be healing for all of us. Understand-ing about and working with this universal power has changed everything for me. It also wasn't a coincidence I met up with my father the weekend before I started my new job. It was like a whole new chapter of my life was starting. I now understand about life and I have a new outlook, a new job, a new man in my life, and a toolkit, and all from being brave and listening and following the guidance and the signs that are there to lead us forward.

I now understand we are living life on Earth for a purpose and we have free will and it is up to us to go forward and overcome any difficult challenges that are put in our way, and we are not on our own but we are connected to the whole. Being spiritually aware is a way of life for me now and I truly am walking the path with all its signposts and crossroads, stopping and taking the time to steer carefully, using this unseen person and force like a satellite navigation system, and being confident enough to know even if I don't know the destination or how to get there, I can still continue the journey.

It is also fascinating to me that people in my workplace who have problems are automatically drawn to me and I can usually provide them with some assistance and I always direct them to Yve's books to help them to help themselves.

15.5 Nicola

I first heard of Yvonne when I was living in Germany but was contemplating whether to relocate with my daughter back to Wales in the UK so we could be amongst my family and friends, who could provide a much needed support network for us. This move would be difficult as I had built up a solid reputation as a Clinical Hypnotherapist in my adopted country and I had my own practice room, together with-- working as part of a hypnosis practice in Munich. When I had arrived in Germany I could not speak a word of German, but I made a real effort to learn the language and I am proud to say I can now speak German fluently, and my work in Munich was all conducted through that language.

A colleague back in the UK suggested I contact Yvonne, as he thought I would be interested in her work and, as she knew many people within the holistic community, she might be able to help me if I relocated back to Wales.   I telephoned Yvonne and spoke with her on quite a few occasions, and in this way we got to know each other. Yvonne sent me her books and they fascinated me. In turn I sent Yvonne my hypnotherapy CD's and background information, and she told me she was very impressed with what I had sent her, and the both of us could see strong links in our work in the arena of the mind.

At the time of speaking with Yvonne I really was very uncertain of what to do as, although I wanted to come home, the obstacles seemed insurmountable and I would need to earn an income from day one to provide for me and my daughter and so it was imperative that I kickstart my business. Yvonne viewed my returning to Wales as the end of a journey that had began when I met the person who was to be my husband.

I am originally from the Port Talbot area of Wales, and in 1994 I was working in Cardiff at the then World Trade Centre, and it was here I met the person who was to become my husband. A year after I met him I was moving to Germany, having fallen in love. Very shortly after that our beautiful daughter was born.

My daughter and I lived in luxury with my husband in a beautiful picturesque village at the foot of the Bavarian Alps. During those early years it was really isolating as my husband was a busy man, with his own family and circle of friends all around him. On the other hand I was a newcomer and I was still struggling to learn German and so was quite cut off from others in a lot of ways.

During this difficult period I was continually reading books on psychology and spirituality, looking to gain some understanding of life. When my German got better I went on to train for two years in a type of prana meditation and I also qualified with a Swiss master in Reiki, which is a form of energetic healing. Throughout this time I understood more about how the unconscious mind worked and was particularly focused on, and drawn to, hypnosis.

It was after nearly eleven years of marriage that my husband announced he wanted his own private life, which didn't include his wife and daughter. The rug was pulled out from under us and we lost everything, as his life was our life. What made it even more of a struggle was that his possessions were not our possessions to share and we were virtually homeless. I was devastated.

After about six months of reeling from the shock I knew I had to pull myself together as my daughter was dependent on me, and so I decided to turn my interest in the mind into my career and I trained as a Clinical Hypnotherapist. It was in this way I was able to help myself deal with the situation and, as you have read, eventually led to me working at an hypnosis practice in Munich as a fully qualified Hypnotherapist.

I had been through so many highs and lows during the fifteen years I had been away from the UK and when I looked back at what my daughter and I had endured I realised I was a strong person, and if I could survive in the way I had when we were left in a foreign country, with no money and no real means of making a living, then I could survive anything. I had trained to be an Hypnotherapist during the most difficult and testing part of my life, and I was reassured that returning to the UK with my new skills would be the culmination of all I had learnt and would see the me going full circle, arriving back to where this particular journey had begun.

I decided I would build a new life and make a success of that life for my beautiful daughter and me. To ensure I was doing the right thing Yvonne advised me to speak in my mind and say 'who ever is working with me, if it is right that I should return to the UK please guide me and I promise that I will listen', and this I did and everything went like clockwork and I was truly guided, even when I had to grit my teeth and take a leap of faith, I listened and followed the guidance and this, together with self-hypnosis brought me full circle.

I have been living back in the UK for two years now and when I first arrived back I immediately signed up for a twelve weeks course with Yvonne. What I learnt in the classroom has strengthened my knowledge on the mind, the universe and the universal language.

In those sessions everyone would have a chance to say what they had experienced during the previous week and this was a learning curve in itself as, without exception, everyone was getting some sort of communication and guidance via dreams, symbolic happenings coincidence etc, which could be interpreted via the style of interpretation taught by Yvonne.

After this Yvonne would then teach for about an hour, and what she taught was absorbing and really did get you thinking outside of the box, which was comfortable for me as I have always thought in this way. We would have a tea break before proceeding with the second part of the class.

This was normally a guided visualisation where, just by following Yvonne's voice, we would quieten our brain waves and enter into a trance like state. Yvonne would then instruct us to visualise certain scenarios, which only she knew the meaning of, so that we could not influence the outcome. She would then instruct us to obtain symbols as we went through the scenario, and the unconscious mind would speak to us via imagery and symbols. When the guided visualisation had finished, Yvonne would explain to us what the scenario represented and then we would work at interpreting the symbols we had received. The guidance received during these guided visualisations was fascinating, as they were so accurate and seemed tailor made for each person. This was really powerful as you realised there was an intelligence possibly outside of you that knew what the scenario of the different guided visualisations meant and somehow this influenced the imagery and symbols received. Once the guidance had been received and understood by the individual they would then understand what areas they needed to work on.

For instance, one guided visualisation we did was representative of what was restricting the mind. During this visualisation a lady who had suffered sexual abuse during early childhood saw a grotesque mummy all wrapped up in bandages and around it were scattered toys from her childhood. This meant she had preserved (mummy) the grotesque events from her childhood (toys), and the guidance was she needed to confront this and work through it, as it was obviously still affecting her as it was in her mind. The lady admitted she had never dealt with the jumbled up thoughts and negative emotions she lived with and just accepted it would always be this way.

The way Yvonne works with this guided visualisation I found fascinating, as it is also working with the symbolic language of the unconscious mind. As a Hypnotherapist I have learnt techniques to induce the 'alpha' wavelength, the hypnotic state. This allows the client's unconscious mind to come to the foreground and speak via imagery and symbols.

The difference with hypnosis is that the client's own unconscious mind is able, in that state, to guide them to an awareness and perspective which allows the unconscious to release the blocked emotion that could have been causing present day issues. This is hypno-analysis and works on a much deeper level moving the client towards their full potential and a more balanced condition. Our unconscious mind is a source of infinite possibilities for guidance throughout our lives and whereby the conscious mind always tries to understand your problems your unconscious mind knows the solution.

The lady who had suffered sexual abuse in her early childhood, whom I have mentioned above, would be an ideal candidate for hypno-analysis as it would be very difficult for her to release what was stored in the mind without expert help.

It has been shown through studies that until the age of seven our brains are in a hypnogogoic or dreamlike state, where the mind absorbs without judgement. As children, over time we are hypnotised through many inherent problems from parents and other influences that create a pattern in the unconscious, hence the saying 'Give me a boy of seven and I will show you the man'. We could say it is not so much about going into trance, but coming out of the trance we are permanently in, and realising we have the potential to be what we want to be. Events which occur in our childhood can have a great effect on our adult lives and can also create stress and anxiety. Throughout our early life we develop veils of perception and build upon our self-hypnosis (self talk) within. Many other events in life can make us feel insecure and lacking in self-esteem.

In other words we are all viewing the world through our own filters and reacting in accordance with our life experiences connected to past emotion.

I agree with Yvonne when she compares the mind to a computer, and appreciate the analogy by cell biologist Bruce Lipton, Ph.D, that the conscious mind operates with the computer processing power of about forty bits of information per second, while the subconscious processes information at twenty million bits per second. The conscious mind is linear processing one thing after another, but the unconscious minds processes everything simultaneously.

Therefore as adults even though the conscious intention is to think positively the unconscious 90% of our minds may still be negatively programmed and actually could be attracting the very situations we most seek to avoid in a bid to release the attached emotion. It's almost as if the subconscious becomes stuck.

We may find in the present day, should we go into situations that hold a similar emotion to the past underlying issues which have been compounded over time, then that present situation triggers the old emotion and the unconscious plays it out. It can take on any form, contributing to panic attacks, anxiety, depression, eczema, phobias, comfort eating and so on. In effect the unconscious is trying to externalise the emotion, which is what we refer to as the 'symptom'. So positive thinking is good, but it's not quite so simple. Therefore it surely makes sense to utilize the unconscious, this amazing part of our mind when making changes and working towards our goals.

The mind really is very powerful, influential and dominant in our lives and it can make us or break us. Any faulty information we absorb into the mind can influence how we perceive life, and any traumatic event at any age can see us processing the event in a faulty way, with the brain waves accelerating to such an extent the actual fact of the event can be lost but the feelings associated with the event retained.

I work with hypno-analysis, which allows the client who has underlying issues to deal with and release the related emotion at the unconscious level. This is different to an intellectual understanding. It supports the person moving towards their true potential.

Yvonne and I frequently refer clients to one another because, if a client has deeper underlying problems, then it is for their benefit they initially work with me with hypno-analysis to relieve the underlying negative emotion. By doing this it is to their optimal advantage and they are then fully able to reap the rewards when they take Yvonne's course and make great progress, wholly benefiting from what is being taught.

Having experienced life from many perspectives, I have been able to have great insight into other cultures and people from many walks of life. Water is symbolic of life, and for me the waves of change crashed hard and fast through my life, washing in new understanding and taking the life I once recognised away. Through all those changes the ocean kept trying to tell me to flow with it, it would show me the way. But it is hard to trust when you feel you are drowning.

To understand the signs of the great ocean; to recognise the changing currents and the rocks which could hurt you; to sense the impending weather comes with experience. The communication between yourself and the ocean develops awareness to what lies beneath, which is the unconscious part of our minds. I learnt to communicate and receive that guidance which came with training and the experience of surviving that period of my life's storm. It is with this knowledge, understanding and professional skills I am able to help and support others, and it is all this put together that enabled me firstly to help myself, as to understand the complex process of what being human means, you can't just talk it, you have to have walked it.   .

15.6 Ryan

I have sat in Yvonne's classes and listened to the stories of other people and some of them have had a really hard time. My story isn't like that, because I have had a really charmed life. I have very loving parents, two gorgeous sisters and we have lived a middle class lifestyle. My parents have always encouraged us to think out of the box, and they have instilled in us that education and work is the key to a purposeful life. Our book shelves at home are filled with books covering a wide range of subjects, and anything that interested me I was able to learn about.

I have always been interested in religion, culture and the beliefs,   values and behaviour of society. Many a night my family have sat around the dinner table and talked about these subjects, and my   parents have taken us on holidays so we could see for ourselves how other people live, and how their particular religion and culture have shaped their society. This led me to study Anthropology at university.

Through my studies I have realised there are so many subjects to consider when seeking to make sense of our world that it can be overwhelming. There is so much to learn and you can go off on a tangent and end up in a tangle.

That is why, when signing up for the very first class with Yvonne, I felt as though I was being fast tracked. From the first lesson and listening to Yvonne tell us we were undertaking a journey of the mind which incorporated a list of subjects I knew were of particular relevance, I was inspired and it left me hungry for more. At last there was a structure to learning of the mysteries of the world that would keep me from being tangled and I couldn't wait for the next class to come along.

The symbols and dreams were a new experience for me and I had a certain amount of scepticism that I could personally experience a seemingly two way communication with an unseen guide or person. Was I wrong!!

From the very first class things began to happen, just little things such as having to park in an area that was always heavily congested. When I said in my mind 'if there is anyone with me can you please get me a parking space?', as I approached my destination a car was pulling out from its parking bay. I said 'thank you' but was only semi convinced. Back home and in the kitchen I was preparing a meal and thinking about this form of communication, and the kitchen light turned itself on. I looked in Yvonne's dream book and it said the kitchen was where you prepared to serve others. In my mind I said 'Wouldn't I have to prepare myself first?', and unbelievably I heard the fan in the bathroom switch on. I knew that the bathroom was where you prepared yourself, and it was as though someone unseen was agreeing with me. It took me a   little while to recover my composure after that one but I could not deny these things had happened and there had to be an intelligence behind them, as they were physical things that were speaking to me in a   symbolic language.

All the things I learnt in Yvonne's classes have opened up a whole new world to me. They have merged with all the things I had already learnt and given me a far greater perspective on viewing the whole.

I wish what Yvonne teaches could be a stand alone course in mainstream education. It would have been such a help to me if I had this knowledge first and then perhaps I had studied anthropology after. I would have understood what I was learning on a far deeper level.

Knowing what I now know I would love to study psychology but this will probably have to wait because I need to earn a living. I have asked in my mind for help and guidance as to what I should do and the next day, through the door was posted a leaflet about adult education at the local college. Reading through the leaflet I realised I could start studying psychology one night a week, and it was as though somebody unseen was encouraging me to do this.

I am going to take up this option and I can't wait to start. Yvonne's course has been invaluable and I am going to build on this new found knowledge and will continue asking for help and guidance to help me experience and achieve what ever I have come on Earth to do.

I am so grateful to my parents for teaching me how to think and not what to think, as this has given me a head start and made it so much easier for me to comprehend the things I am learning and experiencing. There is so little time and so much to do, and I don't want to waste any of it.

15.7 Gill

My name is Gill and I am a forty eight years old woman and have two lovely daughters. I work full time as a Mental Health Social Worker. I have always believed in the afterlife and always felt things around me. I have had life experiences that have made me think 'How could that have happened?' or 'that was meant to be'.

Approximately three years ago my marriage was breaking down and subsequently ended. I was very unsteady at that time, lacking in courage and confidence, and was in extreme pain as the reason my marriage had broken down was my husband was having an affair. We lived together through a period of my sensing there was something wrong and my husband forcefully defending his innocence. My intuition was screaming at me and gave me no peace and my husband was also screaming at me in an attempt to defend himself and side-track me. Even when my youngest daughter asked him if the rumours she was hearing of an affair were true, he continued to deny it. However, it was futile to keep this façade up because my intuition or inner voice, however I chose to describe it, was now being heard. I was listening and I just knew.

I had many readings with mediums over the years and particularly during this time, and I had the urge to want to learn more about things that were sensed rather than seen. One day in work I was chatting to one of my colleagues around this subject and he said 'I have been training with a woman in Cardiff who teaches spiritual education'. Wow, I was so excited and when he gave me Yve's contact details I almost immediately rang her. I remember saying 'I can't explain it but I want to know things and do something different' I told Yve I had always felt different, not superior, just different, and I didn't really know what I meant but I was just surrendering to this.

It took a crisis for me to finally acknowledge this and want to work with it instead of against it, as I knew this was where I would find the answers and this road was right for me. Yve knew exactly what I was feeling and trying to say. I decided to join her classes and although still in pain I felt supported. I realised it may take time but I knew I was going to be OK. This all seemed to be developing at the right time.

Classes began but I was all over the place, preoccupied with my pain but nonetheless gaining strength from the teaching. I benefited greatly from Yve's support and guidance during numerous calls I made to her in sheer desperation. On numerous visits to Yve's home she explained to me what was happening. The vibrations and the aura, our dysfunctions and how we attract dysfunctional others and how we can change this pattern of behaviour.

Here I see a parallel with my work, dealing with depression and its devastating effect. In my work we talk about raising self-esteem and self-confidence and the coping skills to deal with life events. We discuss positive thinking and avoiding negative people and situations and to surround ourselves with people and things that bring us positivity. Although we say these things to people, we cannot bring in the intangible and spiritual perspective and have to work with structured, psychological therapies.

Recently I have been doing work with diagnosis of 'personality disorder'. More specifically, people with a diagnosis of borderline personality disorder come to the attention of the mental health service because they often have more chaotic and dysfunctional lifestyles. Research shows, and as stated in the *International Classification of Mental and Behavioural Disorders* (ICD-10), one of the definitions of a personality disorder is it is usually manifested since childhood or adolescence and continuing throughout adulthood.

Research again shows that dysfunctional parenting from as early as infancy where the child does not get the nurturing reaction from its parent and the stable social context, will impact on the personality.

This research is useful and it would be helpful if we could somehow raise a higher level of awareness of the damage early parenting has on the child and how this can carry forward to adulthood.

From a spiritual perspective there is so much more going on with dysfunctional behaviour. When you consider that the chakras, or wheels of consciousness, are activated by thought and feeling, you can see how we attract people and situations to us that have a pattern. Our thoughts and feelings open and close the valves of the chakras and they filter the world around us, absorbing that which matches how we are feeling, is on our level of understanding, belief systems etc., and you then begin to realize how someone can be in a constant loop that entrenches them deeper into their dysfunction and they have no way of dealing with, or knowing why, they attract this to them and continue to experience the same troubling traits. Also to consider is the universal language that can be mistaken for fantasy, delusion and such like if not understood.

I am not saying this is the answer or even that it is as straightforward as it may sound, but what I am saying is science now understands thoughts and feelings are real and we can attract to us what we give out. This is a part of mental health that is yet to be explored because it is not tangible and lacks sufficient evidence.

The Age of Aquarius is about raising consciousness and I hope globally we begin to wake up to the fact our behaviour will impact on our children whether that behaviour be overt or covert, in other words we do not have to just shout or act badly to affect our children, rather we can be subtle in our approach. As examples, exclusion of a child for what is perceived as bad behaviour, lack of stimulation emotionally, physically and practically, such as in education needs. If you demonstrate to a child by your actions you are fearful, then they absorb that fear and so on, and so on.

We need to understand we have to be robust not just physically, but mentally and emotionally as well, and this has to start from the beginning of life by learning about life, and not just that part of life that is tangible.

As for me, I am now in a good place both mentally and emotionally and I understand so much more about my sixth sense the psychic ability and the universal language. I will never allow anyone to persuade me my ability to sense is faulty, and I work hard to keep myself balanced in every way. I believe my life experience will be of benefit to others and there is so much work to do but I do wonder, how long will it take for us to learn?

15.8 Lois

I attended a course for spiritual and psychic development that Yvonne was hosting in 2003, as I just felt drawn to it. I was nervous about the course because the subject can be quite controversial and can sometimes attract people who seem slightly unbalanced, but I let my instinct guide me. I took a leap of faith and that decision proved to be right and seven years on my life has changed for the better in so many ways.

I am committed to life-long learning. The fact Yvonne's courses encompass science puts the whole spiritual and psychic arena on a different footing and makes solid a subject which otherwise might be considered lightweight. This is a subject that is difficult to quantify, as it cannot be seen physically as it is working with energy, but the results of this energy work can be tangible and since taking that first step I became fascinated with the healing aspect.

I have gone on to study and practice reiki healing, and latterly I have taken a three years crystal healing diploma course. Knowing the big bang probably caused the beginning of our universe, making the leap from energy into matter, from chaos to order, from the un-manifest into the manifest, is awe inspiring. The mineral kingdom has been described as a framework for the universe, extending and connecting out to the whole of the Earth and beyond. Crystals have been formed and created in advance as part of the Creator's plan. They are here to help us and they offer a toolbox for use in life on our planet

It is fascinating when you realise crystals are actually used in our modern world every day. Quartz watches, televisions, computers and mobile phones are just some examples, and some conventional medical techniques would not exist without crystals. The structure of crystals can vary when subjected to changes in temperature and water levels, and they even change colour if you alter their electromagnetic field.

It is an interesting fact that crystalline structures are everywhere - even in the human body, and this is the basis of my healing work. My studies tell me crystalline structures are found on the surface of cells and in the cell 'battery', which is called the mitochondria. Apparently, if the body experiences changes in water, electromagnetic field or temperature, then biochemical traffic across the cell membrane can be altered, as well as the energy production capacity of the mitochondria.

It seems crystals can direct and focus the electromagnetic fields that surround cell membranes and the mitochondria. This means during crystal healing, placing the crystals on nerve clusters usually found around the chakra areas could lead to significant alterations in the traffic of neurochemical messengers within the nervous system and thus affect body wide chemistry. As emotions are often controlled or varied by our body chemistry, you can see how crystals might even affect our moods as well as our physical well-being.

I am now working with crystals for healing and I love my crystals; they have multiplied over the years and spread all over my house. To be fair they live with me now and I care for them, cleanse them, and heal them when they need it but I mainly use these beautifully intricate pieces of minerals to work and help others and me in my healing work.

They have shown me through their colour and vibration where best to place them and how best to use them. They are capable and powerful tools and offer me a firm helping hand with my work. They also show me more than people might dare to share about themselves.

It is becoming clearer the overall climate for spiritual matters has changed dramatically over the years. I believe we are all evolving rapidly spiritually at this time of great change. People have begun to re-assess and re-awaken to new ideas and ways of thinking. People are now ready and willing to try something new in terms of healing.

It is too easy to argue today that these esoteric matters have no place in modern society, for me society cannot call itself modern without it. To simply label these issues as witchcraft or a woman's intuition isn't good enough for me any more. It is a lazy mindset and approaching any subject without the willingness to understand or expand your mind is to hinder your progress and limit your potential.

Working with crystals is to work with the theory that the body is a mass of complex energy, and therefore energy healing and vibration therapies have its place within society.

Modern medicine has already begun to open its arms to complementary therapies and in so doing this the one can only strengthen the other, and whilst one can address certain aspect of the self the other can address the rest.

The minerals and crystals I use in my healing are born from the Earth and they are here for us to use. They are a part of a vast organic toolbox the Earth and all of her creations have to offer.

They have been formed and created in advance to help us and we are beginning to remember their worth, their use and their destiny. They are precious, powerful and beautiful and with the proper and pure intent of the user and healer they can bring great joy and healing in a myriad of ways.

Working in this way is to work on a new level of understanding and it also acknowledges we are so much more than flesh and bones; we are beings of light and more specifically a rainbow of constantly changing colours depending on mood and thought.

We work within a subtle partnership of Yin and Yang energies that are constantly flowing through our energy fields. We are a delicate dance of flow and motion and when we are faced with adversity these canals of energy often become blocked.

Our bodies do respond to crystal energies although one crystal does not suit all. But the mineral kingdom has a vast and colourful family of gems on offer. They are all so different like us and are all singing their own songs, which can aid us in finding our own harmony.

16

Step-by-step guide to expanding the mind and working with the universe

As I have already stated in this book, the key to working with the mind is to challenge our belief systems, as the more restricted our belief systems the more confined our mind is. To enable us to expand and strengthen the mind we need to acquire knowledge, as by doing this it can change the frequencies of the mind just like changing the channels on the radio or television, and this can see us resonating in a different way, attracting different people and situations to us. We also definitely need to understand how to react to and work with the 'gut instinct'.

We need to be totally honest with ourselves about any prejudices we might have, as judgement born out of prejudice is faulty and you will need good solid judgement to analyse the symbols, dreams etc.

If you are worrying, anxious or imbalanced in any way, navigating your way through life using emotions as your navigator, tell yourself it is pointless worrying and life is about the journey and anything we experience, especially difficulties, are obstacles for us to overcome and opportunities for us to develop.

Ask yourself, 'What have I got to learn from this?' If appropriate, take ownership of your problems, for example, if you are in a bad relationship ask yourself what is it about you that attracted you to the person, thereby taking responsibility for your life and problems, as this will empower you and allow you the opportunity for self development. Stand back and be an observer of life for a while and in this way you can better understand what is actually happening around you.

When you encounter situations that provoke any unpleasant feeling, the gut reaction that you might normally respond to, stop before responding and explore what pushed your button and aroused the unpleasant feeling.

Understand as difficult as it might seem you have to change your reaction. For instance, if you have been parented by someone who had concealed and faulty behaviour, you might find when your faulty parent was being secretive you would pick up on it on a gut level, and even though you did not understand they were concealing something, you would react to this gut feeling in a particular way. As a result of this, when meeting someone else who also had concealed and faulty behaviour it could activate your gut feeling and you could automatically respond in the way you reacted with your parent. You might feel you are very comfortable with this person and go on to form a significant but faulty relationship with them.

When that gut feeling comes in, understand it might be telling you something is not right, and it will definitely be telling you something requires more attention. When that feeling comes in, acknowledge it, disengage from the feelings/ emotions and use your mind. And remember the chakras are constantly processing the energy we are exchanging, absorbing, pumping and filtering in line with the frequencies we are tuned into, and this is why it is vital to change the way you react, and stop allowing your emotions to lead you, otherwise you will stay in a constant loop of emotional and irrational exchange, stuck on a channel that is not healthy. You need to train yourself to project your thoughts outwards not inwards, strengthen your mind and gain control of you.

At this stage I need to mention those who have experienced things such as childhood abuse or been the victim of random crime, violence and the type of thing you have no control over because you were at the mercy and free will of others. Please remember this is not your fault and I do not mean to suggest that you attracted this to you in any way. There are things that happen in this life that can be truly devastating to the victim and their families and friends but I am confident mostly you can be helped to overcome adversity in one way or another because you too are connected to the whole by a single organism of interconnected energy fields designed by and connected to a Creator.

With the help of the many trained professionals, such as counsellors, psychologists, hypnotherapists etc you can learn to quiet your emotions and then some level of healing can take place. You can change your status from one of a victim to one of a survivor and your experiences might help you to help others, and in this way you can empower yourself.

Speak in your mind and ask the spirit workers and the universe to which you are connected to help you, as well as the trained professionals, and instead of harbouring thoughts and feelings that are harmful to you and might impact on your body and cause you illness at a later date, work towards leaving it to the universe to decide what is appropriate for the person who has sinned against you. Let the harmful feelings and emotions go and let karma, cause and effect, work its way through, as well as possibly the legal system.

When necessary, use a visualising technique such as imagining yourself full of light, see the light coming from above and pouring through the top of your head and filling you, and once it has filled you see it spill out and fill your aura. You will have read in these pages that light is beneficial and has healing properties and this is the purpose for this visualisation.

Once you are filled with and surrounded by this wonderful white light speak in your mind and say 'I am healing mentally and physically and I accept these healing rays'. Do this exercise whenever you feel the need. It may take quite a few weeks or even months to get to the stage where you feel balanced mentally and emotionally and once you are there you can move on to the next stage. This stage involves meditation.

We know the brain is a mass of electric circuits through which the mind expresses itself. Electrical activity emanating from the brain is displayed in the form of brainwaves and my research tells me there are four categories of these brainwaves ranging from most active to least active.

Apparently, when we are actively engaged in mental activities, it generates beta waves. The frequency of beta waves ranges from fifteen to forty cycles a second, depending on how animated we are.

The next brainwave is alpha, which is said to represent non-animation. Alpha brainwaves are slower and frequencies range from nine to fourteen cycles per second. When we are reflective or meditative we are usually in an alpha state.

The next state, theta brainwaves, is apparently between five and eight cycles a second. Any repetitive task that sees us daydreaming and not remembering the past few minutes is often in a theta brainwave state. Going into and coming out of sleep is when we usually pass into or out from this state.

The final brainwave state is said to be delta, a deep dreamless sleep state with a range of one and a half to four cycles per second. Brainwaves never go down to zero because that would mean that you were brain dead.

In order to meditate we have to quiet our mind and go from the beta wave to the alpha wave. You can use relaxing music to achieve this and just let your mind wander and every time an intrusive thought comes in, push it away. When the music is finished, speak in your mind and say 'who ever is there working with me please help and guide me to achieve what ever it is I have come here to achieve. I want to work with you and I promise I will make an effort to listen'. Try to repeat this exercise every day or at least two or three times a week and always at the end of it say 'who ever is there working with me please help and guide me to achieve what ever it is I have come here to achieve. I want to work with you and I promise I will make an effort to listen'.

Keep reinforcing this to your spirit worker and the universe and even if it takes a good few weeks, eventually the communication will come, as your intention will alter your frequency or channel making it possible for the work and communication to begin.

After a couple of months it might be you no longer need to meditate and reinforce to your spirit worker that you want to work with him/her because the communication might start to flow as you become completely tuned in. However almost every week I confirm in my mind that I am listening to the person who is working with me and I want to achieve what ever it is I have come here for.

The next stage, which can be undertaken a couple of weeks after you start the meditation stage, is to write down a question. Make it simple and focus on just the one question. It might be something you need guidance on such as 'should I change my job?' When you go to bed put the paper with the question on under your pillow and before you go to sleep speak in your mind and repeat the question, i.e. 'should I change my job?' Keep a paper and pen at your bedside and as soon as you have a dream and you start to wake, reach for the paper and pen and write it down.

Using the A-Z symbol section of my forthcoming dreams and symbols book you will begin to understand the style needed to decipher the symbols in your dream. However, it may not be via a dream that you get your answer. It can be in very many ways such as coincidence a symbolic happening or event etc. Whichever way the symbols come, you still decipher them in the same way. Reading the examples I have given you in the chapters of this book entitled 'Examples of dreams and their meanings' and 'Symbolic happenings' should also help you with the style of interpretation. Once you have had an answer to the first question move on to another question and again write it down, put it under your pillow and repeat the question every night before you go to sleep.

Eventually you won't need to meditate or write questions down to get answers, as events occur in your life you can just ask for help with the issues immediately by speaking in your mind. However, please be aware that sometimes the symbol can be interpreted in more than one way and then we have to look at what we need as opposed to what we want, to work out what the guidance is.

This is a form of self-development and is not just about us being told what to do but is also about gaining wisdom, courage, strength etc. and having the free will to decide what is right and wrong, and whether to take the hard road or the easy road. We also always need to check our motives and make sure they are for the right reasons.

It is probable that eventually when you are in bed and start to go into or out of sleep, when you are in the theta state, you might start to have visualization with your eyes closed, as though you are seeing things on your eyelids. This usually starts with colour, and it means you are starting to see the frequencies you are emitting and receiving (remember every thought and feeling has a pitch and a colour associated with it). This comes when the mind is expanding and the third eye is strengthening as these, as well as the chakras, are like psychic muscles that are being worked and are becoming more powerful.

You might go on to see faces, animals, letters, numbers etc. and this means the spirit worker who is working with you is projecting their thoughts, like telepathy, to work with you in expanding your mind and third eye. They are able to do this due to the expansion of your mind, which will change your frequency, and they will be trying to help you to expand the peripheral vision of your third eye so you can sense on a wider and wider frequency. They achieve this by showing you objects that are increasingly wider and wider apart.

Another thing to be aware of is you might find yourself waking up at the same time every night or some nights. Three in the morning is common for most people as this is when you are usually in delta wave, a deep sleep. Spirit workers wake you from delta wave and bring you to theta wave and, again, if you keep your eyes closed upon waking and try to keep your mind placid, looking straight ahead with your eyes closed you might begin to have visualization. It can be like watching a television or a cinema screen. Again, what you are receiving is telepathy, and the spirit workers are continuing to work with you.

Running alongside these things will be the day to day incidents of psychic ability, such as thinking of a person and then you see them in the street, or knowing the phone is going to ring, seeing things in the empty space and that sort of thing. This means your third eye is starting to efficiently process what is being absorbed through the chakras and your gut instinct will get stronger and will tell you when things are not right.

To strengthen the third eye you can do visualization exercise involving touch, taste and smell. For instance, imagine that you have a lemon in front of you, look at it closely and observe the pitted pattern on its skin and the vibrancy of the colour. Using your imagination, smell the skin and breath in the smell of lemon, visualize touching the skin, see your fingers run over the lemon, does it feel chilled as though it has just come out of the refrigerator or is it warm to the touch? Visualize your tongue licking the outside skin of the lemon; does it taste acidic and musty? See yourself place your two hands on the lemon and force the skin apart, exposing the inside of the lemon as the juice bursts out, some of it hitting you in the eye and stinging. With your senses, smell the strong smell of the inside of the lemon and see yourself sink your teeth into the exposed flesh. Does it taste sour and does it make you shudder? Visualize and experience your face tingling and wet from the juice of the lemon. In this type of exercise you are using all of the senses.

To work on the peripheral vision of the third eye imagine a mouse running up the wall in front of you, see it run across the ceiling and past your head so it is running at the back of you. Keep watching it as though you have eyes in the back of your head. See it run down the wall behind you and across the floor, veering off to the left. Run the mouse up the wall to the left of you and then across the ceiling and down the wall to the right of you. This type of visualization will help to strengthen and expand the peripheral vision of the third eye. It is also important to strengthen the seven main chakras to help them work efficiently, and again this is achieved via visualization.

Imagine the main chakras/energy centres as a set of cogs/wheels rather like the workings of a clock or an engine and each cog/wheel needs to move smoothly and at a similar speed for the clock/engine to work properly. It is said the main seven chakras are located at the base of the spine, abdomen, spleen, heart, throat, brow and crown of the head. Concentrate on each chakra, starting with the spine, see it spin efficiently and work your way up each one to the crown.

There are many visualization exercises you can do such as the ones above and they really will strengthen your third eye, peripheral vision, chakras and psychic ability, and so work those psychic muscles! You can also train yourself to see the aura and you can do this by practicing on a friend. Stand your friend against a blank wall, a dark wall is best. Look at the top of your friend's head and keep staring, letting your eyes go off focus. You will begin to see a pencil outline around your friend. Everything that has solidity has this pencil outline, as the solidity is made up of atoms, which are particles and waves. The waves cause a friction with the particles, and the friction gives off a magnetic impulse.

It is this magnetic impulse that healers work on when they channel healing energy from the universe, however this pencil outline is not the aura. Keep staring and in your peripheral vision you might see another, perhaps weird shape. It can be unevenly distributed around the head and shoulder area, and it can extend quite far out. This is the aura. Everything that has consciousness has an aura, and the aura comes from the mind of the spirit and is like a database/storage facility, made up of all thoughts, feelings and experiences we have had in this lifetime. Eventually, with practice, you might be able to see the colour within the aura, which can tell you how a person is thinking and feeling.

Please be practical with your mind expansion and development. Don't be fluffy and fanciful but keep your feet on the ground, constantly check your motives and ask your spirit worker to help you be the best you can be. Good luck and I will be so interested to hear of your development.

17

Join me in my market research

So here you are, you have read this far, and I hope the journey hasn't been too problematic but if you are blistered and weary, don't despair, as the best is yet to come. If you were not already in shape I think you may find your efforts will have been worth it when you realise how mentally fit you are and I want to say – thank you for bearing with me.

In the following pages are my theories answering the chapters you have read, and what the meaning of life etc might be. As you are fit, you too can have informed theories and perhaps your thinking matches mine, perhaps not, but the point is both you and I now have opinions built on firm foundations and we are able to discuss that which cannot be proven, our minds are unrestricted and that is liberating!. One thing I have learnt on this journey is there are plenty of people who express strong views about many things and a lot of these views are restrictive and are based on ignorance, belief, prejudice, fear etc., and this contributes to a mismatch of conflicting information that is 'out there', and such thinking means there are lots of people who are disconnected from the whole.

Recently I was at a function and a woman whom I didn't know came up to me and said within the hearing of others, 'You're a fortune teller aren't you', and it wasn't asked as a question, it was stated as a fact. I replied politely 'No not at all, my work is based on consciousness, the existence of life after death etc' and this lady very forcefully said to me 'Oh I don't believe in that rubbish', and her face was twisted with dislike of me as she said it, and presumably her dislike was because of the opinion she had of me, which was irrational and built on sand.

Being fed up of this type of prejudiced behaviour which has been aimed at me many times before, I replied 'How sad for you, perhaps you should educate yourself about the things you have such forceful opinions of'. Such a smart response didn't make me feel good about myself and I realise I truly am a work in progress and I have a long way to go so please, don't think my summing up of my work is coming from a superi-or stance, as the reverse is true, and I promise I will try to do better, as now I know better I have no excuse.

This book is for the mass public and it is hoped by reading the book it will help to change/shift world consciousness and also inform the world of the lost language of symbols, which I think allows this world to communicate with our higher self, other worlds or parallel universes, spirit workers and ultimately the Creator.

Following on from this book is a large book of symbols and dreams entitled 'Yvonne Bailey's Big Book of Symbols and Dreams', giving hundreds of examples of dreams, symbolic happenings and their meanings, together with an A-Z index of symbols so you can get used to the style of the universal language.

A web site has been created at www.yvonnebailey.co.uk with a database attached to enable you to search for the meaning of your own symbols and dreams, and also with a section to enable you the reader to join with me in market research in this field on a large-scale basis by reporting your experiences as you journey on your road of mind expansion, working with the universe and connecting with the whole. The website will allow you to report occurrences and such like, with the aim of establishing and publishing in a book quantitative data to support the theories in this book. As interest rises in what has been written in this book and more people start to journey with the mind I will be happy to physically travel where ever there is an interest to promote this work by public speaking, hosting courses, seminars and such like.

I also hope to develop and establish training courses online for use worldwide, and it is hoped once sufficient data has been positively analysed this might help to establish links/networks with the education sector. This might then lead to working with the education sector and Governments to assist in policy and educational curriculum changes worldwide.

Also, I intend to promote a series of children's books, based around this book, which might help parents to teach their children not what to think but how to think about all life, the world, universe and the Creator.

Having developed and tested the techniques mentioned in this book and witnessed the life changing results I am confident you the reader as an individual can forge a path through your mind to climb your mountains and in this way you will see more clearly. I am also confident collectively you, me and everyone that meets with us on the road can forge paths through the mind to climb even higher mountains and share an expanded view on life.

It will become easier and easier for others to walk with us as our footprints leave an impression on the road, and they too can benefit from an expanded view and in this way we can collectively see clearly for the benefit of all life, Mother Earth, the Universe and the Creator. In this way all of us joining together can help to raise consciousness, and we can bring about change.

18

My Theories of Everything

"Facts often appear incredible only because we are ill informed and cease to appear marvellous when our knowledge is extended."
                                            Sir Francis Bacon 1561-1626.

Chapter 3 - The plan for our lives

Why our mix (parents, D.O.B, environment etc) had to be as it was, and recognising the universe was somehow orchestrating events at key moments.

Theory
I think there is a plan for our lives on Earth and we have agreed our plan when living in our natural state of conscious-ness/spirit in a parallel universe. I think there are spirit workers in the parallel universe that know our plan and are assigned to work with us and they can orchestrate events to help us achieve our aims. I view our world and some other planets as being like educational establishments we can return to again and again to achieve mental and emotional maturity. Some people might symbolically be at the crèche level, some might be at infant level, some might be at junior level and some might have incarnated many more times and have progressed to University level.

3.1 - Martin Luther King Junior

An example of a modern day Master brought here to help to move humanity on, with the help of the universe.

Theory
I think we are all at differing stages of progression in the 'school or university of life' and whilst some people might be at the stage of having to learn particular lessons, others might have to achieve something and so on. I think when we get to a certain stage of progression

and have mastered the overall aims of progression, then we can focus on a specific thing, to help with the overall plan in moving humanity collectively on.

Chapter 4 - The plan for the Earth and the universe

Astrological ages, which are time periods in astrology, have symbolically paralleled major changes in the Earth's development and the Earth's inhabitants' development.

Theory

A complex magnetic field not only establishes the pattern of the brain at birth but also continues to regulate and control it throughout our lives. I think this field is tuned into the planets that are prevalent at our time of birth and these planets emit an energy form that can influence our thoughts, character traits and such like and is a way of mentoring the individual. I also think the planets are designed to resonate with life collectively, to achieve a desired overall effect and help to move humanity on. For ease of understanding, think of the magnetic field as regulating a symbolic electronic panel that has loads of coloured squares, with these coloured squares representing different aspects of the personality. Where the planets are at the time of birth would light up these coloured squares to a greater or lesser extent. I think it is possible that the planetary influence is monitored and adapted by agents of the Creator so as to influence the magnetic field that regulates the symbolic electronic panel according to what has to be achieved in line with the plan for us as an individual, the Earth and the universe.

4.1 - Age of Pisces

Jesus was said to be born around 2BC in the transitory period, as the Piscean Age was almost fully settled and the Aries Age had practically left. Jesus is known as the sacrificial 'Lamb of God' and 'Lamb' signifies the sign of Aries and Jesus, as sacrificial 'Lamb', therefore, closed the Age of Aries. By closing Aries, Jesus brought in Pisces.

Theory

During the Age of Pisces the truth of our duality, that we are both body and spirit, was revealed and by example Jesus, who I think of as a Master, showed us this. I see him as being a wonderful spiritual healer and also a gifted medium. He had an inner knowing about life and taught those around him how to (symbolically) 'walk on water', or in other words 'stay on top of life'. He did his job superbly well as his life and accomplishments (which were termed by some as miracles) left a lasting legacy, which is how it was meant to be, and I think was an important part of the plan for the Piscean Age. I think he, as well as the spirit workers who were chosen to help him from their parallel universe, must have incarnated and prepared for this important role over many, many lifetimes, and perhaps on other planets, to get to the stage of progression that was needed to fulfil these aims.

4.2 - Age of Aquarius

The things of the air which have shaped our modern day life and would herald the possible 160 years of the coming of this age, have been coming in since about 1870 or thereabouts.

Theory

Aquarius is an air sign and the Age Of Aquarius is to do with all things of the air. In this age man on Earth will achieve a higher state of consciousness and telepathy and psychic ability will be an accepted form of communication, and these abilities are achieved via waves of the air, or frequencies. I think it is probable that a Master will come to close Pisces and open Aquarius and, as this is the age of technological and social advancement, he might come in a way that really gets our attention and challenges science, religion etc. and makes us think on a completely different level. It may be the lengths of the twelve great ages are irregular and so when the actual date to close Pisces and open Aquarius will be is unclear, therefore the Master might appear at any time.

4.2.1 - Things of the air

Telephone 1875
Electricity 1879
Radio 1896
Aeroplane 1903
Television 1924
Internet 1961

Theory

I think these things of the air were part of the Creator's plan to help bring in the air sign of Aquarius, and this seems to suggest the new age has been preparing itself from around the mid to late1800's.

4.2.2 - Helen Duncan - materialisation medium   1897 - 1956

Helen Duncan is known as the 'Medium Martyr', which status helped the phenomena of materialisation via ectoplasm, and the ability of mediumship gain worldwide attention.

Theory

As well as the things of the air, as mentioned in 4.2.1 above, the coming of the Age of Aquarius also brought with it people with rare and exceptional mediumship gifts, including the phenomena of producing ectoplasm which lifted the veil that divides one universe from another, and enabling communicators who it was thought had 'died' to be seen, heard and recognised. This reinforced to us that we are body and spirit and that whilst the body might die, the spirit survives and communication between parallel worlds is possible. I think Helen Duncan was very highly evolved and had agreed to reincarnate on Earth and become a materialisation medium and, like so many of these highly evolved spirits, she suffered for the good of all humanity. I think all of these outstanding and rare mediums were probably as highly evolved as Helen.

4.2.3 - Alec Harris - materialisation and direct-voice medium 1897-1974

Not only was Alec Harris a materialisation medium but he was also a direct voice medium who spoke a variety of languages at his sittings. Like Helen Duncan, his body somehow produced copious amounts of ectoplasm, which enabled these two forms of mediumship to take place.

Theory

Ectoplasm has caused a lot of controversy in our world and I think it was part of the Creator's plan to manifest a tool to enable the pioneering mediums to help bring in this new Age of Aquarius. It was a tool that would get everyone's attention, and this malleable energy was obviously perfect for the job of proving survival of the spirit after bodily death.

These exceptional mediums have done a great service to our world and the legacy they have left for science is perhaps as yet not appreciated but I am sure eventually it will be understood and all the pieces of the puzzle will come together as science progresses. It is interesting to note that Einstein's formula E=mc2 - energy equals mass to the speed of light, shows that mass 'm' is equivalent to energy 'E'. This explains how materialization and dematerialization might operate by matter being transformed into energy. Whilst I myself don't fully understand the formula I do realise Einstein's formula offers possibilities to understanding the process involved in producing a malleable energy such as ectoplasm.

4.2.4 - Lesley Flint - direct voice medium 1911-1994

Lesley Flint was a Direct Voice Medium, which process was activated directly by Spirit communicators, and voices could be almost identical to people's voices before making transition to the Spirit World. Lesley was an uneducated man, yet a variety of languages emerged at sittings and the voices of the dead spoke directly to their friends or relatives.

Theory
Lesley Flint admitted he did not really know anything about the mechanism that allowed the direct voice phenomenon to take place but he knew the voices were located in a space a little above, and slightly to one side of his head. The spirit voices told him they had formed a voice box made from ectoplasm from which they could speak. It is obvious to me the spirit workers living in their parallel universe must know far, far more about science and the atom than we might ever believe was possible. They obviously understood all the components of the atom and how to manipulate those components by using their mind, to achieve the desired results. When eventually we understand this process the possibilities will be endless.

Chapter 5 - The Esoteric Fingerprints here on Earth

The mysteries and unexplained things that are here on Earth can challenge our concept of life and the advancement of man.

Theory

I think this Earth (and other planets) has been used for many billions of years as a place of learning. It is probable over these years' lots of different civilisations have lived in varying stages of progression. Many of us have probably lived in several of these civilisations at different times in previous lifetimes. When eventually the planet becomes severely damaged by pollution etc. and needs to rest to get back 'up to speed' man made/natural disasters could easily wipe out these civilisations, and overtime all records of them could be lost. Most life forms could die out but things such as some sea life, insect life, plant life etc. could be left if they were necessary to help recovery.

When the planet is recovered perhaps humans (aliens, who are also body and spirit just like us) who are living on technologically advanced planets might visit our resting planet. They could come in spacecraft, and eventually might bring the DNA of animals and such like with them if they decided to colonise our planet. When you consider we are sending astronauts into space and building space stations etc on other planets that seem capable of sustaining life, it is not impossible to image eventually we might colonise these planets, and then in thousands of years time the cycle of pollution and resulting disasters might occur and most records of this colonisation might be lost, and those who came after us might be wondering many things such as, 'where is the evolutionary footprint that shows us how these ancient civilisations evolved?'

5.1 - The mystery of the maps

In 1929, a map drawn on a gazelle skin was found. Research showed it was a genuine document drawn in 1513. The geographical detail shown in the lower part of the map agreed very remarkably with the results of a seismic profile made across the top of the ice-cap by the Swedish-British Antarctic Expedition of 1949.

Theory

I wonder who was here 4000 years BC doing things we are only now able to do with our modern technology? Perhaps this is an example of alien spacemen from an advanced planet visiting our planet, and leaving their knowledge to help us at a time when we were less evolved. In the same way we are now mapping other planets who is to say alien spacemen were not mapping ours. Perhaps other more highly evolved and technologically advanced alien planets are sometimes tasked with helping less evolved planets to progress, and perhaps they leave a piece of a puzzle for us to ponder over and try to make sense of. It could even be it is vital for the balance of the entire universe that we are nudged along, and there are probably many different ways of achieving this mentoring.

5.2 - The Nazca Lines

The Nazca plateau has 200 square miles of tableland where hundreds of different figures have been drawn depicting animals, birds and the human form. There are also geometrical devices in the form of trapezoids, rectangles, triangles and straight lines. Viewed at ground level these drawings are little more than grazes on the surface, viewed from above you see them as they really are.

Theory

The human forms that were drawn at Nazca show the heads enclosed in what appears to have been halos of radiance perhaps replicating the aura or even a space helmet, such as our space astronauts wear. Either way, the knowledge and capabilities of the artists were obviously out of place as we still cannot understand the meaning or process of what has been drawn in our enlightened times. The famous spider figure is said to have been devised as a terrestrial diagram of the giant constellation of Orion. Was this drawn to show us the synergy between life on our planet and the wider universe and was this and the other figures and geometrical devices a subliminal message to show us that everything is connected? The artists could have come from other planets or other universes, probably for the purpose of bringing to Earth pieces of a jigsaw for us to consider when evaluating the overall puzzle. I think the possibility of alien artists is compelling. I wonder if there is any link with what had been created at Nazca with things such as ice and sand circles, and the modern day crop circles that appear in fields and since 1990 have evolved into complex geometries? You will read in chapter 6 – Crop Circles – that scientists wonder whether lasers have been used to create the circles and are asking 'Is there a consciousness or intelligence directing an energy form yet unknown to us?' I think this theory also presents a real possibility of how the art and geometrical devices was created at Nazca and perhaps the Nazca artists have been waiting for us to link their historical artwork with the modern day artwork of crop circles etc.,

5.3 - The Inca trail to the past

Through the ancient legends of the peoples of the Andes stalked a tall, bearded, pale-skinned figure. He was known by different names in different places but he was always recognizably the same figure. Viracocha, who came in a time of chaos to set the world to rights.

Theory

Viracocha was said to be a scientist and an engineer, a sculptor and an architect, and he went in various directions arranging many things. He was also a teacher and a healer and made himself helpful to people in need. So where did the white man (or men) so obviously out of place come from? The philosophy of this man was the same as the other Great Masters/Teachers and to me he was obviously of their standard, and he brought with him a technological knowledge not accounted for in those times. Did he (or they) come from other planets, for the purpose of helping to move humanity on and to bring civilisation to an uncivilised society? I think this is probable.

5.4 - San Lorenzo, Mexico - The Olmec Enigma

In San Lorenzo the earliest carbon-dates for an Olmec site (around 1500 BC) had been recorded. However, Olmec culture appeared to have been fully evolved by then and there is no evidence the evolution had taken place in this vicinity. The Olmecs had built a significant civilization yet not a sign of anything that could be described as the 'developmental phase' of Olmec society had been unearthed anywhere.

Theory

Reading the historical facts relating to this Olmec site and then seeing there is no trace of the evolutionary process that led to the advanced civilisation at San Lorenzo reinforces the thought that perhaps the knowledge was brought to the area by alien spacemen from advanced planets. I know some people might think this is nonsense but to me it is highly probable. I would say it is blinkered to think we are the only beings out there in the universe. I think the more technologically advanced a civilisation is, the more spiritually evolved the people would be, and that would be true of aliens. Therefore, if they understood the whole of the universe was connected and the physical form was to enable our consciousness/spirit to progress and was part of a plan, they could easily be influenced by the spirit planners to come to Earth at times of need and help to move humanity on.

5.5 - Children of the First Men, Palenque, Chiapas Province, Mexico

Pacal was a ruler of Palenque in the seventh century AD. His coffin lay buried deep in the bowels of the Mayan Temple and was made of solid stone. The scene carved on top of the sarcophagus lid showed a clean-shaven man dressed in what looked like a tight-fitting body-suit.

Theory

Why was there a clean shaven man dressed in what looked like a tight-fitting body-suit shown operating some kind of machine carved on the lid of the sarcophagus? I think if the Mayans were aware alien space-men came from other planets and brought with them knowledge, technology etc. perhaps the Mayans viewed these aliens as coming from the afterlife. If so, by replicating these alien spacemen and their position whilst flying their spacecraft, perhaps it was thought that would influence their spirit travelling to the right destination after death of the physical body? I think this is highly possible. Also, how was it that what was found in the Mayan Temple seemed to have been modelled from that which had been found in Egypt? Is this evidence the alien spacemen had also visited and influenced the Egyptians? I think this is probable.

5.6 - A computer for calculating the end of the world

The Popol Vuh is accepted by scholars as a great reservoir of unconta-minated, pre-Colombian tradition. It is therefore puzzling to find such similarities between these traditions and those recorded in the Genesis story in the Bible.

Theory

I think it is incredible to see the same message, as in Genesis, rein-forced in different periods of time and in different parts of the world. And yet we have seen this coincidence repeating itself in other situa-tions, such as that which is demonstrated in Nazca, i.e. the spider and the terrestrial diagram of the giant constellation of Orion. Also the Mayan Temple and the Egyptian Pyramids. Even our planet orbiting the sun and the electron orbiting the nucleus of the atom has a syner-gy of connection. I think this is no coincidence and it is another piece of the puzzle for us to put together and is telling us everything is connected and subtly affected by this connection. There is clearly a higher power at work that is orchestrating events, exerting influence where influence is needed and making it possible in many ways for us to acquire knowledge and go forward in life. When you look at Mayan society with its observational astronomy, upon which, through the medium of advanced mathematical calculations was based a clever, complex, sophisticated and very accurate calendar you have to acknowledge that the possibility of this knowledge that connects astrology and geography coming from a higher intelligence to help us here on Earth is feasible. We have been given vital information about the connection between the heavens and Earth and I think this is a significant part of the plan for the Earth and the universe.

5.7 - Knowledge out of place

Glaring disparities were identified between the generally unremarkable achievements of the Mayas as a whole and the advanced state of their astro-calendrical knowledge.

Theory
I think this astro-calendrical knowledge was essential for the esoteric understanding of man and the Creator ensured the knowledge was made available, probably via alien spacemen who came from highly technological and spiritually evolved planets.

5.8 - Someone else's science?

Did the Maya inherit, in good working order, a calendar engineered to fit the needs of a much earlier and far more advanced civilization? Consider the crowning jewel of Maya calendrics, the so-called 'Long Count'. This system of calculating dates also expressed beliefs about the past -notably, the widely held belief that time operated in Great Cycles which witnessed recurrent creations and destructions of the world. According to the Maya, the current Great Cycle began in darkness on a date corresponding to 13 August 3114 BC in our own calendar. It was also believed that the cycle will come to an end, amid global destruction, on 23 December 2012 in our calendar.

Theory

I think the Long Count is the template of the Creator's plan for the Earth and it counts down the time of the plan and I think the prediction for 23 December 2012 is symbolic. I think the whole cycle of the Long Count is about cosmic karma and as everything is connected, what we have given out collectively will find its way back. Imagine the suffering endured by all living things, Mother Earth and the Universe over the last 5125 years, whether caused by thought or action, intentionally or unintentionally, through ignorance or with knowledge. As an example, if you look at the technology that has rapidly grown in the last 140 or so years to bring in the new age, we have unleashed things of the air without a thought to Mother Earth and the Universe. We know a lot of our technology is damaging to the environment and yet, because of our need to keep costs down we continue the damage, even though we do know better. As a result Mother Earth might have to shift different parts of her body to alleviate her pain and suffering and this could cause earthquakes, tsunamis and such like. It is possible that individuals and countries will be more and more influenced by this negative vibe and this might cause more friction and instability to anything we have created that is not stable. And what about the Universe, how has this suffering impacted on the Universe? I have read that scientists at Nasa say a cycle of sun spots, magnetic blasts from the sun, are soon to begin and it is thought these will peak in 2012. This can wreak havoc with satellites and electronic equipment. It could even affect the Earth's magnetic field. Throughout history tribes across the world also predict a cataclysmic event that will occur around 2012, and as mentioned before, here we see the same message reinforced in different periods of time and in different parts of the world. The Creator obviously wants us to get the message and I think this particular message is symbolic. It means we have to consider our actions, become more in-tune with the Creator, the Universe and Mother Earth, and this is what the Age of Aquarius is about.

Chapter 6 Crop Circles

Scientists face real and serious questions in confronting this mystery. Could this be secret laser technology beamed down from satellites? Is it a natural phenomenon? Is there a consciousness or intelligence directing an energy form yet unknown to us?

Theory

When you consider Nazca (see paragraph 5.2 above) with the figures and geometrical devices drawn on the tablelands that, because of the unique conditions in that part of the world, have remained virtually intact for literally hundreds of years, and then you consider modern day crop circles, you cannot help but see the synergy between them. Both the crop circles and Nazca seem to have the same outcome of expression. We appear to be at the receiving end of a transmission that is recorded as accelerating in intensity and content. What is being transmitted includes advanced mathematics, astronomy, ancient symbolism and the spiritual knowledge of our ancestors. It is as though we are receiving subliminal messages that show us everything is connected and there is much more to our world and universe than we realise. I think the artists have come from other planets or other worlds and the theory of laser technology from elsewhere in the universe to me is compelling. I would also like to link in the theories of laser/energy form with chapter 4 – The plan for the Earth and the universe – regarding the complex magnetic field that establishes the pattern of the brain at birth and continues to regulate and control it throughout our lives. This field I think is tuned into the planets that emit an energy form that influences and mentors us throughout our lives, and I wonder if the subjects covered in chapter 4, sub-chapter 5.2 and this chapter 6 are all part of the same mechanism?

Chapter 7 What is religion?

Religion is a set of beliefs and practices.

Theory

Many places in the world are now multicultural and there is a mismatch of cultures and religions rubbing alongside one another. Sometimes this rubbing can cause friction that blisters, and sometimes the blisters erupt. I very much believe in a Creator, but I shy away from the word God, as this word to me has a religious connotation. Religions are man made and have evolved from the legacy of the Masters, whose messages have been open to interpretation. There are many, many religions and offshoots of religions, all with differing rules and regulations, influenced by the different cultures they evolved from. The resulting entrenched and contradictory belief systems can cause problems for a multicultural society. The Masters came here to teach us and were messengers or agents of the Creator, and the core of their messages were the same but they were delivered in a way the people they were teaching could understand, and so were adapted to suit the different and mostly primitive cultures of those times. I think it was intended as we became more civilised and educated we understood the essence of the message and dispensed with outmoded practices. I think it would be wonderful if we could come together as a global community, all singing from the same hymn sheet, and when eventually we understand the composition of consciousness this will probably be possible.

7.1 - The word of the Creator

The word of the Creator can be found in many places, including ancient text.

Theory
Dotted throughout the Christian Bible and hidden amongst the text are scientific facts about this world modern man only just understands. There are many, many other ancient texts that impart knowledge seemingly out of place for the times. The Creator, probably via spirit planners who know the plan for the Earth and the universe, probably provided these pieces of the jigsaw by various means including guiding men to write what was needed to help us on Earth but their written word is open to interpretation and could be influenced by belief systems, culture etc. These writers I would say were working in the same way as mediums work.

7.2 - The Great Masters/Teachers

The Great Masters/Teachers I see as Messengers and Prophets of the Creator who came to impart knowledge and teach the people by example, to help to move humanity on. What the ancient Masters taught has had a huge impact on mankind and their legacy can still be seen today but the interpretation of the words of these Master is at the mercy of man with their cultural differences and differing agendas, and historically this has sometimes caused problems and conflict for mankind.

Theory
I think these Great Masters/Teachers were highly evolved spirits who had mastered the overall aims of progression achieved by repeated incarnations. They were chosen to return to Earth with a specific task,

to help with the overall plan in moving humanity collectively on. The plan for their lives must have been undertaken with military precision, their date of birth being carefully chosen for the planetary influence, the parents for the genes they would inherit and the environment and culture they would be born into. The spirit workers would have been carefully selected to work with these Masters and these workers would have had to be at least as highly evolved as the Masters themselves. As the Masters were then reincarnated in a physical body with the mind locked (so they would not have known they had a particular task to fulfil) they would have had the inevitable human frailties, but probably as they matured they were able to overcome most of these frailties because of their inner knowing and with the help of the planetary influence and the spirit workers who were assigned to work with them. These spirit workers in their parallel universe would have been orchestrating events in many ways, including sending thoughts via telepathy to the Masters in the same way as a medium works, but because of the advanced state of these Masters, they would have interpreted what they were receiving in a balanced and highly developed way. I think all of these Masters were mediums and healers who eventually went on to display all the highest human values such as compassion, empathy, love, courage, wisdom etc. These highest values would have been transparent for all to see and in this way these Masters taught by example. They made an impact on those around them, which was documented in various ways including symbolically, and carried forward to influence future generations. However, what was documented has been at the interpretation of man and some of the highest human values can be diluted and influenced by culture etc.

Chapter 8 - What is science?

In its broadest sense, science (from the Latin scientia, meaning "knowledge") refers to any systematic knowledge or practice. In its more usual restricted sense, science refers to a system of acquiring knowledge based on scientific method, as well as to the organized body of knowledge gained through such research.

Theory
The scientific community is made up of atheists, believers etc, just as you find elsewhere in society. Scientists deal with repeatable experiences but some experiences in life are not repeatable. I think it is probable scientific conclusions might sometimes be influenced by the belief systems and

experiences of the scientists involved in the research and/or experiment they are working on, and as so many experiences are not solid or repeatable, such as an out of body experience, if the scientists had never had an out of body experience and the result of the experiment were not conclusive then the conclusion made might be open to interpretation and therefore could be wrong. A scientist could dissect a human body piece by piece. He could tell you exactly what the physical body of the human consists of but he cannot tell you about the character of that person, whether the person was compassionate or cruel, whether they were a natural mathematician, or if perhaps they had a flair for writing, whether the person loved music or loved sport etc. The human body is solid but the character/spirit that animates the body is not solid, and therein lays the challenge of our duality. It is so much easier to understand and accept that which is solid and we are able to see and touch and is tangible, rather than that which is not solid and we cannot see and touch and is therefore intangible. I think science is only part of the story, albeit a very important part, but we cannot restrict our mental and emotional development by only acknowledging that which has been proven. We need to also acknowledge, in a balanced way, the things that are not tangible but have been experienced by many, many people and we need to continue to search for answers to these things.

8.1 - The unfolding science of the atom

The unfolding science of the atom, with its many different compositions, tells us there is so much more to learn but shows us everything is connected.

Theory
We have learnt atoms contain amongst other things electrons, and electrons give off a negative charge. What if every negative event, thought or emotion was released into the environment via electrons or some such particle, and was ultimately stored universally in the universal database? We have also learnt that atoms contain protons that give off a positive charge. What if every positive event, thought or emotion was also released into the environment via protons or some such particle, and was also stored universally? Supposing there had been more negative events than positive, eventually these electrons would be a force greater than the protons and it could be the Creator timed it so it took a certain period of time to tip the balance of our

Earth and universe? I think the Creator might well have designed the plan in this way and the balance might shift in 2012. By tipping the balance not just Mother Earth but the Universe to which it is connected might have to shift to alleviate its pain and suffering and this could cause earthquakes, tsunamis and such like, the vibrations of which might shatter the clouds of stored electrons and dilute them, making it easier for us to start again. This would mean that good always wins over bad. As a result of the devastation we might then get the message about personal and collective responsibility and karma and in this way we would seek to achieve a higher state of consciousness, and become more in-tune with the Universe and Mother Earth.

8.2 - Quantum physics

Quantum physics is a sub-branch of physics whose subject are phenomena connected with the quantum.

Theory

Quantum physics is the science of the small and deals with the behaviour of matter and energy on the minute scale of atoms and subatomic particles but science has not yet discovered all the minute compositions and possibilities that make up the atom. With quantum physics we now understand what is primary is energy and what we call matter is a special kind of energy – its organized energy, and we are told the trick to creating matter is to organise energy and what organises energy is the mind. I think it makes sense to say that a mind had to come up with this concept in the first place, and is how our complex world and the universe was created and is orchestrated by the Creator.

8.3 - An explanation of the atom by Professor Garry Schwartz

All material things in the universe, including us, are ultimately made from atoms, which in turn are made from subatomic particles – and atoms are pieces of matter. For instance, one type of atom could be hydrogen and another atom, oxygen. They come together and make water. Molecules are made of atoms – cells are made of molecules that are made of atoms – organs are made of cells, which are made of molecules, which are composed of atoms. In simple terms, the atom is the fundamental unit of organized matter.

Theory

When Garry Schwartz tells us about the mind creating a storm, it made me think about the Native American Indians when they did the rain dance. They probably knew how to get their mind to a state where they could connect with the elements and create a storm to make rain in a controlled way. I also thought about poltergeist activity and I think it is the same thing, only whereas the Indians were able to create a storm to make rain in a controlled way, the person creating the energy for poltergeist activity to take place has no control over it and are unaware of their involvement. This activity usually takes place around pubescent teens when their hormones are raging, thus the energy they are creating is wild and raging as well. Also, I wonder if when we walk into a building or any place where we sense a   negative atmosphere, does this mean whoever has been there before has been negative, and have they left behind free floating clouds of electrons that we pick up on? If we ourselves were negative this would probably make us feel much worse and if we believed in evil spirits etc. we could even think an evil spirit had attached itself to us as a result of visiting the building or place and this is how myths are made. Superstition and fear can paralyse the mind and is irrational. And yet is doesn't have to be this way as we all have the means to expand our mind.   Imagine what the mind of the Creator must be capable of, a mind that created the creation and all the tiny pieces of particles and subatomic particles that combine to make the whole, a mind that knew all the ingredients needed and how to manipulate these ingredients to achieve lots of different outcomes, and all realized by just focusing the mind. Now that is some mind and some power!!!

8.4 - The big bang

Not only does the universe have a beginning, but also time itself, our own dimension of cause and effect, began with the Big Bang. That's right -- time itself does not exist before then. The very line of time begins with that creation event. Matter, energy, time and space were created in an instant by intelligence outside of space and time.

Theory

When you consider consciousness exists outside of the physical body and we are all connected by a single organism of interconnected energy fields, and then when you throw into the equation some people are able to harness the energy in the way I think the native American

Indians did, then it is not impossible to imagine that an immense power such as the Creator could have focused its mind, splitting atoms to cause the big bang that created our universe and world. I wonder who or what the Creator is, what is outside of our universe, and where does the Creator live? It is so difficult with our limited knowledge to envisage the answers to these questions but I think if we are living life on Earth to learn lessons and grow in empathy, wisdom etc. then surely there is a goal. Is it the goal that we eventually, through repeated incarnations, reach the highest state we can achieve? Is the Creator this highest state, or in other words is the Creator collective consciousness that has reached the highest state? We automatically assume the Creator is a single entity, either a he or a she, but perhaps this is not the case. It could be the Creator is higher-level collective consciousness that gets more and more powerful as more and more of us reach this higher level and I think that could be the collective aim of progression.

8.5 - The quest for a Theory of Everything

Over the past century, physicists have unlocked the secrets behind radio and television, nuclear energy and the power of the sun. Now they're seeking the ultimate prize: a 'theory of everything' that could reveal a bizarre realm of interdimensional wormholes and time warps. Such a theory would give us the ability to 'read the mind of God'.

Theory

We are told atoms are the basic building blocks of matter that make up everyday objects and there are about ninety naturally occurring kinds of atoms known to man. Scientists in labs have been able to make about twenty five more man-made atoms, probably the best known of which would be the atomic bomb. We are told atoms are composed of electrons that give off a negative charge, neutrons have no charge, and protons give off a positive charge. Inside these protons and neutrons are quarks held together by gluons, and then we hear of neutrinos and other elementary particles and waves. We are also told of superstrings with their tiny loops of string or membranes vibrating in ten dimensions where parallel universes might exist, each with a different law of physics. Can you imagine all these unseen particles dancing about, constantly changing and interchanging, spinning, vibrating and bonding, rubbing against each other and sometimes creating a repulsion or an attraction which will set them off in another direction, but the most mind blowing thing of all is scientists have found some of these particles change when attention is focused upon them. The possibilities to influence and change everything around us must be endless, and I think you can clearly see how we create karma, even when we are able to hide our true feelings, intentions etc there is no escape.

8.6 - CERN, Geneva - the God particle

The instruments used at CERN are particle accelerators and detectors. Accelerators boost beams of particles to high energies before they are made to collide with each other or with stationary targets. Detectors observe and record the results of these collisions.

Theory
One of the things CERN might find as a result of this colossal experiment is the existence of parallel universes. How absolutely thrilling that would be because if they do find these other universes then it would only take a small leap to recognise this is where our spirit or consciousness goes when we 'die'. I think this is probable and if this theory proves to be correct then the death of the physical body and the continued existence of the spirit is a scientific process, not reliant on any belief system, religion etc.

Chapter 9 - Thoughts and feelings are real

It used to be thought we could keep our thoughts and feelings to ourselves, that they were internal. Science is now discovering not only are our thoughts and feelings internal but they are also external, and they have an impact on not just us but everything around us.

Theory
When you think of all people and other living things that have lived on the Earth throughout the Earth's history and then when you realise what science is now telling us, that thoughts and feelings are real, just imagine how this must impact on us, Mother Earth and the universe throughout time. And what about the thoughts and feelings of all living things in the wider universe? It must all be out there in the empty space, populating the universal database. I think grief, sorrow and such other negative events are more prolonged and can have a greater intensity of thought and feeling than that of positive events

such as happiness, ecstasy and such like. Imagine a mother whose baby has died and then imagine a mother who has just given birth. Which feeling would you say is the most powerful and intense? Would the mother experiencing the negative event be releasing electrons in to the empty space? As negative events can be more intense and prolonged than positive events, and as there have undoubtedly been many, many negative events throughout history, does this mean electrons are now more prevalent than protons? I think bad things, evil and such like, also produce electrons but these negative things ultimately never win the fight over good. I think this is because the Creator has planned it so when over a set period of time the meter of the celestial adding machine that has been calculating and recalculating the scale of our growing debt to the universe reaches 5,125, every last penny of that debt is going to be called in, (just as the Mayan calendar tells us) and the increased amount of electrons that are in the atmosphere at that time will tip the balance and everything shifts, a type of universal cleansing the vibrations of which dissipate the free floating clouds of electrons and then we have to start again. Therefore I think attributing bad things to a devil with its own individual personality is wrong, as the negative force of electrons is a derivative of thought and feelings and does not have a life of its own, it is not an entity with its own distinct existence.

9.1 - Matthew Manning - Healer

Matthew Manning is a world famous healer who has participated in a wide range of experiments designed to test what effect, if any, his thoughts would have on a wide range of biological systems.

Theory

When Matthew was attempting to heal the blood cells he placed his hands above the test tubes while imagining the cells surrounded by a brilliant white light. In ancient text we hear of the divine light or inner spark, and there are also many references to the glowing light of God's presence etc. All of this suggests this inner light is a positive thing. Science tells us light contains photons, little parcels of energy that can act like a particle and a wave and does not need a material substance to travel through; it can travel through a vacuum. The size of a wave is measured as its wavelength. I think if you are a kind person then you can be on this wavelength and the more you develop your mental and emotional maturity and achieve inner balance by not being judgmental, critical and such like, banishing restrictive belief systems, the lighter your thoughts and feelings will be, you will be more on this wavelength and the stronger the waves will become. I think that nothing can restrict this positive wave that you can generate. I think you can visualise this white light and harness it by projecting it with your mind outwards to any living thing or any situation, and in this way you can help. I think the Creator designed this mechanism as a tool for good for us all to use, and it is exciting that healers such as Matthew are willing to test their methods and science is now able to offer us   measurable results.

9.2 - Water experiments

The groundbreaking work of Japanese Dr Masaru Emoto has led to a new consciousness of Earth's most precious resource - water. What has put Dr. Emoto at the forefront of the study of water is his proof that thoughts and feelings affect physical reality. By producing different focused intentions through written and spoken words and music and literally presenting it to the same water samples, the water appears to 'change its expression'.

Theory

I think the Creator designed water not just to support life but to mimic life as well. It is absolutely incredible to learn water reacts to not just thoughts, feelings and music, but also to the written word as well. This shows clearly water truly reacts to vibrational energy and we now know that vibration/ energy contains information. Not just our actions but our intention, thoughts etc., impact on everything around us. The human body is made up of around 70% water, and the Earth is also composed of about that same amount, so you can see how collectively we can influence everything. It is interesting to note that again, as observed previously in other things, there is a synergy of connection between the amount of water in a human body and that of the Earth, and also water mimicking life, which reinforces to us we are all connected and affected by the whole. I think the Creator planned that what was necessary for the existence of life was also able to reflect life, giving the Creator, its agents and us the ability to monitor our progression and the level of consciousness of the human race on Earth as a whole. When you look at the state of our world, the pollution, all the fighting and violence, the contradictory beliefs and practices that can result in prejudice, criticism and irrational and judgmental behaviour, we are able to see how this is impacting on our environment and us. If we continue in this way things can get much worse, and when you throw into the mix the fact that we do know better, then you realise it is time for us to change and work towards not just single but collective responsibility.

9.3 - Plant Experiments

Cleve Backster is a leading lie-detector expert who conducted experiments on plants and he learnt the waxy insulation between the cells in plants caused an electrical discharge that mimicked a human stress reaction on polygraph instruments. He went on to realise the plants were displaying an emotional reaction, as they were able to read thoughts and they displayed an emotional reaction to those thoughts.

Theory

I think the Creator designed plants to play an extremely important support part in the cycle of nature. Without plants there could be no life on Earth as they are the primary producers that sustain all other life forms. The oxygen we breathe comes from plants and plants contribute to this life in so many ways, not the least of which is providing a natural remedy to many ailments, and the ailments of Mother Earth as well. Plants are an integral part of the system of life forms that should be in tune with each other and they can tell us when things are not right. To know they display an emotional reaction to our thoughts and feelings highlights how everything is connected and I think we have a lot more to learn from plants, if only we know how to ask and listen for the answer in the way the ancients did. We humans have had such a negative impact on our environment, and I think plants will help us towards righting this if we allow them the opportunity to continue to support us. They cannot right the things we have caused but perhaps they can help to right the effect. As with water, I think plants are a barometer for our environment and the progression of man.

9.4 - Dr Kenneth Ring's NDE research of the blind

Vicki Umipeg was born blind, her optic nerve having been completely destroyed at birth because of an excess of oxygen she received in the incubator. Yet, she appears to have been able to see during her NDE. Her story is a particularly clear instance of how NDEs of the congenitally blind can unfold in precisely the same way as do those of sighted persons. Apart from the fact that Vicki was not able to discern colour during her experience, the account of her NDE is absolutely indistinguishable from those with intact visual systems.

Theory

On my journey of discovery I think some of the most important and influential experiences I have had has been firstly, when I was a child I remember my spirit being out of my body. Secondly, the experiences of sleep paralysis, (which I now think was me waking before my spirit was properly settled back into my body), and thirdly, waking up and shaking violently, (which I now think was my spirit only just beginning the process of entering back into my body and I had woken up too soon), and these have had a huge impact on me. They allowed me the understanding that my body and spirit are separate and the body cannot function without the spirit, but the spirit can function without the body, thereby proving to me the real me is the spirit/conscious part. This has been the main catalyst that drew me to focus on my research about life, and encouraged me down the path of self-development. Many, many people have had similar experiences to me and blind Vicki's story is hugely compelling. The fact that in her physical life she had never seen, having been totally blind from birth, but when her spirit came out of her body she was able to see, is significant. When we look to science to repeat experiences to validate the same, we have to acknowledge that some experiences are random and might not be repeatable, but that does not mean those experiences are false. I think when it is universally acknowledged we are body and spirit living life for a purpose, then we will focus on personal and collective responsibility and in this way we will substantially raise consciousness on Mother Earth for the benefit of the whole.

9.5 - A day in the life of Oscar the cat

Since he was adopted by staff members as a kitten, Oscar the Cat has had an uncanny ability to predict when residents are about to die. Thus far, he has presided over the deaths of more than twenty five residents on the third floor of Steere House Nursing and Rehabilitation Center in Providence, Rhode Island. His mere presence at the bedside is viewed by physicians and nursing home staff as an almost absolute indicator of impending death, allowing staff members to adequately notify families.

Theory

When you consider the role animals have played on Earth, it seems to me they have made huge sacrifices in helping to move humanity toward civilization and yet, even in our enlightened times, we do not understand them and continue to abuse them. The negative and positive aspects of our personality and character traits can be likened to animals. The animal kingdom displays both intellect and emotion, animals are cunning and they show us when they are hurt and in pain, and when they are grieving etc., and they demonstrate duality, as animals are far more tuned into that which is not tangible, such as intuition and picking up on things that are in the empty space. We humans attempt to tame animals, and the most successful examples would be when taming baby animals using respect, love and understanding, and giving firm boundaries. When baby animals in the care of humans are neglected they show signs of trauma and distress, leading to feral behaviour as they grow. And if humans attempt to tame baby animals with violence, the baby animals respond to instructions through fear but in later life lashes out. There are also examples of humans attempting to tame animals when they are grown, and this is a far more difficult undertaking with sometimes only partial success. Recognise anything? I think the Creator designed animals to play a multifunctional role, not the least of which is to see us recognise ourselves in them, to learn about ourselves and to hone our empathy and compassion so that we strive to do better.

Chapter 10 - Universal language of symbols

There is a universal language of symbols beyond the power of words. This symbolic form of communication transcends the spoken language and we can receive these symbols either internally or externally and in our sleep state and waking time. Symbols give a knowledge which concerns the deeper mysteries of man and the universe and helps the universe orchestrate events more easily. It is a language that connects one world to another and allows communication between those worlds.

Theory

Long before I had every heard of a universal language I was experiencing bizarre happenings in the forms of dreams, coincidence, thoughts and physical phenomena. I had no idea all of this formed a language and I was receiving communi-cation from outside of me. When the penny finally dropped it was a eureka moment for me. This symbolic language has been handed down through the ages and I see this language as another piece of the puzzle and a way for the Creator and its agents, spirit workers, the universe and our sub-conscious to communicate with us and give us guidance to lead us forward in life. For instance, if you dreamt of a toilet, you might need to relieve yourself of something, or pass a motion (make a decision). If a coincidence happened there might be a message there for you. For instance, if you were looking to change career you might be randomly handed a leaflet publicising a careers seminar that leads you to your ideal job. If a thought came into your mind that you needed to slow down whilst driving, you might then find there was an obstruction on the road further ahead. If the kettle started to boil without you switching it on, you might be being told that something was coming to the boil. If you suffered bereavement and a butterfly appeared at an improbable time or place, then the message might be the person who had 'died' had made the transition from one life to the next. When you begin to realise these things you experience are sometimes communication it can go a long way to help you on the road to self-development. In order to interpret the guidance correctly you have to be totally honest and open with yourself by acknowledging any frailties that are pointed out to you. In this way you start to become more balanced, letting go of the old belief   systems and ways of acting and being more able to connect to the higher frequencies.

Chapter 11 - Us - the computer

I think the body and spirit is like a computer, which has a wireless connection.

Theory
I think of the body and spirit as being like a computer that has a wireless connection, and just like a wireless/radio we can connect with many frequencies. Our physical body can be likened to the hardware of a computer, (the plastic casing, screen, keyboard etc.). Our spirit, which is the animating force within us and all living things, has a mind. The mind of the spirit is like the hard drive of the computer (where all documents and data is stored) and all our data, (everything we think, feel, experience and learn) is stored in the database of the mind which is located in the storage facility/aura, and we are constantly populating that database with more data. The third eye is like the mouse of the computer and is animated by our six senses and it is part of the mind of the spirit. The third eye interacts with the brain

of the physical body, firing and activating the brain so that our thoughts can be put into action, and our five physical senses as well as the sixth sense, utilised. The brain is a mass of electric circuits through which the mind expresses itself. Throw into the mix DNA, which is like a software programme and contains genetic instructions for the development and functioning of all living things and is programmed to constantly check and recheck for errors that it attempts to repair, and you can see the startling comparisons to all living things and the computer.

11.1 - The database of the mind

We are like a computer and I think our mind is like the database of the computer.

Theory

I think we are like a computer and I think our mind is like the database of the computer. Everything we think, feel, experience and learn is entered, filed and saved in the storage medium/aura of the mind. In our sleep state there seems to be some kind of mechanism that sees the mind retrieving from the storage medium data/memories that it uses to speak to us in a symbolic language of symbols. We have the capacity to translate this language if we take the trouble to learn. Dreams are part of the language that enables the Creator, spirit workers, the universe and our sub-conscious to give us cryptic and subtle messages for guidance and to help us achieve what ever it is we have come here on Earth to experience, achieve etc. It is a language that allows us to communicate from one parallel world to another. The mechanism that allows us to retrieve data/memory from the database in the storage medium/aura of the mind is a mystery to me. However I would use our similarity with the computer to try to find some understanding of this mechanism. Everything we have learnt during our lifetime is not in our conscious memory at any one time. These things when needed have to be moved from the storage medium/aura of the mind to our consciousness, and that's exactly how a computer works. The mechanism is very similar. A computer can have practically any amount of storage attached but when operating all of this information is not being processed, it is waiting to be called upon and moved (loaded) into RAM (memory).

11.2 - The universal database

Every thought and feeling we have is stored internally (in our own database/aura), as well as existing and stored externally 'out there' and it forms a universal database.

Theory

I think every thought and feeling that we have is stored internal (in our own database/aura), as well as existing and stored external 'out there' and it forms a universal database like a big memory bank. I think Mother Earth has her own aura or database that is populated by every thought and feeling of every living thing on Earth, as well as all the information contained in the frequencies that are being emitted by everything on Earth. I think this then connects to a universal database that is being populated by everything in the universe. Science is telling us that a quantum energy field connects everything in the universe, including human beings and their thoughts, and everything emits a type of frequency that contains data. I think it is essential we understand this connection as our world is in a terrible mess. Wars, fighting, violence, prejudice, intolerance and feral behaviour lives alongside all the goodness that there is in this world and, unfortunately, these intense negative things have a greater impact than the positive goodness.

Chapter 12 - We are body and spirit and are here on Earth to learn lessons

The spirit contains a mind and a soul.

Theory

We have seen the Age of Pisces was to teach us about duality, we are body and spirit. I think the parallel universe the spirit inhabits free from the physical body is a world of thought and feeling and as there is no physical body, hate, spite, jealousy etc would be transparent and therefore would need to be overcome. When living on Earth there is no such transparency as we have a body and a spirit. The spirit contains a mind and a soul. The mind of the spirit is for thought and thinking and lies over the heart area of the physical body. The soul is for feelings and emotions and lies over the stomach (gut) area of the physical body. I think the spirit is present at conception, when the sperm and the egg meet, and if it were not present then there could be no life, no animation, but I have no idea by what mechanism the spirit is placed there. I think the mind of the spirit is locked so that everything that has gone before and the reason we have come to Earth is not known to us. I think that portion of the mind that is locked and not accessible to us exists in a parallel universe and is our higher self. When on Earth in the physical body we are at the mercy of those workers in the spirit world or parallel universes who know our plan and have agreed to work with us and help us to learn, experience and achieve what ever it is we have come to Earth for. However, in order for these spirit workers to be effective at their job, we have to be able to listen. When we wake in the morning imagine a periscope rising from the heart area and travelling up to the forehead. The periscope has an eye and this is called our third eye. I think in our sleep state our spirit can leave the body and go to a parallel universe for guidance from the spirit workers. When the spirit returns to the body, if we wake up too soon then we are paralysed, (just like your computer would be paralysed if you disengaged the mouse). This can be a frightening experience but until the spirit is back in place and the third eye is activating the brain then there can be no animation, we cannot move or speak.

12.1 - Mind - Heart/Soul - Gut

The heart is the largest 'brain' of the body and the home of the gut instinct is indeed the gut itself.'

Theory
I think these scientific findings reinforce what I have written in the previous chapter 12, 'We are body and spirit and are here on Earth to learn lessons', and backs up the theory the mind of the spirit lies over the heart area, and the soul of the spirit lies over the stomach 'gut' area.

12.2 - The psychic centres - chakras

A chakra is the wheel of consciousness at each of the seven main energy centres of the spirit and they are activated by thought and feeling.

Theory
I think each chakra can be associated with particular parts of the body and they function as pumps and valves, regulating the flow of energy

(which contains information) through our energy system. Our thoughts (mind/brain) and feelings (soul/gut) open and close these valves and they filter the world around us, absorbing that which matches how we are feeling, is on our level of understanding, belief systems etc. We are consciously made aware of this information when it is expressed via the mind of the spirit to the brain of the body, and soul of the spirit to the gut of the body. If we have any dominant and negative character traits and/or dominant, negative and repeated patterns of behaviour, then we are over-tasking the particular chakra associated with this and the vibration/data will run along the nerve associated with that chakra, and it can have a physical effect on the part of the body to which the nerve connects.

12.3 - The aura

The aura is the database of the mind of the spirit.

Theory
Many, many people are able to see the aura surrounding living things and many of the Great Masters are portrayed as having a halo, and this is probably a representation of the aura. The Native American Indians had their headdress and I think this is also a representation of the aura. I think the aura is of the mind of the spirit and is like a storage facility which contains all our thoughts and feelings, everything we are thinking and feeling now at this moment, as well as every thought and feeling we have ever had in this life, and it contains everything we have experienced or learnt this time around. The aura is the database of the mind of the spirit. Some people are able to see the colour within the aura, and it is now known our thoughts and feelings are atoms which create different colours that can be seen in the aura. For instance, when someone is mentally and emotionally imbalanced they are on the red frequency or channel, and you will see that imbalance in the aura as red. If someone was constantly in that state you could liken this to being tuned into a particular radio channel and you can attract people or situations that are on the same wavelength.

12.4 - Psychics and Mediums

Every living thing in this world is psychic, capable of processing information from everything that's out there in the empty space/universal database, via frequencies/data absorbed through the chakras.

Theory

I think we all have psychic ability, it is the sixth sense and intuition, that gut feeling that when ignored usually sees things going badly for us and we find ourselves saying 'why didn't I listen?' The problem is we process what we absorb via the brain, and our personalities, belief systems etc. occupy the same space. Whilst everyone is a psychic, not all psychics are mediums but most people have the ability to be a medium or at the very least be their own medium just by thinking differently. A medium is able to tune into a higher frequency and communicate with those who have died (discarded the physical body) and are living in a parallel universe in spirit form. The gift can be used to prove evidence of survival to someone who is grieving, or it can be used to provide help and guidance where needed. In a wider sense it can help to move humanity on by influencing the written word, which when read could expand or alter the reader's way of thinking.

Chapter 15 - Case studies

Over the years of working in the spiritual arena I have met many different people, and all of them have a story to tell.

Theory

I have tried to give a cross-section of case studies that might be representative of most people. The case studies highlight how spiritual and psychic development, and development of self, can give you strong foundations enabling you to master the emotions and strengthen the mind. It is then the universal language can guide you. All the stories have a different slant to them but, nonetheless, the outcome sends the same message. Once you start to see life, the world and the wider universe in a different way and you build on that knowledge by self-development, as well as spiritual and psychic development, then you can connect to the higher frequencies. Once you start interacting with the universe via the universal language it is mind-blowing and can change everything. I think if the whole world looked at life in this way and then went on to develop themselves the world would be a much better place. But we could make a start because just by overcoming your own adversity and developing yourself, you can influence others and as we are all connected, eventually this will impact on the whole.

Chapter 16 - Step by step guide of expanding the mind and working with the universe

The key to working with the mind is to challenge our belief systems, as the more restricted our belief systems the more confined our mind is. By doing this we can change the frequencies of the mind, just like changing the channels on the radio or television, and this can see us resonating in a different way, attracting different people and situations to us.

Theory
It is a real challenge to unlearn restrictive and faulty belief systems that can cause mental and emotional problems, and automatic responses that lead to repeated patterns of behaviour. The only way I know to change these faulty beliefs and behaviours is to challenge them by knowledge, and taking down the barriers built on fear, judgement, restrictive opinion and such like. Once you take down the barriers of the mind and it starts to quicken you can connect to different frequencies bringing different people and situations into your life. This in turn will make you mentally stronger and more in control of your emotions and reactions to life. With meditation and visualisation techniques and especially when working with the chakras, you can feel the influence these thoughts have on you. We are body and spirit and this needs to be acknowledged. Spiritual and psychic development can change your life, and can reconnect you to the universe and you can be guided by the universal language to help you experience and achieve what ever it is you have come to Earth to experience and achieve. I think the more people become spiritually in tune, the faster the vibrations on Earth will become and in this way we might raise consciousness.

Chapter 17 - Join me in my market research

The book you are now reading is for the mass public and it is hoped by reading the book it will help to change/shift world consciousness and also inform the world of the lost language of symbols, which allows this world to communicate with other worlds or parallel universes and ultimately the Creator.

Theory

There is a movement globally that is gaining momentum, it is the spiritual movement and more and more people are waking up to the fact of our duality, that we are all body and spirit. It is hoped this book might help fill in pieces of the puzzle for those who are journeying with the mind, and introduce them to the lost universal language. A web site has been created at www.yvonnebailey.co.uk with a database attached to enable anyone to search for the possible meaning of their own symbols and dreams, and also with a section to enable you the reader to join with me in market research in this field on a large-scale basis by reporting the experiences you have as you journey on your road of mind expansion, with the aim of establishing and publishing in a book quantitative data to support the theories in this book. I think if the contents of this book, the supporting web site etc. is meant to gain momentum then nothing can stop it. It will journey where it is meant to journey, and will influence who ever it is meant to influence, and I am releasing it back to the universe with much love.

xxx

19

Some final thoughts

Albert Einstein said *'God does not play dice with the universe'*

The reason for not writing a conclusion to end this book is because there is no conclusion, just some final thoughts. There is so much about us, our world, everything that inhabits and makes up our world, the universe and beyond we still do not know about. The things we do know sometimes alter when we try to combine them or make them fit with other things, and so we might have knowledge of many things on a stand alone basis but not how they interact with, or what it means for, the whole.

We are left with theories of everything, but there are so many different pieces of the jigsaw to consider we have immense problems in bringing it all together, as there are many alternatives branching out in different directions. However, for me I am more than satisfied there is a Creator at the heart of it all. I know I am more than just a physical body, I am a spirit occupying that physical body for a reason and I think so are you.

Our world and the wider universe could be likened to halls of learning and the Creator has planned an opportunity for all to experience, achieve and learn singularly and collectively. We have been given the means to communicate with the whole via the universal language, and we are born with free will and are at the mercy of random and /or accidental happenings and the free will of others. We have personalities that are built on our date of birth, our genes, environment, culture, religion, and so forth.

All these things combined have a significant effect on us as we have a basic programme that is personalised by these things as well as the things we cannot see, our own spirit that animates the physical body, our soul growth arguably achieved over other life times, the planets that establish the pattern of the brain at birth, and the chakras that are constantly processing the energy we are exchanging, absorbing, pumping and filtering in line with the frequencies we are tuned into.

Our physical body we can see, these other things we cannot see, and this is our duality.

As we are a living being so is Mother Earth, she is a living planet, and there are other living planets out there with spirits living a life in differing physical bodies, adapted according to the environment their planet provides. We ourselves in different lifetimes might have lived on some of these other living planets which are probably at different stages of evolution, to enable us to have different experiences, lessons etc.

Our planet is a living thing and everything that happens on her is happening to her. If we create things that damage her, such as bombs, then we are hurting her. If we make it difficult for her to breathe, such as cutting down and not replacing trees, then we are hurting her, and if we continue to inflict hurt and pain on all living things then we are continuing to release an abundance of electrons or some such negative particles that contribute to the imbalance. Just like we humans might flex our body to get more comfortable and alleviate pain, so Mother Earth will flex her body to get more comfortable, and this will have an effect on the whole to which she is connected, out there in the universe and probably beyond.

When natural disasters occur some people can be heard to ask 'why did God let this happen? Or some people might say 'There is no God otherwise this would not have happened'.

I think that we come to Earth with free will and, as a single organism of interconnected energy fields connects us all, then there has to be cause and effect or karma. In other words, I do not think that God is responsible for natural disasters rather we need to look to man.

When you look at the solar system and you see our planet orbiting the sun, and then you look at the atom and you see the electron orbiting the nucleus, you cannot fail to see the synchronicity. When you consider the human body and the spirit that animates it, I think of the Earth and her ley-lines, and how they cross and interconnect. We know if we are in pain and are anxious we feel it in the chakra associated with the part of our consciousness experiencing the anxiety. When the anxiety continues over a period of time, or to a particular level of intensity, the person creates a symptom on the physical level.

Is this what happens to Mother Earth? Does that mean she has her own chakra system running through her body absorbing and emitting frequencies of information via her lay lines? If one country is doing something harmful to Mother Earth does this then mean another country might eventually experience the effect if it is in the path the frequency is travelling? And does this then extend to everything that is out there in the wider universe?

I think that karma, cause and effect, can be experienced by the individual in this lifetime and I do not think it carries through to other lifetimes when in a physical body. I think it is probable when we die we have plenty of opportunity to work through past deeds not accounted for once we pass in to a parallel universe of spirit/consciousness. I think it is this lifetime we have to concentrate on and what ever we do both singularly and collectively, be it good or bad, eventually it will find its way back to the source. Karma collectively is subject to the cycle of the cosmos and thus we can inherit the sins of the fathers collectively. Perhaps one of the lessons for us as a person, group and/or country is that of personal responsibility to the whole that we are connected to.

We are connected to the whole of the universe and somewhere out there in the universe someone is contacting us now via images on the Earth. I wonder if whoever or whatever is contacting us wants to tell us of the effect our actions are having on them as well, the whole, and if this is so, are we yet ready to listen?

As the frequencies and energies of the departing Pisces are ending and The Age of Aquarius final prepares to stand alone, I wonder if the Creator has planned to send a Master to close the one and open the other, and is that Master born yet or is he already here walking amongst us? Will he come from another planet or perhaps another universe? And if he comes, I wonder if we have sufficient awareness to recognise, understand and accept him, as I am confident he will not be self-proclaimed. Perhaps that is the purpose of this book, to help to raise consciousness so when he comes we will know him and will understand he is not part of any particular religion, culture etc., but he is part of, and belongs to, all.

It could be when we reach 2012, and if the cycle of the Long Count is linked with cosmic karma and what we have given out collectively finds its way back, there might be enough people on Earth with sufficient awareness to influence change. Perhaps that is when He can, and will, come?

This is the beginning of the Age of Aquarius and it is concerned with a higher state of consciousness. It will be with us for the next two thousand or so years. I wonder what it would be like to be reborn towards the end of this age, living with more evolved humans. However, I would not want to be born within the final one hundred and sixty years of its time in power as whilst the frequencies and energies of the Age of Aquarius were winding down and the new frequencies and energies of Capricorn were coming in, conflict and chaos will be the inevitable transitory merger of these great forces.

And so it will continue.

20

Noah's Ark and 2012

Noah's Ark I think means the spiritual light.

And the animals went in two by two – the male and female of us humans with our differing looks, personalities etc,

Because there were floods – floods of tears and the people were drowning as the times were so wicked and in order to be saved they turned towards the spiritual light,

It took Noah years to finish his ark – it has taken years for the spiritual movement to gain momentum,

A great rain then lasted for forty days and forty nights – it will probably take a significant event, or a series of events, of enough gravitas that creates such an impact we will be forced to change.

www.yvonnebailey.co.uk

Some other titles from Capall Bann

Everything You Always Wanted To Know About Your Body, But, So Far, Nobody's Been Able To Tell You by Chris Thomas & Diane Baker

"...easy to understand...insight into how you can heal yourself...comprehensive guide" Here's Health Have you ever wondered why some people become ill and others do not? Why some people recover from illness and others do not? Do you know how your body really works? Is there an alternative approach to treating symptoms of illness instead of using prescriptive drugs? This book leads you through the body, organ by organ, system by system, and explains in clear language how illness arises and what to do about it, explaining the workings of the human body in simple language and clear illustrations; which elements are connected together and why they can influence each other. It also relates each region and organ to its associated chakra and how our day-to-day lives have an influence on our health and wellbeing. Every part of the body is dealt with in these ways and the major underlying causes for most of our illnesses explained with details and suggestions on how to heal yourself by working on the root cause issues. This book also takes a look at how some illnesses are brought about by past life traumas and looks at ways of healing the symptoms of illness without the need for prescriptive drugs. Several forms of healing practices are used to achieve this: Bach Flower Remedies, Reflexology, Herbalism, Biochemic Tissue Salts and Homeopathy are the main approaches used, with a further twenty seven therapies fully described. A comprehensive look at the body and illness and one of the most comprehensive guides to alternative treatments currently available.
ISBN 186163 0980 £17.95

Can't Sleep, Won't Sleep - Insomnia, Reasons and Remedies
by Linda Louisa Dell
This book gives some of the many reasons for sleep problems and sets out some of the many remedies, therapies and techniques that can help you to re-train your sleep patterns to your very individual needs. Starting with an explanation of what insomnia is, the author progresses to cover the purposes of sleep, dreaming, sleep posture, depression, chronic fatigue, women's problems, stress, SAD, relaxation techniques, hands-on healing, and much much more. Problems and possible remedies are blended here making fascinating reading and a real help for anyone experiencing sleep problems - and so many of us have for all sorts of reasons. Help yourself get a good night's sleep - read this!
ISBN 186163 238X   £13.95

Reaching For the Divine - How To Communicate Effectively With Your Spirit Guides & Loved Ones On The Other Side by Phillip Kinsella
A serious manual for anyone remotely interested in Life After Death. For anyone who has lost someone close to them, this can be a very traumatic experience. This book, is designed to help you communicate with your loved ones who have passed into the Spirit World. It also enables you to work with your Spirit Guides and helps you understand the mechanics of clairvoyance and how it works. It not only covers subjects on how to understand the Spirit World's language, but enables you to become a conduit between the two worlds too. The author is a professional working medium and teacher on he subject of After Life Communications. This book is a must for anyone searching to establish the true power of themselves and how they can Reach For The Divine. ISBN 186163 2800 £10.95

FREE DETAILED CATALOGUE

Capall Bann is owned and run by people actively involved in many of the areas in which we publish. A detailed illustrated catalogue is available on request, SAE or International Postal Coupon appreciated. **Titles can be ordered direct from Capall Bann, post free in the UK** (cheque or PO with order) or from good bookshops and specialist outlets.

A Breath Behind Time, Terri Hector
A Soul is Born by Eleyna Williamson
Angels and Goddesses - Celtic Christianity & Paganism, M. Howard
The Art of Conversation With the Genius Loci, Barry Patterson
Arthur - The Legend Unveiled, C Johnson & E Lung
Astrology The Inner Eye - A Guide in Everyday Language, E Smith
Auguries and Omens - The Magical Lore of Birds, Yvonne Aburrow
Asyniur - Women's Mysteries in the Northern Tradition, S McGrath
Beginnings - Geomancy, Builder's Rites & Electional Astrology, Nigel Pennick
Between Earth and Sky, Julia Day
The Book of Seidr, Runic John
Caer Sidhe - Celtic Astrology and Astronomy, Michael Bayley
Call of the Horned Piper, Nigel Jackson
Can't Sleep, Won't Sleep, Linda Louisa Dell
Carnival of the Animals, Gregor Lamb
Cat's Company, Ann Walker
Celebrating Nature, Gordon MacLellan
Celtic Faery Shamanism, Catrin James
Celtic Lore & Druidic Ritual, Rhiannon Ryall
Celtic Sacrifice - Pre Christian Ritual & Religion, Marion Pearce
Celtic Saints and the Glastonbury Zodiac, Mary Caine
Circle and the Square, Jack Gale
Come Back To Life, Jenny Smedley
Company of Heaven, Jan McDonald
Compleat Vampyre - The Vampyre Shaman, Nigel Jackson
Cottage Witchcraft, Jan McDonald
Creating Form From the Mist - The Wisdom of Women in Celtic Myth and
    Culture, Lynne Sinclair-Wood
Crystal Clear - A Guide to Quartz Crystal, Jennifer Dent
Crystal Doorways, Simon & Sue Lilly
Crossing the Borderlines - Guising, Masking & Ritual Animal Disguise in the
    European Tradition, Nigel Pennick
Dragons of the West, Nigel Pennick
Dreamtime by Linda Louisa Dell
Dreamweaver by Elen Sentier
Earth Dance - A Year of Pagan Rituals, Jan Brodie
Earth Harmony - Places of Power, Holiness & Healing, Nigel Pennick
Earth Magic, Margaret McArthur
Egyptian Animals - Guardians & Gateways of the Gods, Akkadia Ford
Eildon Tree (The) Romany Language & Lore, Michael Hoadley
Enchanted Forest - The Magical Lore of Trees, Yvonne Aburrow
Eternal Priestess, Sage Weston

Magical Lore of Cats, Marion Davies
Magical Lore of Herbs, Marion Davies
Magick Without Peers, Ariadne Rainbird & David Rankine
Masks of Misrule - Horned God & His Cult in Europe, Nigel Jackson
Medicine For The Coming Age, Lisa Sand MD
Medium Rare - Reminiscences of a Clairvoyant, Muriel Renard
Menopausal Woman on the Run, Jaki da Costa
Mind Massage - 60 Creative Visualisations, Marlene Maundrill
Mirrors of Magic - Evoking the Spirit of the Dewponds, P Heselton
The Moon and You, Teresa Moorey
Moon Mysteries, Jan Brodie
Mysteries of the Runes, Michael Howard
Mystic Life of Animals, Ann Walker
New Celtic Oracle The, Nigel Pennick & Nigel Jackson
Oracle of Geomancy, Nigel Pennick
Pagan Feasts - Seasonal Food for the 8 Festivals, Franklin & Phillips
Paganism For Teens, Jess Wynne
Patchwork of Magic - Living in a Pagan World, Julia Day
Pathworking - A Practical Book of Guided Meditations, Pete Jennings
Personal Power, Anna Franklin
Pickingill Papers - The Origins of Gardnerian Wicca, Bill Liddell
Pillars of Tubal Cain, Nigel Jackson
Places of Pilgrimage and Healing, Adrian Cooper
Planet Earth - The Universe's Experiment, Chris Thomas
Practical Divining, Richard Foord
Practical Meditation, Steve Hounsome
Practical Spirituality, Steve Hounsome
Project Human Extinction - The Ultimate Conspiracy, Chris Thomas
Psychic Self Defence - Real Solutions, Jan Brodie
Real Fairies, David Tame
Reality - How It Works & Why It Mostly Doesn't, Rik Dent
Romany Tapestry, Michael Houghton
Runic Astrology, Nigel Pennick
Sacred Animals, Gordon MacLellan
Sacred Celtic Animals, Marion Davies, Ill. Simon Rouse
Sacred Dorset - On the Path of the Dragon, Peter Knight
Sacred Grove - The Mysteries of the Forest, Yvonne Aburrow
Sacred Geometry, Nigel Pennick
Sacred Nature, Ancient Wisdom & Modern Meanings, A Cooper
Sacred Ring - Pagan Origins of British Folk Festivals, M. Howard
Season of Sorcery - On Becoming a Wisewoman, Poppy Palin
Seasonal Magic - Diary of a Village Witch, Paddy Slade
Secret Places of the Goddess, Philip Heselton
Secret Signs & Sigils, Nigel Pennick
The Secrets of East Anglian Magic, Nigel Pennick
A Seeker's Guide To Past Lives, Paul Williamson
Seeking Pagan Gods, Teresa Moorey
A Seer's Guide To Crystal Divination, Gale Halloran
Self Enlightenment, Mayan O'Brien
Soul Resurgence, Poppy Palin
Somerset Faeries and Pixies - Exploring Their Hidden World, Jon Dathen
Spirits of the Earth series, Jaq D Hawkins

Stony Gaze, Investigating Celtic Heads John Billingsley
Stumbling Through the Undergrowth , Mark Kirwan-Heyhoe
Subterranean Kingdom, The, revised 2nd ed, Nigel Pennick
Symbols of Ancient Gods, Rhiannon Ryall
Talking to the Earth, Gordon MacLellan
Talking With Nature, Julie Hood
Taming the Wolf - Full Moon Meditations, Steve Hounsome
Teachings of the Wisewomen, Rhiannon Ryall
The Other Kingdoms Speak, Helena Hawley
Transformation of Housework, Ben Bushill
Tree: Essence of Healing, Simon & Sue Lilly
Tree: Essence, Spirit & Teacher, Simon & Sue Lilly
Tree Seer, Simon & Sue Lilly
Torch and the Spear, Patrick Regan
Understanding Chaos Magic, Jaq D Hawkins
Understanding Second Sight, Dilys Gater
Understanding Spirit Guides, Dilys Gater
Understanding Star Children, Dilys Gater
The Urban Shaman, Dilys Gater
Vortex - The End of History, Mary Russell
Warp and Weft - In Search of the I-Ching, William de Fancourt
Warriors at the Edge of Time, Jan Fry
Water Witches, Tony Steele
Way of the Magus, Michael Howard
Weaving a Web of Magic, Rhiannon Ryall
West Country Wicca, Rhiannon Ryall
What's Your Poison? vol 1, Tina Tarrant
Wheel of the Year, Teresa Moorey & Jane Brideson
Wildwitch - The Craft of the Natural Psychic, Poppy Palin
Wildwood King , Philip Kane
A Wisewoman's Book of Tea Leaf Reading, Pat Barki
The Witching Path, Moira Stirland
The Witch's Kitchen, Val Thomas
The Witches' Heart, Eileen Smith
Treading the Mill - Practical CraftWorking in Modern Traditional Witchcraft by Nigel Pearson
Witches of Oz, Matthew & Julia Philips
Witchcraft Myth Magic Mystery and... Not Forgetting Fairies, Ralph Harvey
Wondrous Land - The Faery Faith of Ireland by Dr Kay Mullin
Working With Crystals, Shirley o'Donoghue
Working With Natural Energy, Shirley o'Donoghue
Working With the Merlin, Geoff Hughes
Your Talking Pet, Ann Walker
The Zodiac Experience, Patricia Crowther

FREE detailed catalogue

Contact: Capall Bann Publishing, Auton Farm, Milverton, Somerset, TA4 1NE